THE
COUPLE'S
COMFORT BOOK

A Creative Guide for
Renewing Passion, Pleasure
& Commitment

JENNIFER LOUDEN

HarperSanFrancisco
A Division of HarperCollinsPublishers

To
Christopher Martin Mosio,
my beloved

ALSO BY JENNIFER LOUDEN

The Woman's Comfort Book
The Pregnant Woman's Comfort Book
The Woman's Retreat Book
Comfort Secrets for Busy Women

THE COUPLE'S COMFORT BOOK: *A Creative Guide for Renewing Passion, Pleasure & Commitment.* Copyright © 1994, 2004 by Jennifer Louden. All rights reserved. Printed in the United States of America. No part of this book may be used or reproduced in any manner whatsoever without written permission except in the case of brief quotations embodied in critical articles and reviews. For information address HarperCollins Publishers, 10 East 53rd Street, New York, NY 10022.

HarperCollins books may be purchased for educational, business, or sales promotional use. For information please write: Special Markets Department, HarperCollins Publishers, Inc., 10 East 53rd Street, New York, NY 10022.

HarperCollins Web site: http://www.harpercollins.com

HarperCollins®, ■ ®, and HarperSanFrancisco™ are trademarks of HarperCollins Publishers, Inc.

Library of Congress Cataloging-in-Publication Data

Louden, Jennifer.
   The couple's comfort book : a creative guide for renewing passion, pleasure
& commitment / Jennifer Louden. — 1st ed.
      p.   cm.
   Includes bibliographical references.
   ISBN 0–06–077669–2
   1. Man-woman relationships. 2. Nurturing behavior. 3. Self-help techniques.
I. Title.
HQ801.L6516   1994
306.7—dc20   93—20733
                                                                CIP

05 06 07 08 09 RRD(H) 10 9 8 7 6 5 4 3 2 1

Contents

A New Foreword—
Ten Years Later

I have been married now for fourteen years. We have a daughter. She will soon be ten. We have survived the death of a parent, financial pressure, a major move, parenting, intense travel schedules—not to mention coming to terms with the startling truth: we really do marry our opposites.

My parents always told me that marriage is hard work. They never told me there would be days when you hate your spouse. Days? Sometimes weeks. No one told me what a cold war marriage can be. Not that I would have listened. At twenty-three, looking into those big green eyes of my husband, I would have said (and probably did, if I could remember), "Not us. We'll be different."

Darby tells her version of the relationship saga. "Almost ten years ago, very early on in my partner's and my relationship, I found *The Couple's Comfort Book* at a local bookstore. Being dopey in love, I picked it up and ended up stretching my limited grad-student budget to bring it home. Dopey in love from time to time gave way to conflict (sound familiar?), and one night I grabbed the book and scrambled to the chapter on how to have a fair fight. 'We're gonna do it this way!' I said, waving the book. 'You'll be Carlos, and I'll be Martya!' We aired our views, and we really listened to each other (see pg. 285). We didn't interrupt, snipe, or manipulate. We learned to argue 'by the book,' and both of us firmly believe that if we hadn't learned how to play fair in our times of difference, we would have called it quits long ago. I really appreciate the book's recognition that love wears many emotional hats (delight, neediness, desire, ennui, anger, etc.)—that is its greatest strength. Ten years later, we still pull this book off the shelf."

Maybe some people don't have to learn to fight by the book. Maybe some relationships are blessed. There do seem to be couples who inhabit what I call the nirvana of relationships—married or not, parents or not, straight or gay—they have found someone with whom they are complete. Okay, yes, they fight, they may mutter petty, flinty-hearted things under their breaths, but somehow, these couples have an I-can't-live-without-you connection, some extra reserve of magic patience and grace. One couple I knew could spend five minutes saying goodbye—and all they were doing was driving across town in separate cars, all of a ten-minute trip!

For the rest of us, mere mortals, we must face the astonishingly difficult spiritual work of being in a relationship without that magic. We must face the worst and the best in ourselves, over and over again, if we choose to stay together, if we choose to create real intimacy. Face it—the hardest spiritual path in life is being in a committed relationship. Yes, I can say parenting is a close second, but the really hard years of parenting do end. You still worry, you are still connected, oh yes, but the everyday rub up against it, that ends. The children move out (hopefully). Your partner doesn't (hopefully).

I wish I could find a magic pill to make my marriage easier. The only thing I have found, which I return to over and over, is the idea that by being together, we create a third something: the relationship. This third something needs love, attention, and feeding. As much as I may hate my partner at any given moment, I value and treasure this third thing with my whole being. It is very precious to me. It deserves to flourish. So most of the time, I can do something to nurture the relationship, even when I'd like to find subtle and crafty ways to torture my husband. Usually, any step I take away from my usual routine, from, "If he would only do _____, then I would be able to do _____," away from our tangled, sour power struggles, and into serving the relationship, then the funniest thing always happens. He does something nice for me. Then I look at him across the kitchen counter, and suddenly, he's cute again. I scoot over to his side of the bed. I say how nice it would be to go away for a weekend together, alone. We talk—about important things or mundane things— but we talk. In those moments, we are one of *those* couples; we are graced and living in relationship nirvana.

Nurturing your relationship is certainly not mandatory. Most people don't do it. You can certainly avoid it, keep meaning to do it, talk about doing it without actually doing it. Nobody will die. You may even stay together.

Yet I wager that you will feel you are missing something, something juicier, richer, more intimate, more real, more alive. I'd never suggest that taking this step toward one another is easy, but I can declare that the reward is what we all yearn for, in the words of the late Raymond Carver: to call myself beloved, to feel myself beloved on this earth.

Jennifer Louden
November 2003
Bainbridge Island, Washington

Introduction

How to Read and Use This Book

You've had an awful week at work, and to top it off, as you drive home you feel a cold settling into your chest. You can't wait to tell your mate, who you know will comfort and soothe you, but five minutes after you arrive home, you find yourself battling with your partner over who is the most exhausted and overworked. Disappointed and angry, you crawl into bed, completely baffled by what went wrong.

or

You're bursting with love and appreciation for this great person you share your life with, but you can't think of how to show it, so you rely on the nice but slightly stale rituals of making dinner or giving flowers.

or

You look across the pile of bills at the face you cherish and try hard to remember the last time you did anything fun, wild, or spontaneous together. A fantasy begins to form, but the baby wails and your mirage of frisky fun disappears in a whiff of dirty diapers.

Now, what do you do?

A. Sigh and do nothing? (The most popular choice.)

B. Let your relationship grow stale? (The second most popular choice.)

C. Move to Tahiti and open a breadfruit stand? (Good fantasy.)

D. Pick up *The Couple's Comfort Book* and start renewing passion and love in your relationship? (You've got nothing to lose.)

What Does "Nurturing a Relationship" Mean?

Nurturing a relationship is an act as familiar as kissing hello, as flamboyant as a surprise birthday party, as unique to your relationship as a love note written with your pet names, or as universal as regularly voicing your appreciation for your partner. Nurturing your relationship means keeping it current, warm, juicy, sparkling with gratitude, burnished with respect. Nurturing your love means you give it the same attention you do your career, your children, or your commitment to your community. *It is the act of creating an environment in which the relationship, and each person, can flourish.*

To nurture another human being is to accept that person for who he or she is. To nurture is to honor your lover as the magnificent human being she or he is inside. It is to support your partner's growth toward wholeness. It means you honestly care about your partner's thoughts, feelings, wants, and especially needs. It is *always* a reciprocal process. One partner does not do all the nurturing: that is excessive caretaking, and that eventually leads to resentment, burnout, and finally bitterness and alienation.

It is very important that you realize that nurturing your relationship never means tolerating an abusive or destructive situation. Physical, emotional, or verbal abuse is not acceptable at any time. Learning to live with a destructive relationship is not nurturing; it is martyrdom.

Why Nurture the Relationship?

Many of the most common problems couples have are based on a lack of nurturing. You may not call it that. Instead, you may say, "He never talks to me" or "She doesn't appreciate anything I do for her" or "She hardly ever initiates sex" or "He wants to have sex all the time, and sometimes I just want to be held." These are all signs of insufficient nurturing. The solution for the chronic frustration, boredom, or disagreements you may be experiencing lies in small acts of appreciation, acceptance, celebration, letting go, and, above all, conscious and constant communication.

Psychologists and researchers recognize the importance of nurturing each other in order to sustain a healthy relationship. In their book *Going the Distance*, Dr. Lonnie Barbach and her husband, David Geisinger, write, "A relationship is a complex living organism. As with all living things, if it is to thrive it must have what is basic to life itself: adequate protection and nourishment." They go on to say that keeping your connection alive doesn't require tremendous amounts of time and energy but "ongoing, thoughtful attention to the things that nourish a relationship." Discovering those nourishing moments and weaving them into your life is what this book is about.

Everyone knows what happens if you don't nurture each other, because we've all experienced it. Static sameness, drab days and passionless nights, nitpicking each other's faults, highlighting the disappointments, and downplaying the delightful moments. Why nurture the relationship? Because it will die if you don't.

Consider what a friend told me over lunch recently: "I'm trying to give him a chance. I want to stay together. But he has no idea how to take care of me. I spend my time and energy on him, but when it's my turn, he doesn't have a clue. After nine years, I'm sick and tired of it. I want some nurturing too."

What Is the Difference Between Nurturing and Comforting?

While writing *The Woman's Comfort Book* and teaching workshops, I discovered comforting and nurturing are two different things. To comfort your partner is to pamper, stroke, and care for him or her. We most often need this type of comforting after a bad day, a big disappointment, or during a grieving or healing process. Nurturing your partner can be more difficult. It can involve stepping back and letting go, getting out of your mate's business, even if it means he or she may fail. It can mean sacrificing to the relationship some of your own desires. It can mean accepting the parts of your partner that you simply do not like. Nurturing can be painful or uncomfortable at times, but the final result is always warm, embracing, and affirming.

See "Divine Sustenance: Sacrificing to the Marriage" for a description.

Gender and Nurturing

Because of the present limitations in our society, you may have been taught that only women are capable of nurturing and that nurturing is only for children or other dependent beings. *Nothing could be further from the truth.* It is crucial to separate nurturing from mothering, to strip it of its label as something only women do. Men are just as "naturally" capable of nurturing as women, and the need to be nurtured does not diminish with age, nor is it a sign of weakness. To have needs, to be needy, is a part of being human. The problem arises when we deny our needs, especially such a powerful one as our need for a nurturing relationship. When we deny this need, over time we wound our core self, and our ability to relate honestly to each other becomes skewed.

See "Women and Men Nurturing Each Other."

Why I Wrote This Book

I wrote this book for the same reason I wrote my first book: because I needed it. I have found writing to be a rich process of self-discovery. At first, I thought *The Couple's Comfort Book* would simply make a good sequel to my first book. But as I began to write, I started to have trouble. It was not flowing as easily as the woman's book. I began to panic. At the same time, my husband, Chris, and I began counseling together. It took several months to put the two together. Oh so painfully slowly, I discovered why I was writing this book—not for career reasons, but *because Chris and I had no idea how to stay connected in a healthy way.* We were "showing up" less and less for our own marriage, losing ourselves in our careers or in front of the TV. It hit us both like a ton of bricks: we were afraid to be vulnerable and open with each other. We were losing the battle with entropy and familiarity. It terrified us.

After nine years, Chris and I had come to a crossroads, a crossroads I believe most couples come to. There are two choices. You can stay connected and conscious, or you can choose what most people choose and what our culture encourages, which is to check out. Hide behind having children, being career obsessed, watching TV, or negative thinking. Whatever the choice, the sum effect is lack of soul connection. A colorless, often increasingly bitter, existence results.

Children

Couples with children read this book as it was being written and consistently said two things. One, "We don't have time to do any of this!" Two, "If we don't take time for this stuff, we won't have a relationship left." Whitney Kershaw, a mother and an activist for mothers, said, "Almost the best thing you can give your kids is a good relationship. By modeling a loving, happy, healthy relationship, your children will see they can have this too." Anne Mayer, in *How to Stay Lovers While Still Raising Your Children*, says, "There is great harm in overcommitting ourselves to our children and not spending the time necessary to maintain our marital relationships. . . . When we neglect our needs, not only do we suffer, but more importantly, our children suffer. They suffer from our resentments, our frustrations, and our troubled relationships." Yet there is no denying how difficult it becomes to nurture your relationship, or even to have ten minutes alone together, once you have children. But it becomes even more important because now you, your partner, *and* your children need your intimate connection to be healthy and thriving. A burned-out marriage fosters a burned-out family.

How to Use This Book

This is a reference book. Chapters are cross-referenced by notations in the margins. In addition, you will find a chart in the middle of the book with a list of common complaints, followed by possible solutions and the page on which to find them. The structure is meant to complement your busy lives and allow you to browse and sample only what appeals to you. If you want to explore a subject further, references are given at the end of each chapter.

Don't get hung up on the "You'll Need" part of each chapter or on doing things exactly the way I describe. This book is a creative incubator to awaken your own passions on how to keep your love flourishing, *never* a rigid set of instructions.

I have compiled this book as an offer of water for the parched earth that our lives can become, as one way to dig yourselves out before you become buried under an avalanche of obligations, before your faces become blurs because you are running so fast to get it all done, before you lose your soul because you don't have time to do anything that matters to you. Ultimately, what nurtures a relationship is finding the time to stay connected without losing yourself. I hope this book helps you do that a little more often.

I believe this book will make you feel good, will deepen your respect and appreciation for each other, and might just spice up your sex life. *It is the first step that is most difficult.* After that, you may actually want to play with this book even more than you want to watch TV. (I know, that might seem hard to believe.) Take one small step. Read the next chapter together, right now. . . .

Bringing the Book Home

When you bring this book home, your partner might have many possible reactions: delight that you care enough to strengthen your bonds of intimacy; anger that you believe the relationship isn't perfectly perfect the way it is right now; derision because you ventured into the self-help section of the bookstore and actually purchased one of *those* books; fear that you aren't happy coupled with fear of becoming closer; or arousal because a book about nurturing each other must have some good sex stuff in it. Fill in your own reaction: _____

Realize that even if you usually buy books about personal growth, bringing home a book that suggests even the smallest need for improvement or change in your partner is bound to set off *some* reaction, even a very muted one. So here are some suggestions for presenting this book to your lover.

Note: Even if you both bought the book on the same day and brought it home to surprise each other or you picked it out together in the library, glance over the ideas below. It is a good way to get your new or renewed phase of nurturing off to a clear, well-communicated start.

Explorations: Expectations

Take five minutes to examine your hopes and fears. If you aren't aware of what they are, you can set yourself up to be disappointed in your partner and not even be sure why. If you do these questions alone, ask your partner to do them *after* you have brought the book to his or her attention and generated a little interest.

Finish the sentences either by writing as many completions to each question as you can think of (try for ten for each question) or by facing each other and verbally giving your answers. Say or write *whatever comes into your mind,* as quickly as possible, without self-criticism or censorship. The less you ponder, the more easily you can get past the obvious. Accept that

you will feel resistance. You might feel you have nothing more to say.
Keep going.

> When we read this book, I hope . . .

> When we read this book, I expect . . .

> If we read this book, I'm afraid . . .

Broaching the Subject

Here are some suggestions from couples I have interviewed for ways to
introduce the book or encourage resistive partners:

From Ken in Evanston, Illinois: All that it would take to get him to read
the book would be "a direct request from Helen, a desire to deepen our
relationship, and a belief that the book would help with that." From
Helen: "An explanation of how to fit the exercises into my busy day."

*See "Togetherness Time"
for help.*

Perhaps the best way to introduce this book is to state as clearly as possible *why* you want to deepen your relationship, what your needs, feelings,
and desires are. Example: "I found this book in the bookstore today, and I
thought it would be fun to experiment with together. I love you very
much, and I want to be closer to you. I'm excited about sharing this with
you." Choosing specific, "I" statements without suggesting fault make this
less threatening and more successful.

*See "Daily
Communication:
The 'I' Statement."*

Communicate to your partner that nurturing your relationship *isn't* about
fixing it. This isn't a book for snarled relationships but a book filled with
beneficial, playful ideas for maintenance, like a how-to manual for a For-
mula One engine. It is not about psychobabble or, as my mate says, "New
Age couple theroputogames."

From another couple: Don't put too much emphasis on the book as the
only means to nurture the relationship, but instead use it as a starting
point.

From Christina and Steve: "'Defruitify' (make a little fun of) by joking
about the book. Even at the expense of the author." (Fine with me.)

Tell your mate, "This book was recommended to me by a bookseller today. It is on the *New York Times* best-seller list, and everyone is talking about how wonderful it is." (I can hope.) Seriously, your partner might be more inclined to try it if it is recommended by an expert, a doctor, or another couple. (So give a copy to your resident expert; have him or her read it and recommend it to your mate.)

Share the book for the first time at a special, quiet moment.

From Sophie and Ben in Chicago: "Tell your partner about the book. Leave it at that. A day or so later, ask them if they would consider reading it. Another day or so later, ask them to read a certain section. Then, maybe the next day, ask them to do an exercise."

Many of the men I polled said they would participate if they knew it would lead to more sex. This is a loaded gun. (Pun intended.) Trading favors, "You do this for me, and I'll do that for you," leads to resentment and isn't a good practice to get into, especially around nurturing. The reason: we all want to know that our partners do things for us because they love us, not because they expect something in return. On the other hand, it is true that greater intimacy (which is created by nurturing each other without tit-for-tat conditions) can lead to more frequent and passionate sex. (Test couples who did these exercises reported just such an occurrence. And there *are* chapters about enhancing your sexual life.)

Start small. Tell your mate you just want to spend ten or fifteen minutes connecting. You are not asking for a weekend retreat.

Nancy said her husband, Bob, was interested because he very much wants to nurture her but lacks specific ideas. This book gives lots of specifics, so for the partner who lacks creativity, energy, or time, voilà! The creative part has been taken care of.

From a couple in Virginia: "Just ask."

Stress the rewards—greater intimacy, communication, less stress, whatever feels right for your situation.

BRINGING THE BOOK
HOME

*See "When I Think of
Nurturing the
Relationship:
Resources."*

From Faith Boyle: "The satisfaction you get out of the relationship is directly related to what you put into it. Think about the investment of time and energy you would put into a new relationship—planning dates, buying new underwear, sending cards—and put that energy into your present relationship. Have an affair with your spouse."

If He or She Says No

If your mate says no, you have several options: you can do the exercises alone (not as absurd as it sounds); you can incorporate the exercises into your life together without making a big deal about where they came from; you can throw the book away (recycle it or give it to a friend); you can ask yourself why your partner won't participate.

You always have alternatives. Think positively, and know you have the power to meet your own needs at all times. Try not to limit yourself with negative thinking.

Fear

It is not unusual to be afraid of learning more about your relationship and your partner. "What if I discover we are incompatible?" "What if I find out she doesn't love me?" "What if I find out we are actually separate individuals with separate needs and desires?" I found in my interviews with couples that many people don't want to peer too closely at the person they live with. This may be the safe path, but it is also deadly. The nature of relationship, the nature of humans, is to want homeostasis, routine, stale comfort as in, "Let's make sure everything stays the same forever." Change is scary, even traumatic, but it is inevitable. Change *is* the reality of life.

Don't be surprised if at the beginning of nurturing your relationship, resentments surface. A familiar pattern: you start doing sweet things for each other, and suddenly a few days later you have a fight about how she never initiates sex or he never buys thoughtful gifts. This fight may seem to have come out of nowhere, but it hasn't. When we begin to nurture each other, we touch on unmet needs. An angry voice rises up and says,

"This feels good. Why hasn't he done this for me before?" Or, instead of resentment, our internal voice might say, "This feels too good. I can't handle it," and we pick a fight to distance ourselves because we are afraid this good stuff will be cut off.

How do you deal with fear, fights, and resistance to change? *Recognize they exist*. Discuss your fears about changing, acknowledge your resistance to trying anything new. Too often we start beating ourselves up and throwing ourselves headlong into a project *before* we have given any attention to our reluctance and fears. Don't deny your resistance and fear; it won't go away, it will only get bigger. Instead, make room for it. Write down your resistance, and name your fears. Or try designating a chair or box in your house where you store your resistance to exploring new things. Refer to it, or mimic adding to it when you feel the overwhelming need to stay the same or are afraid to try something new. Tune in to your feelings and the voices in your head. Talk about your feelings as they come up. Go slowly. Try to link fears and overwhelming feelings of neediness with your new self-nurturing activities. Do nice things for yourself when your partner slips back and the nurturing from him or her falters.

Whatever you do, avoid perfectionism. *Perfect* translates directly to *failure* where nurturing is concerned. All change is a give-and-take process, two steps forward, one step back. Words of appreciation and intimate dinners in front of the fireplace instead of the TV might happen for a few days, and then it is back to *Star Trek* and a mumbled "How was your day?" Real change takes time, patience, and what feels like an endless number of reminders, both to yourself and your partner. If you accept this at the outset, you will succeed in polishing your relationship to a fresh, healthy luster of passion, respect, and connection—a heady mix!

About Relaxing

Throughout the book you will see the word *relax* like this:

Relax

I have used it as a shorthand throughout the book so you won't have to reread the same relaxation instructions over and over. When you see **Relax,** refer back to this section, or relax your body and mind in any way that feels good.

The instructions below can be used before any exercise or on a daily basis. Stress has become an enduring, overwhelming part of life, one that erodes love steadily and destructively. Controlling stress, together and separately, is the first step in nurturing yourself and your love. Just a few minutes spent relaxing will produce immeasurable results.

If the technique below makes you nervous or agitated, you may be someone who needs to relax by doing something physical. If so, see "Moving into Your Bodies" for relaxing movement ideas.

Relax

If the idea of recording your own meditation tape overwhelms you, I've listed a couple of guided relaxation tapes at the end of this chapter.

Take turns reading the instructions to each other, or record them on tape while playing relaxing music in the background, like *The Source* by Osami Kitajima. Read v-e-r-y slowly, pausing for twenty seconds to a minute at the ellipses (. . .). It helps to imagine yourself doing the meditation and pace yourself accordingly.

Lie or sit down in a comfortable position. Make sure your body is fully supported. Uncross your legs and arms. Close your eyes. Begin to breathe deeply, as deep into your chest as you can, exhaling slowly. . . . Allow yourself to breathe more deeply, down into your belly. . . . Exhaling slowly. . . . Taking your time. There is no place else to be but here, nothing else to do but relax. . . .

Now as you breathe in, imagine you are inhaling a color. Any color you choose. . . . Imagine this color flowing through your body. . . . Gently pouring into any tense or blocked areas. . . . Dissolving tightness, heaviness. . . . As you exhale, feel all unwanted feelings leaving your body. Continue releasing and letting go, breathing in color, breathing out any tension in your body.

Now see your beautiful color beginning to fill your mind. . . . All unwanted thoughts are pushed out. . . . As you exhale, feel all your worries, all your harsh judgments about yourself, all your severe expectations, flowing out. . . . Until your mind is still and tranquil as a rock at the bottom of a clear lake or as quiet as a museum on a Monday morning. . . .

Direct your color to your heart. . . . Feel the color's loving, healing action massaging your heart, warming and releasing any blocked emotions. . . . Softening old hurts. . . . Again, with each exhalation, letting go of whatever tired or heavy emotions you wish. . . . Allowing yourself to breathe even deeper, open and easy. . . . Free and relaxed. . . .

You are now filled with a sense of well-being and peace, feeling centered and ready for whatever you wish to do next.

Resources:

Breath Sweeps Mind: A First Guide to Meditation Practice, edited by Jean Smith (Riverhead Books, 1998). Essays by various well-known authors offering easy-to-follow advice on all aspects of meditating.

Instant Calm, by Paul Wilson (Dutton/Plume, 1999). Quick-fix solutions to relieve the stress of daily life.

Personal Reflections and Meditations, by Bernie Siegal. Audiotape. Harper Audio, available in bookstores. Four guided meditations.

The Art of Breathing and Centering, by Gay Hendricks, Ph.D. Audiotape. Order from Audio Renaissance Tapes, 5858 Wilshire Blvd., Suite 205, Los Angeles, CA 90036. Simple and effective breathing exercises.

The Blooming Lotus: Guided Meditation Exercises for Healing and Transformation, by Thich Nhat Hanh (Beacon Press, 1993). Simple calming exercises to open the heart and restore inner balance.

Music:

Inward Journey: Music from Health Journeys by Steven Mark Kohn, *Detaching the World,* Vol. 1: *Ambient Music for Massage/Relaxation/Meditation.*

Websites:

Health Journeys—visit the Desk Spa
http://www.healthjourneys.com

Seven Masters
http://www.johnselby.com

Your Daily Affirmation
http://www.yourdailyaffirmation.com

When I Think of
Nurturing the Relationship...

When to Do It:

- When you have no idea what the word *nurture* means when applied to relationships or adults.

- When you think nurturing is something only women can do.

- When one person feels she or he always instigates change within the relationship.

- When one partner wants to play a greater role in nurturing the relationship.

What Is It?

Each person and each couple has a different definition, a different set of parameters, of feelings, of dos and don'ts, around nurturing. Define the concept of nurturing for yourself. Defining moments are ripe moments, teeming with insight. Also, defining nurturing eliminates confusion and untangles expectations; what you think of nurturing and what I think of nurturing will inevitably be two different things. And, like all the exercises, it offers an opportunity for you to perceive more nuances, further gradations of desire and sensuality, about each other.

As a wise woman once said, "To me, any good relationship, any working relationship, is inherently a nurturing relationship." Recognize what you are already doing to nourish each other, and then pinpoint what you might experiment with in the future.

You'll Need:

Your beliefs about relationships.

Paper or your "couple's journal" (described in a following chapter), and pens.

Small, self-sticking labels. (Little sticky labels found in office supply stores.)

Time needed: Two sections require ten to twenty minutes, but it is not necessary to do them together. One section takes only a minute or two a day.

See "Introduction: What Does 'Nurturing a Relationship' Mean?" for more.

What to Do:

Explorations: Nurturing the Relationship

Complete each sentence stem as many times as you can. You can do this in writing or by verbally giving your responses. Be empathetic and listen carefully to your partner.

When I think of nurturing the relationship, I think of . . .

When I think of intimacy, I think of . . .

When I think of compassion, I think of . . .

When I think of tenderness, I think of . . .

When I think of commitment, I think of . . .

When I think of sacrifice, I think of . . .

These questions open up a dialogue about an area few couples ever discuss. Talk about what you learned with your lover.

Signs of Nurturing

The aim of this checklist is to help you identify areas in which you and your lover show caring now and areas you don't, pinpointing places you might want to improve. There is *no right or wrong way to do this*, no scoring afterward. The exercise is designed to make you more conscious of your own strengths as an individual and as a couple. It is not meant to make you feel inadequate or to start a fight.

Read and rate each question. If the question doesn't apply, skip it. If you want to do it alone, that's up to you. Proceed in your own way at your pace.

1 = never	2 = occasionally	3 = most of the time	4 = always

PARTNER 1   PARTNER 2

_____ _____ How often do you relax with your partner?

1 = never	2 = occasionally	3 = most of the time	4 = always

_____ _____ How often do you show your partner you care?

_____ _____ How often do you experience a moment of conscious connection?

_____ _____ When is your relationship your first priority?

_____ _____ How often do you spend time alone with your partner?

_____ _____ How often do you give your partner alone time?

_____ _____ Can you say no to your partner without feeling guilty?

_____ _____ Can you see things from your partner's side, even when you disagree?

_____ _____ Do you help when your partner is overwhelmed or anxious?

_____ _____ Can you appreciate the rhythms of your relationship, the ups and downs, the changes, without getting upset?

_____ _____ Do you consider your partner your equal?

_____ _____ Do you use pet names or other endearments?

_____ _____ How often do you show physical affection (holding hands, hugs, and so forth)?

_____ _____ How often do you remember to care for yourself and your own needs?

_____ _____ Can you welcome your differences of opinion?

_____ _____ Do you accept your partner's weak points?

1 = never	2 = occasionally	3 = most of the time	4 = always

_____ _____ How often do you nurture your support team:
friends, family, community?

_____ _____ How often do you indulge your sensuous side?

_____ _____ How often do you play together, get silly,
have fun?

_____ _____ How often do you nurture your spiritual selves?

_____ _____ How often do you let go and totally trust
each other?

_____ _____ Can you forgive your partner when he or she
hurts you?

If you like, talk about the questions where your and your partner's ratings differ widely. Can you deduce anything from these discrepancies? Are the questions you answered "never" areas you would like to improve? Don't forget to congratulate each other on the number 4s!

Recognize What You Are Already Doing Well

We tend to ignore the good things about our relationships and focus on the negative aspects. This exercise helps to overcome the obstacles that may be preventing you from noticing your partner's good deeds. It is based on the work of Mark Kane Goldstein, a psychologist at the University of Florida.

Get your little sticky labels. For one week, each time your lover does something you consider nurturing, take a sticker and stick it in your "scoring" area. Each partner needs a separate "scoring" area. The wall by your office phone, over the kitchen sink, and inside your briefcase or appointment calendar are possibilities. At the end of each week, count your stickers. Then take turns expressing your appreciation for each nurturing act that caused you to "stick a sticker." (Don't turn this into a competition. Make it a feast of appreciation instead.)

What Couples Wrote

Here are some excerpts in answer to the question "What does nurturing your relationship mean to you?" asked of couples across the United States.

"Nurturing means working every day to support each other, to listen, to be loving." LYNN AND PAUL STUBENRAUCH

"The water and nutrients that keep it healthy and growing—the garden of your life. You can cultivate weeds or flowers." MELINDA AND VINCE

"Individuality within a relationship."

"Being present in the relationship is very important." CHRIS MOSIO

"Understanding your relationship, knowing that each is unique, and not trying to force your relationship into someone's ideal mold. To nurture it is to believe in it as it is."

"My concept of nurturing is one of acceptance and appreciation. . . . Remind them and compliment them on their strengths all the time." MIKE VOSBURG

"Taking time for just us! We're all so programmed to be productive, yet after problems arise from not taking time for us, everyone looks at you and says, 'You've got to stop being so productive and take time for yourself and your relationship.'" JENNIFER TAYLOR

"Letting the stiff urban guard down. Talking honestly about all things. Especially moments of undigested past trauma." BEN AND SOPHIE

"Working at coming to grips with our differences and supporting each other's career dreams/goals. Trying to get to know each other better in terms of what we feel and think. Making time for physical intimacy (sex, cuddling). Also, giving each other space, accepting each other's moods."

Answer the question "What does nurturing your relationship mean to you?" Post your answers where you can see them easily. Feel free to add to them or rewrite them as you change and expand your idea of nurturing each other.

Resources:

Busy but Balanced: Practical and Inspirational Ways to Create a Calmer, Closer Family, by Mimi Doe (Griffin, 2001). An elegant, realistic how-to manual.

Conscious Loving, by Gay Hendricks, Ph.D., and Kathlyn Hendricks, Ph.D. (Bantam Books, 1990). Excellent relationship guidance and exercises.

Fifty-two Simple Ways to Say "I Love You," by Stephen Arterburn and Carl Dreizler (Oliver-Nelson Books, 1991). Easily digestible ideas to help you grow stronger together.

Loving What Is, by Byron Katie with Stephen Mitchell (Harmony Books, 2002). Learn how to use a process called "The Work" to transform negative feelings into a new reality.

Lovingkindness: The Revolutionary Art of Happiness, by Sharon Salzberg (Shambhala, 1997). A compassionate guide.

Soul Mates, by Thomas Moore (HarperCollins, 1994). An exploration of relationships of all kinds and how they enrich us.

The Five Love Languages: How to Express Heartfelt Commitment to Your Mate, by Gary Chapman (Northfield Publishers, 1992). Guides couples toward a better understanding of their unique love languages.

Music:

The Silent Path by Robert Haig Coxon, *Seven Metals* by Benjamin Iobst, *Canyon Trilogy* by Carlos Nakai, *Silence Follows Rain* by various artists, *Lux Vivens: The Music of Hildegard von Bingen* by Jocelyn Montgomery, *And the Stars Go with You* by Jonn Serrie.

Website:

Conscious Loving
http://www.consciousloving.com

Ease into Nurturing Each Other

When to Do It:

- When your heart is thudding in panic at the idea of caring for your partner.

- When time constraints often waylay your more elaborate plans.

- When you are clueless about what your partner likes or wants.

What Is It?

Does the idea of nurturing each other mystify you? Overwhelm you? Make you feel slightly fearful or uneasy? You are not alone. Several couples interviewed expressed fear about nurturing each other and fear around reading this book. "What if I find out something I don't want to know?" or "If it ain't broke, don't fix it."

People fear change. We fear expressing our needs and desires to our lover. Making a clear request means that I am a separate person, not part of the comfort and protection of the royal "we" where we find such delicious refuge. The dynamics of personal relationship are such that when change does occur, there is an equal move by one or both parties to return to the status quo. All of this makes the seemingly uncomplicated and pleasurable act of caring for each other more fraught with difficulties than is at first apparent.

So start small. Small is beautiful. Melt into having a more conscious, appreciative connection. Forgo the gung-ho, "our relationship will be perfect by noon tomorrow" attitude. Share your anxiety. Give it some space. Glide (don't charge) into the glow of a nourishing, deeply rooted relationship.

You'll Need:

Specific items called for by your partner, perhaps a kind word, a loving back rub, a juicy kiss, or a pat on the shoulder.

Time required: Two minutes to however long you like.

See "Bringing the Book Home: Fear" for more.

What to Do:

Make a List

Complete the sentence stem below. Come up with as many conclusions as you can—ten, twenty, or even thirty. Focus on specific, positive items, but don't censor yourself. Record *all* your reactions, even if they seem too wild or impossible.

I feel loved and nurtured when you . . .

Hold my hand in a movie.

Initiate morning lovemaking.

Catch my eyes across a crowded room and wink.

Dance in sexy underwear.

Trade lists with your partner. Once a day, even if you don't feel like it, choose one item from your partner's list and carry it out. Don't tell your partner which one; surprise him or her. If there are items on your sweetheart's list you don't feel comfortable doing, skip those. Feel free to repeat pleasures that go over particularly well. After two weeks, set aside fifteen or so minutes to talk about what this has been like. Concentrate on imprinting into your consciousness the likes and dislikes of your best beloved.

See "Recognizing Your Needs: Investigate Complaints" and "Reminisce and Rekindle: Remember When We Used To . . ."

See Your Partner Anew

Do you ever find yourself looking at your lover and not really seeing him or her? It is an awful, dull feeling. Open your heart and behold your mate by focusing on one aspect of his or her being at a time. Examine hair, nose, a little finger. Listen to your mate talk with your eyes closed, and memorize her voice. Study the wrinkles on his hands. Study your lover from across a crowded room. Reacquaint yourself with your partner's unique beauty. Get past the blur of familiarity.

See "Creative Connection: Sex and Painting."

Express Your Love

Compliment your partner in specific, particular, singular ways. Tell your
lover you delight in the way he or she giggles, makes a cup of chocolate
mocha coffee, wraps her legs around you when you make love, grows
sweet peas, or makes potato soup. Daphne Rose Kingma writes, "Compliments invite the person who is complimented to embrace a new perception of him or herself. And just as layers and layers of nacre form a pearl
over an irritating grain of sand, so compliments collect around us,
developing us in all our beauty."

*See "Everyday Rituals"
and "Gratify and
Delight" for more ways
to express your love.*

No Change for the Day

For one day, accept your partner. When you find yourself opening your
mouth to preach, cajole, push, or complain, close it and your eyes.
Imagine your partner wrapped in a soft, golden light. Or imagine your
partner as an innocent child. Spend thirty seconds with this image in
your mind's eye.

See "Acceptance."

Do It by the Alphabet

Each week, nurture each other according to the letter of the week. For
example, begin at A (a logical place) and work your way to Z. The first
week you might bake your partner an Apple pie, Applaud your partner
(also known as a Standing ovation, so you can use it again during the S
week), or give your sweetheart an Antidote to stress (a hug and dry
martini, or a cold compress and fifteen minutes alone listening to Bach).
There is plenty of room for humor and inventive play. Keep it simple to
avoid being overwhelmed. (Remember, you are starting small.)

*See "Writing Your Own
Comfort Book" for more
ways to dream up shared
merriment.*

Queen or King for an Hour

Flip a coin to see who will go first. The partner who wins the coin toss
rules for the next hour. Agree ahead of time that no request is out of
bounds; the person of the hour is to be treated to whatever he or she
wishes. When the hour is up (use a timer), the next person is crowned for
his or her hour of royalty.

*See "Gratify and
Delight" for queenly and
kingly raptures.*

Support

Next Monday, when you wake up or over breakfast, ask each other,
"What can I do this week to support you in your goals?" Decide on one
simple, small action from what your partner tells you and carry it out.

Give Each Other Permission to Do Nothing

See "Daily
Communication:
Breathing Together."

Find ten minutes to cuddle each other, look into each other's eyes, and do
nothing else. Start your do-nothing time by giving each other permission.
"Herb, I give you permission to lie here and do nothing." "Diana, I give
you permission to lie here and do nothing." Concentrate on breathing
and being together. When (not if) worries, pressing concerns, or a yard-
long to-do list intrudes on your relaxation, focus back on your partner's
eyes and cuddle closer.

Take Advantage of Differences

See "Acceptance."

Instead of turning a difference of taste into a power struggle, use it as an
opportunity to be sweet to your beloved. My friend John likes to watch
the TV news. His wife Anita prefers playing environmental tapes. So
instead of flipping the TV on, John pops in an ocean tape. "I make a
special effort a few times a week to initiate listening to what I know she
likes. So she knows I'm happy to subordinate my preferences to hers."
Simple as flossing your teeth but just as difficult to remember.

Dealing with Being Closer

See "Winds of the
Heavens" and "Self-
Care in Relationships"
for more.

After doing one of the activities in this chapter (or anywhere in the
book) or after a period of intense closeness, take time away from each
other. Be gentle and conscious by talking about your fears around being
open and intimate. Try to communicate to your partner how you feel
about nurturing him or her—good and bad feelings. Allow yourself to feel
ambivalent and to pull away, but do it consciously. Being close brings up
lots of intense reactions, and you need rest time away from each other to
prevent distancing fights.

Resources:

How to Be in Adult Relationships, by David Richo (Shambhala, 2002).
An honest perspective on becoming a more loving and realistic
person.

1,001 Ways to Be Romantic, by Gregory J. P. Godek (Casablanca Press,
1993). If it isn't in here, it probably doesn't exist.

Opening to Love 365 Days a Year, by Judith Sherven and James
Sniechowski (Health Communications, 2000). Page-a-day reflections
offering direct, uncomplicated guidance.

The Couple's Tao Te Ching: Ancient Advice for Modern Lovers, by William
Martin (Marlowe and Company, 2000). Extraordinarily rich and nurturing.

The Romantic's Guide: Hundreds of Creative Tips for a Lifetime of Love, by
Michael Webb (Hyperion, 2000). Another creative romance
resource.

*True Love: How to Make Your Relationship Sweeter, Deeper, and More Pas-
sionate,* by Daphne Rose Kingma (Conari Press, 1991). Witty little
book; works well as a reminder to stay in touch and work on your
love.

Website:

Loving You
http://www.lovingyou.com

A Couple's Journal

You'll Need:

A sturdy bound book. I like the black ones from the art supply store. Three-hole notebooks are okay, but they can encourage editing via ripping out pages. Find a journal with pages that lie flat. I don't recommend fancy books, because you may feel you can only write polite, fancy things inside.

You can also use a file folder and write on loose paper and collect the pages.

Pens you find easy to write with.

Time required: Five to ten minutes to write, then an occasional verbal check-in.

When to Do It:

- When you want to communicate but you can't find the time.

- When you need to discuss touchy issues and it would be easier to do so in writing.

- When you and your partner keep fighting every time you try to discuss a particular subject.

What Is It?

A couple's journal is a safe and creative place in which to share uncensored thoughts and feelings as well as express and sometimes transform anger, frustrations, and fears. It is a territory where you can discover intimate knowledge about your best beloved. Although keeping a journal is usually thought of as a solitary pursuit, it is an unparalleled tool for improving communication between lovers.

Writing can allow you to detect deeper feelings, feelings that talking can't always uncover. By using different techniques, like writing with the non-dominant hand (the hand you don't usually use), stream-of-consciousness writing (writing whatever occurs to you without editing or stopping), or timed writing (using a timer to build tension), you can bypass your internal censors and discover ideas and feelings that were below the surface.

Keeping a journal together is also a satisfying way to keep in touch when your schedules are in conflict. There are days when my partner comes home from working all night and our day together consists of a quick hug in bed, as he lies down and I get up. Still, we can each find five minutes in our separate days to connect in our couple's journal. It keeps our love from getting lost in life's shuffle.

Finally, your couple's journal offers a place to chronicle your relationship. You can create a memoir of your shared life. Capture how you survived building your house or remember the epiphany you had about why you always get angry when he drives. Recording your answers to the various Explorations and other writing exercises in this book is a great place to start this history of your commitment.

What to Do:

Journal Guidelines

Keeping a couple's journal is an act of courageous communication. A balance is needed between the free-flowing I-can-write-anything of personal journal writing and the need to respect your partner's feelings. This balance can be achieved with a few guidelines.

1. Never make fun of what your mate has written. Don't bring up material from the journal during a fight. Don't share what is written in the journal with another person.

2. Remember that this is *raw* material. Written words on a page can take on a powerful, permanent quality. Try to remember the words are coming straight from the heart, unedited. Keep your sense of humor, and remember, nothing is written in stone.

3. If you are in doubt about whether to write something, consider this question: What is my hoped-for result? If it is to manipulate, injure, or impress, reconsider.

4. Above all, aspire to be honest and caring in what you write.

When and How

Decide *together* how often and approximately how long or how much you will write in your journal. Once a day for three months? Twice a week for a month? Once a week for six months? Make a defined commitment to each other, and write this in the front of your journal to avoid confusion.

One way journal keeping could work: You come home from work and spend fifteen minutes relaxing before making dinner. This is the time you like to write in the journal. Your partner prefers to write just before bed. You pick a topic and write it across the top of the page, then write as long as you feel like it (although you have agreed to always try to write at least a paragraph). You put the book back in its special place by your bed. That night, your partner reads what you wrote, then writes. The next time you write, you read what she or he wrote and either respond or add to it, or you pick a new topic and start a new entry. And so your journal grows.

Talking About What You've Written

Decide ahead of time how you will discuss what you've been writing. Will you have a weekly check-in, or will you bring up insights or questions based on journal entries anytime? Be clear. Some couples feel that writing their innermost thoughts is okay, but discussing them face-to-face is too touchy. If this is the case, it helps to make a small ritual out of talking about journal material. Other couples like to weave the journal stuff right into their lives. Decide *before* you start writing.

Dealing with Resistance

For additional topics to write about, see "Bringing the Book Home: Explorations"; "When I Think of Nurturing the Relationship"; "Recognizing Your Needs"; "Women and Men Nurturing Each Other"; "Nurturing Your Relationship Through Money"; "Self-Care in Relationships"; "The Art of Gift Giving"; "Erotic Delights"; "Nesting"; and "Divine Sustenance."

Keeping a journal together does require commitment and effort. The first or second week, one of you will most likely hit some resistance. Use this resistance. Write about why you don't want to write. Stream-of-consciousness writing works well for exploring resistance, as does timed writing. *Immediately* after making an entry, reward yourself with something that makes you feel good—a baseball game with your son, frozen yogurt, or a favorite old movie.

Journal Topics

Here are some possible topics to get you started. If you find these topics boring or overwhelming, by all means, ignore them or adapt them to whatever you would like.

Sentence Completion

Complete each sentence as many times as you can. Push past the obvious, the polite, the mundane. Each sentence can function as a journal entry. These are good entries to use when you are feeling blocked or are especially busy.

I feel good when . . .

I feel afraid when . . .

I feel angry when . . .

I feel happy when . . .

When you are ill, I feel . . .

When you brag about me, I feel . . .

When I yell or nag at you, I feel . . .

When you take care of the children, I feel . . .

When we make love, I feel . . .

One of the things I would like to be appreciated for is . . .

One of the things I wished you understood about me is . . .

When we go out with other people, I like you to . . .

One of the things that first attracted me to you was . . .

All my life I . . .

What Does Comfort Mean?

What childhood memories do you have of being comforted? To help you focus, think back to a specific age. When you think of nurturing, what comes to mind? Do you have any fears around being comforted? Would you rather be comforted by someone or comfort someone else?

See "Getting to Know You: What Did Mommy or Daddy Do?" for additional insight into patterns of childhood comfort.

Delight

Do you have enough pleasure and delight in your life? What are your beliefs about pleasure, sensuality, enjoyment, ecstasy? Is it okay to please yourself? Do you always come last? Does work always come first? How hard is it for you to relax and let go? Using your nondominant hand, quickly list twenty ways you could get more pleasure into your life. Then, have your journal companion respond with twenty ideas, also using his or her nondominant hand.

See "Ease into Nurturing Each Other: Do It by the Alphabet"; "But There's Nothing to Do"; and "Writing Your Own Comfort Book" for more pleasure possibilities.

When the World Is Moving Too Fast

Write about the stress you presently feel. Tune in to the feelings in your body by writing very, very slowly. Feel your hand forming the words. Breathe deeply, and slow everything down.

You can **Relax** before doing this.

Appreciation

Do a timed writing for five minutes listing everything you love about your partner. Pour out all the appreciation you haven't had time to share.

See "Ease into Nurturing Each Other: Express Your Love"; and "Everyday Rituals: Evening."

Make a list of everything you have to celebrate in your life—accomplishments, happy days you've shared, health of family members. Add to it when you feel down, and reread it when you feel defeated. Or make a list of everything you love in your life or everything that gives you satisfaction or everything that turns you on or everything that gives you joy. Create a record of shared joy and bliss.

Details

We can forget to recount to our loved one the nuances of our day. This can erode trust and communication. Record the details of today: what jokes you heard, what the baby did, who stepped on your feelings. Get into the minutiae.

Becoming Intimate

Sages, mystics, and lovers have written volumes trying to define love.
What is your definition? What were your childhood messages about love?
Did your family openly display affection? Are you more inclined to
communicate your love by personal sharing or by doing things for your
beloved? How often do you say "I love you" to your partner when you
mean something else, like "I appreciate you," "I want you to do this for
me," or "Thank you"?

*See "Couple Customs:
A World of Your Own."*

Celebrate a specific erotic experience by describing it in detail. It doesn't
have to be intercourse: it could be eating a tart, luscious apple in the sun
or the feel of warm, clean towels against your skin as you fold the laundry
or a hard, firm welcome-home hug. Share a sensual experience with your
partner.

Conflicts

Name what you are frustrated about in your life right at this moment.
Name what frustrated you yesterday. You can name more than one
thing. Name the last infuriating thing your partner did. Can you take any
action to transform or avoid any of these frustrations? How can your partner help you?

Pick a recurring argument that has never been resolved. State your version of it and what you would like to have happen. Avoid blaming your
partner; stick to how *you* feel, what *you* want to have happen, and why.

*See "Releasing
Resentment."*

Support Systems

Is it okay for you to ask others to help you? Do you feel that when someone does you a favor, you must hurry and balance the scales? Are there
areas of your life where it is more difficult to ask for help than others?
What are they? Are there certain things you can ask your partner to do
and others you can't?

*See "Community
Context: Exploration."*

Continuing Journaling

Pick up a book about journal writing, and adapt it to your couple's journal. See "Resources" for ideas.

Use timed writing, especially when you are busy. One partner picks a topic. He or she writes the topic at the top of the page and also how long to write for, say five minutes. Take turns picking topics and times.

Have one journal companion write a stream-of-consciousness piece. Then have the other person keep going with it. To get started, pick a headline from today's paper or a sentence from a favorite book. You can write about the state of your relationship, love, your children, how you feel today, your job, your house, your body, the garden, last weekend, the last fight you had. The trick is to just let go and see where the writing takes you.

Generate a list of topics in the process of living your life—global concerns, vacation plans, a movie you saw together. List them on the inside of the journal whenever they occur to you, and use them when you need something to write about.

Most important, write about what is currently happening in your life. Spend a few minutes recording what you would like your partner to know about your concerns, your inner life, your hopes. Focus on nurturing the relationship by communicating *frequently.*

Resources:

How You Do Anything Is How You Do Everything: A Workbook, by Cheri Huber (Zen Meditation Center, 1998). A workbook that encourages you to write, draw, color, paint, cut, and paste your way to inner discovery. Do it together, or take turns doing sections and then share them.

Putting Your Heart on Paper, by Henriette Anne Klauser (Bantam Books, 1995). Communicate your deepest thoughts and feelings.

SoulCollage: An Intuitive Collage Process for Individuals and Groups, by
Seena B. Frost (Hanford Mead Publishers, 2001).

Sunbeams: A Book of Quotations, edited by Sy Safransky (North Atlantic
Books, 1990). A gem of a quote book. Use this to find quotes to
express your feelings.

The Healing Journey for Couples: Your Journal of Mutual Discovery, by Phil
Rich and Stuart Copans (John Wiley and Sons, 1998). Sixty journal-
ing exercises.

The Secret of Staying in Love, by John Powell (Thomas More, 1995). An
excellent section in the back on keeping a journal together.

Soul Strokes

You'll Need:

Time alone.

Patience to practice.

A timer that doesn't tick loudly.

Time required: Anywhere from ten minutes to however long you wish to speak.

When to Do It:

- When you feel lonely in the relationship.

- When you often find yourself complaining, "We never talk about anything!"

- When you believe honest communication between men and women is fundamentally impossible.

- When you are so wrapped up in your job, you walk right past your lover when you go to meet him for lunch. Or you are so busy with the kids, she comes home from work and you automatically yell at her to do her homework before she goes out to play.

What Is It?

The most important thing you can do to keep your relationship alive is to listen to your partner. We all want to be heard. It doesn't mean we have to agree with each other, but it does mean that we are willing to listen with an open heart.

Unfortunately, this simple and profound gift is often severely neglected or complicated. The purpose of soul strokes is to provide you with straight-forward guidelines to help you connect on a *daily* basis through clear communication. Soul strokes are designed to help with that nasty gender problem, "He never talks" or "She never listens." Soul strokes are *not* about problem solving or about fighting. Soul strokes are about being heard and validated, *without having to agree or solve anything*.

The most effective way to nurture a relationship is to communicate regularly and openly. Or as award-winning writer and mother of six Tamera Smith Allred says in her book *On the Homefront*, "We try to spend 30 minutes a day, every day, talking and sharing our feelings alone. When we are talking we do not try to fix, change, or challenge the other person. We seek to listen, to understand the other's feelings.

We have learned that the deepest longing of the human heart is to be heard and understood." Couples that thrive spend time alone talking on a daily basis. Yet studies show most couples spend less than thirty minutes a week talking about intimate subjects. Nothing destroys a healthy relationship faster than lack of communication.

If you are muttering to yourself, "I don't have time for this mushy nonsense," consider the question, *How important is your relationship to you?* Is it worth an hour of your time a week? Fifteen minutes a day? You find time for exercise, TV, and countless other things. Find time for your relationship.

Use soul strokes for keeping in touch daily and for dealing with the "I want to talk but he (or she) doesn't" blues. Used regularly, it is the most effective tool in this book for staying in touch and building intimacy.

What to Do:

Soul Strokes, the Foundation of Nurturing a Relationship

Below is a six-step plan for improving communication. Don't skip a step. It may seem complex at first, but it will quickly become second nature. There is an overview of the steps at the end of the chapter. Use that for quick review until the process becomes your own.

Step 1: Pick the right time and place. A discussion should not be broached as one person is rushing around the house searching for the keys and hyperventilating about being late for an appointment. The right time means no one is exhausted, doing something else, angry, or otherwise distracted. The right place means you can give each other your full attention and open your hearts without being interrupted or inhibited.

Step 2: Show up. Communication is possible only if both partners are present. This is what is meant by having a "conscious relationship." Showing up is hard work. Before you begin, take a few deep breaths, concentrating on breathing out your worries and distractions. You can also **Relax** together before stroking each other's souls.

See "About Relaxing" for instructions.

Concentrate on staying present while your partner is talking. Your attention might wander, you will want to yawn or squirm, or you will be stricken with a sudden burning desire to jump up and get some ice cream or wash the dog or organize your sock drawer. These are all internal indicators that what is being talked about is hitting a cord with you. Take a deep breath and focus on your partner.

Watch your language. Soul strokes are not about fighting, blaming, or problem solving. Watch out for statements that point a finger at your partner. Stay away from "you" statements ("You always do that and it drives me crazy"). Stick to "I" statements about how *you* feel.

Empathy. Before you begin, close your eyes and ask yourself, "How does my partner feel right now?" Open your heart and see the upcoming discussion from his or her point of view. Whenever you feel yourself getting bored or resisting what your mate is saying, close your eyes and ask yourself, "How does my partner feel right now?"

See "Empathy" for additional insight.

Step 3: Pick a subject. What is happening in your life right now is a favorite, but anything goes as long as it isn't about blaming.

Stay on the subject, and talk about the same one. One partner states the subject to be discussed. Then the other person restates the subject the way he or she understands it. If necessary, keep doing this back and forth until you both agree on what you are talking about. *Stick to that subject only.* This step is important because huge globs of frustration are produced in conversations between lovers because of subject skipping. No one feels heard if one person talks about one subject, then his or her partner responds by talking about something completely different.

Step 4: Start with an appreciation. After getting clear on what you are talking about but before you start in on what you are going to say, state something you appreciate about your partner today. "I appreciate your taking the kids out this afternoon," "I appreciate your kissing me good morning," "I appreciate the way you smiled at me in the car."

Note: It is wonderful to start any conversation or discussion with a tender, thankful statement.

Step 5: Have your say. Use your time to say anything you wish about the subject at hand. Express yourself. Luxuriate in being heard.

The person listening *does not interrupt.* The person listening *pays attention.* This can be very difficult, yet it is the most important part of the process. Stay present and maintain eye contact. Soul strokes do *not* work if one partner is filing fingernails, flipping TV channels, sighing repeatedly, or finishing sentences for the other.

When the time is up, switch roles. The partner who has been listening now receives the same amount of time to talk about his or her side of the same subject. Try not to stray into other subjects.

You can continue switching back and forth, reacting to what has been said by your partner in the previous round.

Step 6: End with a big hug. Try it, even if you don't feel like it. The aim is to say, "I still love you," even if you don't feel very loving in this moment.

To sum up:

1. Pick the right time and place. Not when you are exhausted or distracted.

2. Show up. Take some deep breaths. Watch your language. Not blaming or problem solving, but expressing and being heard. Empathize.

3. Make sure you are both talking about the same subject.

4. State something you appreciate about your partner before you begin.

5. Have your say. Listen *without interruption* and *with full attention.*

6. Big hug. (Kisses are good too.)

Can't Talk?

There are times when one person can't think of anything to say during his or her time. There are several things you can do:

Stick to nonthreatening subjects.

Be patient and be an example by opening your heart up first and taking a risk. Sometimes one person has to give more, a lot more, before the other person can start.

Do the meditation in "Reminisce and Rekindle" before you begin.

Clear your resentments doing the exercises in "Releasing Resentment."

Use the suggestions below to jump-start the conversation.

What to Talk About

For daily or weekly check-ins, here are some suggestions for what to talk about.

Many couples use soul strokes around the daily subject of "What Happened in My Life Today" without getting into complaining or fighting.

Do the "I feel, I need, I want" exercise in "Everyday Rituals: Transition Rituals." This works nicely as an opener.

Tell your lover five specific things that make him or her a pleasure to live with or three things he or she did today that you cherished.

To combat the "I want to talk but he or she doesn't" syndrome, use the sentence stems below. Finish the sentences by facing each other and verbally giving your answers. Say *whatever comes into your mind*, as quickly as possible, without self-criticism or censorship. The less you ponder, the more easily you can get past the obvious and into more personal revelations. Accept that you will feel resistance. You will feel you have nothing more to say. Keep going.

Topics for deepening intimacy can also be found in "Bringing the Book Home"; "When I Think of Nurturing the Relationship"; "Recognizing Your Needs"; and "A Couple's Journal."

You could help me talk about my feelings more by . . .

If I weren't concerned about what you thought . . .

Sometimes, I become frightened when communicating with you because . . .

One of the things I would like you to know about me is . . .

One of the things I would like you to appreciate about me is . . .

If I were more able to let you see how much I love you . . .

If I were able to be more open about my feelings . . .

I've noticed recently about myself . . .

A Little Twist

Some couples like to add an extra step. After each person has had his or her turn, they do a round of talking using one of two sentence stems. This can be useful if soul stroking feels too one-sided for you.

As I listened to you, I felt . . .

As I expressed my thoughts and feelings to you, I felt . . .

Practice

Keep doing it. Make a shared goal to have a soul stroking talk every day for a week. The more you do it, the easier it gets. Don't give in to boredom and status quo! *Seize the Relationship!*

Resources:

365 Questions for Couples, by Michael Beck (Adams Media Corp., 1999).
Grow closer by asking and answering thought-provoking questions.

Website:

PAIRS
http://www.pairs.com

Topics for deepening intimacy are also in "Women and Men Nurturing Each Other"; "Nurturing Your Relationship Through Money"; "The Art of Gift Giving"; "Getting to Know You"; "Nesting"; "Erotic Delights"; and "Divine Sustenance."

Daily Communication

You'll Need:

A sense of humor.

Time needed: All sections require three minutes or so to read, then practice in daily life.

When to Do It:

- When you find yourself arguing heatedly over one partner's driving ability, what kind of trash bags to buy, what color to paint the living room, or any other minor difference of opinion.

- When you are regularly convinced your mate is trying to force you into the mental ward with his or her obtuse articulations.

- When you learn what your weekend plans are by overhearing your mate on the phone with a friend.

What Is It?

Imagine your mate coming through the door at the end of a long day. You've both been working overtime. The baby is whining or the dog is whining or the phone is whining. You are starving. Your beloved flops onto the couch and announces, "I am exhausted!"

What happens? Perhaps you take off her shoes and rub her feet, asking about her day? Or do you demand he makes dinner because doesn't he know you work just as hard as he does and you're exhausted too? Or perhaps you reply, "I'd love to go out to dinner. How sweet of you to ask. Just let me get my coat."

Daily communication between intimates too easily turns into a deadly gauntlet of misunderstandings, headaches, and unmet needs. Stockpiled resentments, critical internal voices, unrealistic expectations, fears of engulfment, and simply not enough time spent keeping each other up-to-date muddy our interactions, making it almost impossible for us to communicate clearly. Add a liberal dash of stress and you can see why a simple statement like "I'm exhausted" can be interpreted as anything from an accusation to a cry for help to an invitation to dinner!

How do you deal with the black hole of communication? Practice soul strokes at least twice a week, and use the exercises in this chapter for smoothing daily interactions. The essence of a committed relationship is found in dealing with the details of life. Approaching these details in a loving, clear manner can eliminate an awful lot of hassle and pain.

See "Soul Strokes."

What to Do:

Developing an Open Heart

Cultivate an open-minded, loving attitude. Believe your mate has good intentions. How often do you conclude your partner is opening his or her mouth only to annoy you, is being deliberately dense, or secretly hates you but won't admit it? *Give your sweetheart the benefit of the doubt.* Let's say you are at a party. Your partner spots you and mouths, "I want to go home." But you're having a great time. Instead of thinking he or she is trying to squelch your happiness, take a deep breath and believe "I want to go home" is simply a straightforward request, nothing more. Forget mind reading. From here, it is easier to offer acknowledgment or open a dialogue for compromise. *Assume your partner is innocent and has good (or at least neutral) intentions!*

See "Empathy" and "Acceptance" for more about being open.

Keep in Touch

Life is too complex. One of the simplest things you can do to nurture your partner is let her or him know what is going on with you on a day-to-day basis. Create a message center in your home where you not only record phone messages and leave mail, but where you also post your shared calendar. On this calendar you may schedule things to do together but also make notes about important things going on in your life, and even not-so-important things. Get in the habit of leaving each other notes saying, "Remember my interview on Friday" or "Eric gets his report card Thursday."

See "Togetherness Time: Putting It All Together" for one way to construct a shared calendar. See also "Ease into Nurturing Each Other: Support" and "A Couple's Journal: Details."

Schedule daily check-in sessions. Include more than dry information. Name one feeling you had today or one bodily sensation or one personal revelation.

See "Everyday Rituals: Transition Rituals" for a great ritual, "I feel," "I need," "I want."

Watch Out for Generalizations

Leave generalizations for bad sitcoms. Avoid statements like, "He or she never listens." Just because he didn't listen to you when you told him about the concert on Friday night does not mean he didn't listen to you when you told him how much you hate your boss on Tuesday morning. According to the men and women I interviewed, nothing is more hurtful than to have all listening (or *all* anything) thrown out because of an occasional attack of early senility or because you were engrossed in *Championship Wrestling*.

Forget Could and Can

When asking for support from either sex, it helps to use the words *would* or *will* instead of *could* or *can*. With the questions "Could you help me wash the dog?" or "Can you help me wash the dog?" your mate might feel you are questioning his or her ability to help and may also feel there is no choice in the matter. "Would you help me wash the dog?" and "Will you help me?" are better; they are clear, personal, and offer a choice.

No Leading Questions

"Are you excited about this weekend?" she says as she blissfully packs for the six-day, sixty-mile desert hike she is dragging you on. Have you noticed that people use the word *excited* in different ways? How often has one person had their feelings bruised after asking the "are you excited about" question and not hearing the answer they want? (The only correct answer is something like, "Of course, I'm excited. I can't wait! I'm so excited I'm going to wet my pants!")

Instead of setting your sweetheart up for failure, try using the all-important *I*. For example, "I am very excited about our survival trip in the desert. I hope you are too, but I am willing to hear how you honestly feel." Or, "I am excited. How do you feel?" Leading a lover to excitement doesn't mean he or she will want to drink.

Nonverbal Communication

Using words to communicate feelings is something most women do better than most men. Women are trained to talk about feelings, to understand the language of emotion and relatedness. Men are not. Women want men to meet them on their turf of talking about feelings. But many men can't because they've never learned how. Yes, men must learn, and many are, but why should all the learning be on men's shoulders? Can't women try to understand, appreciate, and converse in the communication modes men use at the same time men are learning how to express and verbalize their feelings? Try:

See "Women and Men Nurturing Each Other" for more about men and women communicating.

Breathing together: Sit back to back, skin to skin if possible. Close your eyes and **Relax.** Focus on your partner's breath. Begin to breathe with her or him. Establish a pattern together of a slow inhalation, followed by several seconds of holding your breath, then a slow exhalation, and finally a moment's pause before beginning again. Visualize your breath coming in through your nose, going down into your lungs as you inhale, then out through your back and into your partner's lungs as you inhale, then back into your lungs and completing the circle as you exhale. When your mind tries to distract you, simply focus back on the circle of life you are creating together.

See "About Relaxing."

This is a great five-minute "happy hour" after a hard day at work.

Actions: Agree verbally to express your love in deeds, not words, for one week. At the end of the week, get together and list everything your partner did to say "I love you." Then inform your partner (lovingly) of everything you did that he or she missed.

Appreciate the other's silences: Silence does not make intimacy impossible. When one of you feels like talking and the other doesn't, try sitting in silence, holding hands, with your eyes closed. Be in the silence for as

See "Creative Connection: Creative Communication"; "Empathy"; "Reminisce and Rekindle"; and "Moving into Your Bodies: Dancing" and "Moving into Your Bodies: Release" for more nonverbal communication tools.

long as it takes to "communicate" what you are thinking about or to feel "heard."

The "I" Statement

Memorize the all-important "I" statement. Saying "I am feeling happy" instead of "you make me happy" means you take responsibility for your feelings—both good and bad. Avoid "it," "you," "we," "everybody," "always," and "all" statements, especially "you." "You" statements are almost always accusatory and lead to a defensive reaction. "You made me late again today" versus "I was late today and I feel upset about it." "We need to fix the garage" versus "I would like to fix the garage. Would you help me?" "You always ignore me at parties" versus "I felt ignored tonight." Consider your tone of voice and body language as well. If your voice says, "I can't stand you right now," but your words say, "Honey, how wonderful to see you," your partner is going to believe your tone of voice over your words any day.

"Why" Is for Two-Year-Olds

When asking a touchy question, avoid starting with a "why." Instead, begin with an "I" statement, followed by a neutral inquiry. For example, "Why are you late?" triggers a defensive answer while "I was worried. Would you tell me what happened?" sets a more neutral tone.

And And And

Avoid either-or and "This is great but" statements. Forgo "Either you start doing your share of the dog walking or I'm going to get rid of him!" and try instead "I would like you to share equally in taking care of the dog and I will do my share too." Instead of "Thanks for cleaning the bathroom *but* you forgot the toilet," offer "Thanks so much for cleaning the bathroom *and* would you clean the toilet too?" Strive to create win-win situations instead of adversarial or blame scenarios. (If this sounds too Pollyannaish, remember that changing always seems much more impossible than it is.

Consider the rewards for not changing: more miscommunication, needlessly hurt feelings, and alienation.)

Catching the Inner Dialogue in Action

Our inner dialogue is the committee of voices we all have in our heads. This exercise is for clearing up miscommunication *in the moment.* If used regularly and with love, it can drastically improve your outlook on the human race. If unchecked, your inner voices can cause you to be judge, jury, and executioner with your mate without either of you realizing what has happened.

It works like this. Jack comes home from work and says,

JACK: I'm so tired, I really don't feel like cooking tonight.

In a split second, Zoe's inner dialogue spits out a variety of reactions:

ZOE: (in her head) He's trying to make me feel guilty for not cooking. He wants to go out, but he knows we're saving for a new car. He wants to be alone tonight and not talk or cuddle with me. He hates his job, and he's blaming it on me.

Zoe is pretty much unaware of her inner dialogue, and so when the accompanying feelings of guilt, anger, and abandonment bubble to the surface, they are disconnected from the thoughts that caused them. She might start a fight or withdraw or become defensive without being aware of why these reactions are happening.

Stop! When you begin to overreact to a statement made by your partner, indicate you believe you are experiencing distortion and would like to check in. Use the sentence stem "Do you mean. . . ." For example, Zoe asks Jack,

ZOE: Do you mean you wish I were June Cleaver and cooked dinner every night in pearls and nylons?

Jack can answer *only* yes or no—no explanations, no rolling of eyes, no accusations of "How silly can you be?" Zoe keeps asking "Do you mean . . ." until she gets a yes. At this point, she could say, "I'm glad I understand." Or she could ask for a short soul-stroking talk to further discuss her assumptions. Yes, this example is pristine and fairly impossible. Life is never as neat and clean as it is for Zoe and Jack, but this is an effective tool that *does* work in messy, real life. Stop these miscommunication mishaps, because they are the buggers that fester into major arguments. If you can't remember to do this, put some notes around the house to remind you.

Finally

See "Ease into Nurturing Each Other: No Change for the Day" for a related idea.

Many minor disagreements and communication breakdowns happen because one person is feeling unloved. The more often you can start a conversation with "I appreciate you and I love you," the less often you will end up in a misunderstanding.

Resources:

Talk to Me Like Someone You Love: Flashcards for Real Life, by Nancy Dreyfus, Psy.D. (Celestial Arts, 1996). In a moment of pain or miscommunication, you grab this ring of cards, find one that applies, and present it to your partner. Very useful.

The 30 Secrets of Happily Married Couples, by Dr. Paul Coleman (Bob Adams, 1992). Lots of good tidbits, especially about communication.

Nonviolent Communication: A Language of Life: Create Your Life, Your Relationships, and Your World in Harmony with Your Values, by Marshall B. Rosenberg (PuddleDancer Press, 2003). Simply the best! Guidance on identifying and articulating feelings and needs, expressing anger fully, and exploring the power of empathy.

You Just Don't Understand: Women and Men in Conversation, by Deborah Tannen (Random House, 2000). Explains the profoundly different ways men and women communicate, and what to do about it.

Recognizing Your Needs

When to Do It:

- When you or your partner is complaining about feeling unsupported, misunderstood, or undervalued.

- When you feel frustrated with your partner, but you can't put your finger on why.

- When you can't distinguish between what you need and what you want.

- When you have no idea what you need.

What Is It?

A need is something you cannot do without. A want or preference is something you would like to have, but you can do without. Our wants can be meaningful and powerful but sometimes frivolous, and they are almost always negotiable. Our needs are important, both universal and deeply personal, and they are almost never negotiable.

Recognizing wants and needs is the easy part. From here, things get complicated. How do you fill your needs without ignoring your partner's? Aren't needs something we got rid of in the seventies? Aren't needs something only selfish, "me generation" people worry about? Isn't this meaningless psychobabble?

No! Understanding everyone's needs is the cornerstone of couple nurturing, not a descent into pop psychology hell. Read on for needy enlightenment.

What to Do:

Explorations: What Are Needs?

Beyond our physical needs for safety, food, shelter, and rest, we have emotional needs that are just as crucial to our survival. Consider the following list of basic personality needs.

You'll Need:

Your couple's journal or paper, and pens.

Relaxing music and candles (optional).

Time required: Ten to twenty minutes per section. Parts can be done alone or used all together for a total exploration.

To be heard, understood, and known by someone we love

To be touched

To be authentically ourselves

To be accepted for ourselves

To be supported and nurtured

To be trusted and trust others

To be sexual

To have fun

To know our life makes a difference and has a purpose

To be loved

Explore your needs by writing as many completions to each question as you can think of. Or face each other and verbally give your answers by completing each sentence as many times as you can. Say or write *whatever comes into your mind,* as quickly as possible, trying to avoid self-criticism or censorship.

I am a person who needs . . .

Ever since I was little, I have needed . . .

I feel good about needing you to . . .

I am afraid of needing you to . . .

For my partner to nurture me, I need to . . .

To nurture myself, I need to . . .

See "Winds of the
Heavens: Boundaries"
for related issues.

You may learn you have many needs in common. Discuss what you discover.

Permission to Need and to Meet Your Own Needs

You can't fulfill your needs or allow your partner to fulfill them if you don't give yourself permission to have them in the first place. The very word *need* can stir up uncomfortable, intense reactions. To need has become labeled as improper, ugly, grasping. Self-sufficiency has become the badge of honor. But to deny what we need from other people is to trap ourselves in a desperate paradox: if you don't allow yourself to have needs and take action to meet those needs, you end up more needy. This creates more fear and an even more urgent set of needs. And so a vicious cycle ensues, one where your relationship spirals down into blame, alienation, and lack of caring. You accuse your partner of not caring for you and your partner keeps saying, "I'll do what you want but what is it you want?" To stop the cycle, affirm to each other it is okay to have needs. Take turns looking into each other's eyes and saying, "I am willing to have needs." Next, say to each other, "I am willing to let you meet my needs." Finally reiterate, "I am willing to meet my own needs." Discuss how this felt. Repeat this exercise whenever you are feeling fearful of being needy.

Get in the habit of asking each other, "What does your deepest self desire?" This question allows your dual nature, the opposites that push and pull inside of you, to express itself to your partner. Don't be alarmed if your adult or ego self wants one thing and your deepest self another. There is an essential duality, "a tension of opposites" as Jungian analyst Marion Woodman calls it, to life. Creating a way to respect this tension in your relationship encourages a whole, mature relationship and opens up the opportunity to integrate your unconscious needs.

See "Creative Connection: The Inner Relationship."

Investigate Complaints

Another way to pinpoint unmet needs is to unmask chronic complaints. The following exercise is based on the work of Dr. Harville Hendrix, the author of *Getting the Love You Want* and founder of the Institute for Relationship Therapy. On your own, make a list of frequent gripes. Think back to statements you made starting with "you always," "you never," "why can't you," and "why don't you." Examples of habitual grievances:

You never acknowledge me when I speak to you.

You always want to go out on Friday nights.

Why can't you be more like Barbara's husband?

Why don't you do something physical for a change?

When you've collected your complaints (it might take you a few days to think of more than one or two), get a clean sheet of paper. Transform each complaint into a stated need. For example:

I need you to acknowledge me when I speak to you.

I need to stay home with you on some Friday nights, cuddle, watch a video, and spend time with the kids.

I need you to touch me at parties and act like I'm with you. (Barbara's husband obviously does this.)

I need you to care about your health because I worry about the history of heart disease in your family.

Avoid nonspecific statements like "I need you to help me around the house" or impossible requests like "I need you to make love to me every night for the rest of our lives." These types of statements give your part-ner the opportunity to misunderstand you, feel overwhelmed, and there-fore not be able to meet your needs. A better choice would be to say, "I need you to sit down with me and discuss household responsibilities. Could we do this on Wednesday?" or "I would like to make love twice a week. Can we discuss this?"

See "Negotiating" for
help discussing disputed
complaints.

Take your newly stated needs and plug them in the next section. Doing this exercise might raise some anger or resentment (it did for us). If so, do the resentment-clearing exercise in "Releasing Resentment."

Compromise

Your most basic needs cannot be compromised. You can't give up your need to be loved, understood, or supported by your lover. So, where can you compromise? What happens when your needs clash? How can you balance what you need with what your partner needs? By determining the difference between a true need and a preference or desire, you can find a healthy give-and-take.

Our modern culture is based on wanting. The din of wanting can drown out the sound of our inner voice telling us what we truly *need*. Couples get stuck when they mix preferences up with basic needs. Figuring out what is negotiable and nonnegotiable helps you know when you can compromise without losing yourself or triggering a nasty wave of insecurity.

Spend a few days observing what arouses your interest, what compels you. Listen to your language for phrases like "I want," "I need," "I have to have," "wouldn't it be nice," "I couldn't resist." Each time you pinpoint a desire, write it in your pocket notepad.

If you have done the sections "Explorations: What Are Needs" or "Investigate Complaints," plug in the needs you discovered here to complete the process.

Decode each desire to see what it really is. Do this by asking yourself, "Do I honestly need this?" If the answer is yes or maybe, then ask yourself, "What does this need represent?" Finally, "Can I compromise and if so, how?"

An example: You state, "I need you to help me around the house more." You then ask yourself, "Do I honestly need this?" The answer is yes. You then ask, "What does the need (to have you help me) represent?" Allow an answer to pop into your mind. Maybe it occurs to you, "I need to know I am not in this relationship alone. I need to know you care about our home." Finally, ask, "Can I compromise, and if so, how?" In this case, the answer could be, "I can recognize and appreciate you more for what you already do. I can stop nagging and start taking direct action to make myself happy, which could include asking for help at the appropriate time."

Another example: You feel you need more solitude. Inquire of yourself, "Do I honestly need this?" The answer is "most of the time." "What does this need for solitude represent?" You realize, "I need to be able to hear myself think, to play with my paints and writing, to spend some time getting centered." Finally you ask, "Can I compromise, and if so, how?" You decide, "I know we are both overwhelmed with work and raising our child, so I am willing to give up eating dinner out to pay for a baby-sitter once every two weeks for three hours so I can be alone." (Okay, once again, this is a neat example from a book. Your life is more complicated, I know; so is mine. But I also know that if you don't give some thought to these things called basic needs, your relationship and your well-being will suffer. So try to consider it.)

Resources:

Everything You Know About Love and Sex Is Wrong: Twenty-Five Relationship Myths Redefined to Achieve Happiness and Fulfillment in Your Intimate Life, by Pepper Schwartz (Perigee, 2001). A fresh look at a lot of sacred cows, including never going to bed mad.

Getting the Love You Want, by Harville Hendrix, Ph.D. (Owl, 2001). Clear explanation of the unconscious agendas in our relationships.

His Needs, Her Needs: Building an Affair-Proof Marriage, by Willard F. Harley, Jr. (Revell, 2001). Relevant if you are afraid of straying.

The Further Reaches of Human Nature, by Abraham Maslow (Viking Press, 1971). Maslow's definition of needs is the best I have ever found.

The Good Marriage: How and Why Love Lasts, by Judith Wallerstein and Sandra Blakeslee (Warner Books, 1996). In-depth study of fifty couples married for nine years or more, revealing what we each need to do to have a successful marriage.

The Love Test: Romance and Relationship Self-Quizzes, by Pepper Schwartz and Virginia Rutter (Perigee, 1998). Self-diagnose your relationship.

Unconditional Love, by John Powell (Thomas More, 1995). Back to basics about the needs of people and relationships. Very grounding and wise.

Website:

Couple's Place
http://www.couples-place.com

When Life Is Too Crazy

When to Do It:

- When you've got your hands around your beloved's neck and you are starting to squeeze.

- When you find yourself wanting to scream every other sentence.

- When you believe nurturing your partner in this lifetime is not possible.

What Is It?

The phone is ringing, your mate is late, the four-year-old just spilled her milk all over the dining room rug, the teenager is sulking about not getting to go out Friday night with his friends, you are stressed out over an upcoming performance review at work, the breakfast dishes are still in the sink, dinner looks like pizza, *again*, the roof is leaking, you've got a headache, did I mention the phone is still ringing. . . . Okay, on an evening like this, how is anybody going to nurture anyone, let alone connect in a meaningful way with one's partner?

No one is. It is important to remember that nurturing each other *is not always possible*. If you read this book and think that some ideal couple somewhere lives the examples in this book each and every minute of each and every day, forget it. Wipe that out of your mind. This book is not meant to make you feel inadequate. There are plenty of TV commercials and magazine ads to do that. Being realistic about your life and your relationship is crucial. Realizing that the suggestions in this book won't always work is equally important. By seeking perfection, we set ourselves up for failure.

So with a nod to reality, what can you do when life throws you a huge sack of poop? How can you help each other cope? Here are a few suggestions.

You'll Need:

A good memory (when we're under stress, we forget everything that might make us feel better).

Failing a good memory, keep this book around.

Nature.

Friends.

Angels.

What to Do:

Time-Out

Football coaches know the wisdom of stopping the play when things get out of control. Take a tip from Don Shula and institute the principle of time-outs in your relationship. This is especially valuable with children, when traveling, or during the escalation of an argument. All action, talking, agitating, and screaming halts when "time-out" is called. *Before* life gets crazy, discuss how time-outs will work with everyone in your family. Agree to abide by this time-out no matter what, just like a football player.

See "Soul Strokes" or "Negotiating" for skills to use in discussing the craziness. See "Moving into Your Bodies: Release" for a tension-loosening exercise.

Anyone can call a time-out (sports are very democratic). After a time-out is called, everyone freezes and takes thirty seconds to breathe deeply. Then whoever called the time-out opens a dialogue with the purpose of changing the present course of craziness.

One-Minute Vacations

See "Erotic Delights: Getting in the Mood" for the standing sweep—a great hug recipe. Also see "Everyday Rituals: Connecting Throughout the Day" and "Rhythms of Rapport: A Reconnecting Ritual."

Develop a proclivity for inviting each other to take one-minute holidays. Again, do it *in the moment* of stress and disconnection. Look into each other's eyes and repeat together, "I am at the center of myself" or "Everything will be all right." Rub each other's necks for thirty seconds apiece. Give each other a full body hug. Close your eyes and remember a happy, peaceful moment you shared in the past. Put on a piece of music, hold hands, and do nothing for one song.

Nature

Touching nature is the best one-minute vacation of all because it gives you perspective and grounding. When life is disintegrating around you and the last thing you want to do is be nice to each other, take a moment and step outside. Look at the sky. Look at a tree. Look at a bush, a rock, a flower. Just look. Maybe hold hands. You do not have to live in the Rockies to do this; your backyard or terrace will do nicely.

Physically Slow Down

When we are tense, we speed up. We start moving faster, talking faster, and this only compounds our tension. Remind your mate when he or she is a high-speed blur to slow down. Actually slow down. Talk a little more slowly. Move more mindfully through the craziness at hand. Take a moment to smile at each other.

See "A Couple's Journal: When the World Is Moving Too Fast" and "Daily Communication: Breathing Together."

Spell Each Other

Couples are strong because often when one is down, exhausted, at the end of her or his rope, the other has at least an ounce of energy left. Offer it like the amazing gift it is to your lover. Take the kids out for ice cream and let him soak in the tub. Send her to bed early and do the dishes. Give your extra energy without strings attached.

See "Ease into Nurturing Each Other: Express Your Love."

Call an Angel

What to do when both of you are at the ends of your ropes? Call in help. Excessive self-sufficiency hurts. Develop a small emergency support system for these moments. When life is not crazy, sit down together and make a quick list of the moments that fray you both: when the kids are sick, when one partner is very late from work three nights in a row, when there is no food in the refrigerator. For each problem, brainstorm at least two solutions. Collect a file of take-out menus so you don't always have to order pizza. Collect two friends or neighbors with whom you trade emergency baby-sitting—just an hour for a breather. Think of comforting, perspective-giving places you can visit when you are at each other's throats. Write these down! Don't rely on your memory.

See "Writing Your Own Comfort Book" for help in creating a sourcebook for nurturing in all sorts of situations.

Learning from an Anxious Moment

Perhaps it is the everyday moments of craziness that wear away at us the most. Next time you feel tortured by life, stop, ask yourself or your partner, "What's right about this situation?" or "Why am I so anxious?"

Listen for the first thing that occurs to you, and act on this idea if you can. It is *in the moment* of anxiety that we can learn most about what we can do to make ourselves and our partners feel less crazy.

Resources:

See "Nurturing Merriment: Dealing with Conflicts"; "Tea and Sympathy"; "A Sensory Banquet: Relax the Senses"; "Moving into Your Bodies: Inner Calm"; and "Music: Making Beautiful Music Together" for more in-the-moment nurturing ideas.

Checklists for Life: 104 Lists to Help You Get Organized, Save Time, and Unclutter Your Life, by Kirsten M. Lagatree (Random House Reference, 2000). Help with all those nagging little uncertainties, from organizing your closet to choosing a lawyer.

Let Go of Clutter, by Harriet Schechter (McGraw Hill, 2001). Get less cluttered and more organized, now.

Ready for Anything: Fifty-two Productivity Principles for Work and Life, by David Allen (Viking, 2003). A boiling down of goal and time management that works great for people who love systems.

The Power of Full Engagement: Managing Energy, Not Time, Is the Key to High Performance and Personal Renewal, by Jim Loehr and Tony Schwartz (Free Press, 2003). A more integral approach to dealing with time—and the lack of it.

Time Management from the Inside Out: The Foolproof System for Taking Control of Your Schedule and Your Life, by Julie Morgenstern (Henry Holt, 2000). No one-size-fits-all guidance.

Websites:

Getting Things Done
http://www.gettingthingsdone.com

List Organizer
http://www.listorganizer.com

Miracle Organizing
http://www.miracleorganizing.com

Togetherness Time

When to Do It:

- When you get depressed or overwhelmed by how impossible it seems to find a moment with your sweetie.

- When you feel like you've worked so hard to be independent, you hardly ever see each other.

- When your relationship has been put behind kids, careers, and projects for too long.

- When the only time you see each other is over a crying baby, across a load of dirty laundry, or as one of you runs out the back door while the other one is crawling in the front.

What Is It?

You can't nurture the relationship if you don't see each other. You may chuckle, but the sad truth is that finding time to be together has become the primary obstacle impeding many couples from keeping their relationship out of the morgue. Leisure time has declined sharply over the last decade, as much as eleven hours for working parents with two children.

We are in a national and, in some ways, a global time crisis. People wear their lack of time like a badge. Conversations become a competition to see who is the most tired, the most overcommitted, the most needed, the most stressed. We are impoverishing ourselves, squandering our most basic, precious, nonrenewable resource.

Yes, there are very real reasons why time is shrinking. The most glaring is our need to compete globally for shrinking resources and jobs. Yes, it is harder than ever to make a living. Yes, there are more working poor

You'll Need:

A calendar you can share. (A wall calendar posted someplace you can see it often works well.)

Personal calendars.

Couple's journal or paper, and pens.

A timer.

Time required: For the entire exercise, about thirty minutes. Parts can be done on your own in ten minutes.

people. Yes, living in single-family homes and raising children with only one or two parents is ridiculously inefficient and hard.

Yet, when something is important to you, you find time for it. Period. If you don't know what matters, you tend to waste time and clutter your life with things and activities that mean little and then complain about how little time you have, which in turn gives you no time to figure out what is *really* important to you! The only way you or me or anyone is going to get enough time is if we get off this crazy treadmill long enough to examine our lives, decide what is important to us, and simplify our existence to make it happen. Perhaps no other modern crisis is so insidiously ruining our world than our perceived lack of time. Lack of time is helping to cause the erosion of family and community, our ability to help those in need, our inner lives, and our intimate relationships.

Start to change by affirming to each other that time is not money, time is much more precious, *time is your life*.

Next, consider, "How important is this relationship to me?" How do we find time to watch so much TV (the American average is six hours a day) if time to be together is so lacking in our lives? *How important is your relationship to you?* Nothing will change until you face the answer to that question.

What to Do:

What Do You Need from Time?

See "Recognizing Your Needs" for more.

Find out what each of you needs from time with each other. Do this exercise separately. Get a piece of paper and a pen. Set a timer for *five* minutes. Write everything that pops into your head in answer to "When it comes to time with my lover, what I need most is . . ." The timer encourages you to keep thinking past the most obvious ideas. The last minute is the hardest. Try writing with your nondominant hand (the hand you don't usually write with) or breathing deeply or visualizing a usual day in your life to help you come up with more ideas. Keep going!

What Are You Willing to Do to Get More Time Together?

Do you make the erroneous judgment that caring for your relationship is a flexible and elective time requirement while caring for your career is fixed and nonnegotiable? If so, now is the time to change.

Do this exercise separately and in the same manner as the first question. Set a timer for *five* minutes. Write everything that pops into your head in answer to "What am I willing to change in order to spend more time with my partner?"

What Do We Want to Do?

Do this exercise together. Set the timer for *ten* minutes. Designate one person as the recorder. He or she writes down everything both of you can think of in answer to the question, "I would like to _____ with you." Brainstorm, get silly, say anything, no matter how nonsensical, expensive, or seemingly insignificant. Invent a catalog of merry, simple, and wacky things to do together.

See "But There's Nothing to Do" and "Writing Your Own Comfort Book" for help dreaming up things to do.

See "Ease into Nurturing Each Other"; "Everyday Rituals"; "Couple Customs"; "Nurturing Merriment"; "Gratify and Delight"; "Natural Nurture"; "A Sensory Banquet"; "Erotic Delights"; "Massage"; "Moving into Your Bodies"; "Creative Connection"; "Ruts"; and "Co-creators" for more fun things to do.

Putting It All Together: Scheduling

I've observed three ways couples use their time together. One is to talk about all the things they like to do, then never make specific plans, frittering away most weekends (that's us). Another is to schedule every free minute so efficiently, there is little time for spontaneity or just being together. Third is the couple where one person does most of the planning and motivating, believing that time spent together having fun is essential for renewing their relationship; this causes regular attacks of resentment and anger and helps enforce a passive-aggressive relationship. None works well.

Get your shared calendar. *Don't initiate big projects in the first month.* Start small and simple. (I repeat, start small or you might be disappointed.)

Our Shared Calendar: November

When it comes to time with Chris, what I need most is to know he is listening

SUNDAY	MONDAY	TUESDAY	WEDNESDAY
	1	**2**	**3**
7	*Big day for Chris— extra support needed.* **8**	**9**	*I am willing to bring Jennifer to the set.* **10**
14	*Chris calls about music tickets.* **15**	**16**	**17**
21	**22**	**23**	**24**
Schedule next month. **28**	**29**	*J's Birthday— Don't forget J needs extra attention.* **30**	
		OCTOBER	

OCTOBER

S	M	T	W	T	F	S
					1	2
3	4	5	6	7	8	9
10	11	12	13	14	15	16
17	18	19	20	21	22	23
24	25	26	27	28	29	30
31						

Our Shared Calendar: November

When it comes to time with Jennifer, what I need most is to not be interrupted

THURSDAY	FRIDAY	SATURDAY	TO BE DONE
		Should be in sync. 5	*Discuss holiday gift buying.*
4		6	
		End of big shoot—Chris needs space.	
11	12	13	
	I am willing to cook dinner with Chris.		NOTES AND MEMOS *Try to work at Shelter together.*
18	19	20	
Thanksgiving with John and Julie. Watch holiday expectations 25	*J's deadline. See music.* 26	27	

		DECEMBER				
S	M	T	W	T	F	S
			1	2	3	4
5	6	7	8	9	10	11
12	13	14	15	16	17	18
19	20	21	22	23	24	25
26	27	28	29	30	31	

Share your responses to "When it comes to time with my mate, what I need most is . . ." Listen carefully as your mate shares his or her needs. Agree for the next month to honor one each. Write these across the top of your calendar.

Next take turns reading and listening to your responses to "What am I willing to do in order to spend more time with you?" Pick one idea from each person's list. Decide when during the next month you will carry out these activities. Write them on your shared calendar on the agreed-upon dates.

Next check out the list of fun things you compiled, and schedule one thing to do together over the next month. Remember to consider each of your schedules and the demands on your time.

Note: If your fun ideas require planning, say planning a skiing trip, decide *now* who will do what to make your happiness happen. Divide up duties *in writing* to be clear.

See "Daily Communication: Keep in Touch" and "Winds of the Heavens" for explanations of all examples on calendar.

Finally, pick a day near the end of the month to schedule the next month. After you've done this process once, it only takes a couple of minutes to plan the next month. Save your lists because you can draw from them for many months. Putting it all together, our shared calendar one month looked like the one on pages 60 and 61.

Post this calendar where you can both see it daily. Transfer any necessary reminders to your own system of organization. Try it for a month, see what works, then sit down on the agreed-upon day and schedule the next month. You might find that at first you forget or revert back to old patterns. *This is perfectly natural.* We scheduled racquetball, a music concert, and a day of cross-country skiing our first month (I know, I said start small). Racquetball was postponed because Chris was sick. Music was out because Chris was filming a music video (very funny). Cross-country skiing was preempted by my parents' surprise visit. We didn't get discouraged, we just sat down the next month and tried again. You might be tempted to give up. Ask yourself, "Are we spending more time together in ways that we both enjoy?" If the answer is yes, *keep using this process.* If the answer is no, find one that works better for you, anything that helps you stay conscious of how you spend your time.

Children

If you feel guilty about taking time away from the kids to be together, consider this: if you always put your needs aside in order to care for theirs, you will probably end up with nothing between you. Also, if your children see you have each other, they will learn they aren't responsible for you, that your happiness does not depend upon them. Finally, children who grow up watching parents who honor each other—who actually like each other enough to spend time together—are much more likely to keep their own priorities straight and to develop their own healthy relationships.

Boundaries with Others: Saying No

If time together is at a premium because you can't say no to others, especially your mother and father, consider this little fable (a true story): Once upon a time, there was a daughter who couldn't say no to her mother. The mother insisted, pressured, whined, and cajoled her daughter, with her family in tow, to have dinner with her every single Sunday night of every single week of every single year. To be sure, the daughter's husband hated it. "My dear, this is the only time we have alone. Let us sip cider and watch the sunset. *Alone*." But the daughter said, "But I can't say no. We have to go. After all, she's my mother and she's not going to live forever." And this went on and on for years and years, Sunday night after Sunday night—precious nights when they could have sipped cider and watched the sunset. But the daughter said, "I can't say no. We have to go. After all, she's my mother and she's not going to live forever." But the daughter's husband was the one who didn't live forever. He died of a heart attack. And the daughter is still having dinner with her mother every single Sunday of every single week of every single year.

You have to compromise on this issue. You cannot satisfy everyone because if you try, you won't satisfy anyone, especially yourself. Saying no as a couple can be less threatening than saying no alone. Use each other as an excuse. Put your relationship first. Be clear that if you keep giving to everyone else, you'll have nothing to give to each other. Your commitment to each other has to come first.

See "Winds of the Heavens: Boundaries" for more.

And

There will always be plenty of good reasons why you can't spend time together. Try to remember, life is not a dress rehearsal.

Resources:

Busy but Balanced: Practical and Inspirational Ways to Create a Calmer, Closer Family, by Mimi Doe (Griffin, 2001). A superb how-to manual. Highly recommended.

Life Matters: Creating a Dynamic Balance of Work, Family, Time, and Money, by Roger Merrill and Rebecca Merrill (McGraw-Hill, 2003). From the coauthors of *First Things First,* an excellent approach to balancing family life.

Sabbath: Finding Rest, Renewal, and Delight in Our Busy Lives, by Wayne Muller (Bantam, 2000). Be inspired to create one day of rest for yourself and each other.

Slowing Down to the Speed of Love: How to Create a Deeper, More Fulfilling Relationship in a Hurried World, by Joseph Bailey (McGraw-Hill, 2003). About "deep listening"—wonderful.

The Art of Talking So That People Will Listen: Getting Through to Family, Friends, and Business Associates, by Paul W. Swets (Simon and Schuster, 1986). An excellent guide to communication and the art of listening.

The Family Calendar, edited by Julian Ross and Ruth Porter Ross (Polestar Publishers, every year). Many special features. Families I know swear by this calendar.

Everyday Rituals

When to Do It:

- When everyday life is dragging you down.

- When eating dinner in front of the TV every night is turning you into Roseanne Arnold or Barney Fife.

- When you crave a meaningful connection between your inner world of depth and emotion and your outer world of endless business demands and errands.

What Is It?

My parents have a ritual. I can count on it so consistently that once when I flew home to surprise them, I knew right where they would be sitting at five o'clock and what they would be doing: talking about their day, talking about their kids, talking about the world while sipping a glass of wine.

What makes my parent's daily act a ritual and not a routine? The manner in which they approach it. Routine conjures up mindless repetition—not necessarily tedious, but not particularly conscious or connected. *Much of our lives is spent is daily routine*. And unless we are aspiring Zen Buddhists, we welcome a certain amount of this automatic behavior. It frees us so we don't have to think about each detail of life. But the other extreme is chilling: if we spend so much of our lives, separately and together, in a mindless, repetitious state, what does that do to our relationships with ourselves and each other?

A solution is to introduce simple rituals to transform some of our routines into conscious moments of recognition and support. The ideas listed here are offered as a means to instill renewed life and grace in the acts of daily living and to change the arid patterns you may find yourself locked into. They are also offered as jumping-off points for creating your own rituals.

You'll Need:

Couple's journal or dream journal, and pens.

Melodious music, twinkling candles, inspiring literature, glowing compliments, ambrosial massage oil.

Time required: A few minutes in daily life.

What to Do:

What Makes It a Ritual?

Conscious intent turns routine into ritual. You can step outside the customary and state, "This is a moment for connecting with each other, not just for doing the dishes." Symbolic gestures indicating a beginning and an ending help establish *living* ritual: lighting a candle together, then blowing it out afterward; playing a certain piece of music to go with a particular ritual; breathing deeply and maintaining a moment of silence beforehand; holding hands and smiling into each other's eyes afterward.

Beginning the Day

The Buddhist monk Thich Nhat Hanh states that every morning "we have twenty-four brand new hours to live." Try saying that to each other upon waking.

See "Music: Morning Music" for suggestions.

Use music to start your day. Take turns choosing a piece of music to play, surprising and communicating with the other person through the music. You could develop a "morning collection," adding to it as you hear selections that you like. Or wake up to the classical music station and lie in bed for a few minutes, hugging and listening.

Whenever you have a powerful or haunting dream, tell it over breakfast. By doing so, you step beyond logic and reveal your unconscious, a glimpse of your soul. Your partner listens carefully, then retells it to you the way he or she heard it. Refrain from analyzing. When a dream seems particularly relevant to the relationship, write it in your couple's journal or in a special dream journal. The point is to give your unconscious life conscious recognition in the relationship.

Share your plans for the day. Then take turns affirming to each other how wonderful the day will be. For example, you tell your mate you have a big meeting to lead. He replies, "You will be so articulate and creative, they won't know what hit them. I love you, and I know you are going to do a great job." Expand on the "have a good day" by thinking for a minute what you would wish for your partner's day and then putting that idea into his or her head.

Connecting Throughout the Day

When things get crazy, stop, look in each other's eyes, take a deep breath, and repeat silently or aloud:

> Breathing in, we are connected.
>
> Breathing out, we are peaceful.

You can also do this over the phone. Sounds corny, but try it when the kids are screaming, the doorbell is ringing, and the spaghetti pot is boiling over.

A different version: simply listen to each other breathe deeply. Again, this works great over the phone as well as in person. (The first time you do this, one of you might breathe heavily and giggle uncontrollably. It is still a connection.)

Together pick a sound you both hear a few times a day (church bells, children laughing, birds chirping). Whenever you hear this sound, you agree to stop, take a deep breath, and think a positive, loving thought about your beloved.

When you anticipate an upcoming busy time at work, fill a few postcards or greeting cards with words of love, stamp them, and keep them handy to mail to your lover at work (or at home if he or she works there) when you feel the need to connect but don't have time for it.

See "Gratify and Delight: Notes."

For couples who have phone problems (one partner has the phone personality of Lurch or your jobs make you so crazy you tend to be short with each other), try calling and telling each other one thing you appreciate about the other (or find a sexy or other compliment *du jour*), then say good-bye. Nothing more is said, and nothing more is expected.

If talking on the phone is out of the question, keep in touch the way one Orange County, California, couple does. They keep a chalkboard in their

For more connecting
ideas, check out "When
Life Is Too Crazy."

garage. In the morning, she leaves first, but before she drives off, she jots a
message to him on the board. When he departs later, he reads the message
and writes one for her to come home to. The same thing could be accom-
plished in your shared journal or with sticky notes on the refrigerator.

Transition Rituals

It's vital to address transition tension in your relationship. You are in one
mode during the day, another at night, and switching gears is something
many people don't do well. "Men may have a fear of connection at the
end of a day because to them it means more responsibility, more performance. Women have different fears, based on security issues; they fear
separation. So at the end of a day or week women may want to be loved
and listened to and men may want quiet and privacy. Having different
needs at the same time can set us on edge with each other, and we end up
passing each other in the hall on the way to bed," explains Jennifer James
in *Women and the Blues.* What to do?

Have a talk about what you each need when you come back together
after a workday apart. Use these questions to spark your conversation:

> In your original families, how did members greet each other at the end
> of the day?
>
> How did your family make transitions from week to weekend?
>
> What do you currently do to make the transition?
>
> How would you ideally like to make the change between work and home?

Be gently honest and specific. Realize that your needs will be different on
different evenings.

See "Negotiating:
Either-Or Day Ritual"
for more.

If you have different "transition styles" and can't agree on a compromise,
take turns doing it both ways.

Take turns creating a relaxing environment for the other person to come
home to. A two-lawyer household I know has a loving competition going
to see who can create the best atmosphere on Friday nights. They race to
be the first one home and plan ahead how they can surprise each other

with a house lit only by candles, a bath drawn and waiting, or an especially naughty gift. (No, they don't have children.)

Unwind *before* encountering each other. Listen to relaxing music during the last ten minutes of the commute, breathe deeply, and imagine the faces of people you love waiting for you at home. If you're extra stressed, stop someplace peaceful before you go home (an empty church to light a candle) or a park (to watch the sunset or meditate).

When you do encounter each other, don't dump your frustrations with work and/or your kids on each other first thing. Bring the best of yourself to the evening, and put off sharing your problems for later. Yes, extraordinarily simple but how often we forget simple gifts.

Kay Hagan, author of *Fugitive Information* and four other books, and her partner use Kay's wonderful check-in method whenever they've been apart or are feeling disconnected. They take turns completing the sentences "I feel," "I need," "I want." For example, once when Deborah picked up Kay at the airport, Kay told Deborah, "I *feel* jittery. I *need* to eat. I *want* to take a bath, while you make me tea and then talk to me while I bathe." Deborah responded, "I *feel* pressured because of my exam. I *need* to go home to study, and I *want* to be alone." Directly opposed, yes, but instead of a fight erupting, their separate needs were clearly expressed and a healthy compromise was reached. Highly recommended.

You can include this check-in as part of a daily debriefing session, which my parents call teatime. You could meet in a relaxing, private space and use the soul-strokes method, five minutes for each partner, starting with the check-in.

See "Shared Sanctuary" for ideas about creating a relaxing space and "Soul Strokes" for how to stroke each other's souls.

Do something physical to make the shift. A meditation walk is a possibility; walk more slowly than usual while coordinating your breathing with your gait. You might take four steps with an inhalation and five with an exhalation. Experiment to find your rhythm. Concentrate on lifting each foot as a unit, heel and sole together, and letting your arms swing loosely at your sides, all in time with your breath. After a block or two, talk to your partner about your day or hold hands while staying in tune with your breathing.

See "Moving into Your Bodies: Inner Calm."

Take a shower or bath together.

See "A Sensory Banquet" for bath-enhancing ideas.

"Minimize passive ways of tuning out. Maximize active transitions." Jennifer James stresses that if, for instance, you drown your transition time in alcohol you just have to deal with your feelings later, like the next morning. Examine this thorny issue *consciously*, and half your work will be done.

Dinner

Plan a once-a-week or once-a-month ritual dinner. Buy a special glass for each other (and other members of the family if needed) to use only at these dinners. Begin the meal by toasting each other, naming something each of you appreciates about the other. End the meal by asking each other for a quality you would appreciate receiving more of in the coming week or month, for example, patience while you learn the new computer system at work. The beginning and end qualities can be changed: name something you are thankful for and then a quality you want to bestow on others, like more understanding. Experiment!

"Bring yourself wholeheartedly to the dinner table," says Stephen Levine, author and teacher of mindfulness. Hold hands, take three deep breaths, and smile into each other's eyes. Take a moment to feel your whole body as it is. Hold your eating utensils with the hand you don't usually use. Chew slowly, tasting all the flavors of the meal. During dinner, don't say anything negative, about yourself or anyone else. End the meal with another smile and three more deep breaths.

Practice a simple way to begin your meals together. You could recite a short poem together, chant alleluia in a round (great with families), or bow to each other. Once, long ago, I visited a Club Mediterranean where they played the introduction to "Upstairs, Downstairs" to signal meals. You could play a few chords on a guitar or chime a bell, then observe a moment of silence.

Evening

Sit facing each other, close enough to hold hands if you feel like it. One partner goes first, completing the sentence "Something I appreciate about you today is . . ." The listening partner maintains eye contact and *does not interrupt* (or make any type of noise, especially sarcastic snorting). The partner talking does so for about a minute. Switch and repeat. Experiment with additional sentences, like "I respect you today because . . ." or "You made me proud today when . . ." (Do this without the TV on.) Finish with a foot or hand massage for ultimate nurturing.

If completing sentence stems seems too rigid, contemplate writing an appreciation note. Once a week express all the positive things you admire about your partner and your relationship. Go to bed early and read your letters to each other while sharing a bowl of ice cream or glass of wine.

See "A Couple's Journal: Appreciation."

Date nights are time-honored rituals I've heard about from many couples. The crux is to make a firm commitment. Set aside one evening a week for being alone and nurturing the relationship. If you have tried this in the past (which we have) and failed (which we did), then start with one hour one night a week. Build from there. Keep in mind your stumbling blocks: baby-sitters, no money (our biggest excuse; fun doesn't have to cost anything), conflicting business appointments, or the big G, guilt. If you don't take time out to recharge your love life, you will end up grouchy and less able to be a good parent/employee/employer; even the president takes vacations. Plan ahead (I keep saying this, but it bears repeating). Make date plans you can do at home, with the kids asleep or watching a movie (something educational on PBS, of course). Work on your list of reliable baby-sitters, and schedule one in advance to baby-sit, say, every Thursday night for three hours. Or work out a barter arrangement with another couple (every other Tuesday night you watch their kids, every other Wednesday night they watch yours). In your personal comfort book, add to your list of cheap and free pleasures. Devise a ritual way to begin and end your date evening, to set it apart from other fun times. Don't talk about work, kids, or problems. Or set aside a "venting" time at the beginning, say five minutes each, and rattle off your concerns, then concentrate on reviving the dying art of conversation. Discuss current events, a book you are reading, a moment of beauty you witnessed recently, the wine list, the fact you are wearing a studded leather teddy.

See "Writing Your Own Comfort Book" and "A Couple's Journal: Delight" for how to come up with date night ideas.

Bedtime

Emerson wrote, "Finish each day and be done with it. You have done what you could." Institute a ritual for leaving the day behind. You could massage each other's faces or take a shower together and imagine the day's worries going down the drain. Or try what one couple from North Carolina does. They acquired a beautiful wooden box. When they are plagued with worries, they get the box, open it, speak all their frustrations into it, and firmly shut the lid. Then they place the box outside their bedroom. You could also write your concerns on paper (example: I'm going bald; our child is flunking math; I'll never sell another book), also listing what you imagine as the worst thing that could happen (my wife will leave me because I'm bald; our child will never work in aerospace; I'll have to get a new career) and if it is within your control to do anything about it (not much, bald is bald; work with him after school; work on promotion and keep my sense of humor). Then put the paper in the box *outside* the bedroom.

See "Bringing the Book Home: Fear."

See "Couple Customs: Reconnecting."

Read something beautiful to each other before bed. Nancy and her husband, Bob, a very nurturing couple who live near Chicago, read Wendell Berry's poetry to each other in bed. Visit a bookstore together to find a book that appeals to both of you.

See "Daily Communication: Nonverbal Communication" for more about this, or "About Relaxing" and "Rhythms of Rapport: A Reconnecting Ritual" for variations.

Try sitting back to back and breathing deeply for one minute.

Look into each other's eyes, take a deep breath, and repeat, silently or aloud:

> Breathing in, I welcome sleep,

> Breathing out, I let go.

See "Letting Go" for more.

"I choose this day to be married to you" is a phrase a couple I interviewed learned from an elderly couple. In the elderly couple's long marriage they had never gone to bed until they could honestly say this to each other. Imagine hugging and saying, "I choose this day to be committed to you" instead of a mumbled "'night."

Designate a regular massage night. Prepare the area by straightening up, lowering the lights, spraying relaxing scents, and preparing essential oils for massage.

See "Massage" and "A Sensory Banquet."

Transforming Present Rituals

Examine places in your life where you feel bored or stuck or times when you tune out. Check out what you do now when you get home from work (turn on the TV, make a drink, change clothes) or how you wake up in the morning (buzzing alarm, hardly speak, grab a muffin). Use the soul-strokes method to talk about one routine you would like to make more meaningful. *Start small and easy.* Baby steps are the best way to overcome resistance to change. *Be gentle with yourself.* Nurturing is about delight, giggles, healthy connection, *not* striving for perfection.

Resources:

Inner Work, by Robert Johnson (HarperSanFrancisco, 1986). My favorite dream book.

Peace Is Every Step: The Path of Mindfulness in Everyday Life, by Thich Nhat Hanh (Bantam Books, 1992). Beautiful to read together (like all his books), plus lots of ideas.

The Book of New Family Traditions: How to Create Great Rituals for Holidays and Everydays, by Meg Cox (Running Press, 2003). The best book on creating rituals for every occasion.

The Heart of a Family: Searching America for New Traditions That Fulfill Us, by Meg Cox (Random House, 1998). Thoroughly researched, filled with amazing stories.

The Joys of Everyday Ritual: Spiritual Recipes to Celebrate Milestones, Ease Transitions, and Make Everyday Sacred, by Barbara Biziou (Griffin, 2001). Another excellent and creative resource.

Website:

Loving You
http://www.lovingyou.com

Rhythms of Rapport

You'll Need:

Your personal calendar or journal.

Your couple's journal or paper and pens.

Time required: From two to twenty minutes a day.

When to Do It:

- When you believe you should always be in step together.

- When after a period of being away from each other, you wish to synchronize.

- When you are struggling over the timing of a major decision.

- When the pace of your partner's life is driving you batty.

What Is It?

Life is a rhythm. You and me is a rhythm. Unfortunately, sometimes those rhythms become a cacophony of clashing cadences. (Say that three times fast.) For example, a person who jumps out of bed at six o'clock. ready to ski the Matterhorn is married to someone who loves to watch "Creature Feature" until the wee hours. A woman who takes three hours to pack for a trip lives with someone who dumps the underwear drawer in a suitcase and is ready to go. A man eager to start a family is mated to a person not yet moved to tears by a display of Baby Gap clothes. What can these people do with each other, besides scream?

"Time is the very fabric of a relationship," says clinical psychologist Peter Fraenkel, Ph.D. "People living under the same roof but in different time zones, so to speak, may be more distressed than those that are geographically separated but on the same schedule. Time often goes unnoticed—or unacknowledged—as a source of conflict in a relationship."

Each life has its own beat to dance to, a beat that is so strong it may be difficult or impossible to alter or rearrange. But living with someone else means you must discover the middle ground (or live with the resulting chaos). Nurturing the relationship entails dealing with these rhythmic conflicts: recognizing your cycles, communicating about how they affect you, and appreciating and accepting your differences. (Doesn't that sound easy on paper!)

What to Do:

Overview

To become aware of where your rhythms might diverge, consider the checklist below. Once again, there are no right or wrong answers. Simply check yes or no for each statement.

YES   NO

_____ _____ I consider myself a turtle—slow but steady.

_____ _____ I consider myself a rabbit—fast but sometimes I burn out or get overwhelmed.

_____ _____ I consider myself a morning person.

_____ _____ I consider myself a night person.

_____ _____ I consider myself neither, sort of in-between.

_____ _____ I need to take my time making a decision.

_____ _____ My mind works quickly, and it makes me impatient to wait after I've made up my mind.

_____ _____ If I'm late, it makes me tense and nervous.

_____ _____ If I'm late, it doesn't really matter to me.

_____ _____ When I was little, I was punished for hurrying and doing tasks in a sloppy manner.

_____ _____ When I was a child in school, I was often the first one done with an assignment or test.

_____ _____ One or both of my parents were slow and meticulous.

YES   NO

_____ _____ One or both of my parents made decisions quickly.

_____ _____ Sleeping late is a sign of laziness.

_____ _____ Going to bed early is a sign of a boring person.

_____ _____ It takes me awhile to get started doing a project (for example, painting the bedroom), and I like to pace myself when doing it.

_____ _____ When I know I have something to get done (like painting the bedroom), I like to get it done as quickly as possible without stopping midstream.

These statements are pretty transparent; they are meant to help you glimpse your partner's "time style." Your partner has not devised a devious strategy to drive you mad; it is simply how he or she has learned to use time. Use this quiz as a jumping-off point to explore the question "Where in our relationship is time a source of conflict?"

Read on for specific help for different timing conflicts.

Battle Over Body Clocks

A person who needs an intravenous java infusion every morning just to stand up is mated to a person who plays eighteen holes of golf by ten o'clock. Too late, you did it, you love one of *them*. Now what do you do?

Compromise is the all-important concept in "dyssynchronous" relationships. (But then, when isn't compromise all-important in any relationship?) Realize that your partner is not grumpy in the morning just to tick you off, but because of the very real influence of his or her internal time clock. *Your internal body clocks cannot be substantially changed.* Once you embrace this fact and stop making it a moral judgment, you are on the home stretch.

Meet halfway by pinpointing and then sharing your peak times. To find out when your peak time is, simply notice for two or three days when you feel most energetic, awake, and alive, then schedule time to be together when your peak times overlap. If you can't be together during your peak times, note where your second-best time occurs, and schedule nurturing activities then.

Little rituals help. Christina and Steve, a very loving couple I interviewed, have developed a lovely way to deal with their morning differences. Steve gets up first and makes coffee. He then wakes Christina very gently, tempting her with "I have the best cup of coffee you have ever tasted right here." He continues to lure her into the day with superlatives about java, and a compromise is reached between Christina, who hates to get up, and Steve, who is raring to go.

Reframe the disparity in your internal clocks by stressing the attributes (accentuate the positive). Jim Thornton writes in *Men's Health* about how he and his wife "put a positive spin on our situation. We manage to discover advantages where less happy couples see only time incompatibilities. When Debbie and I drive long-distance, for instance, we get sleepy at different times, making it easy to spell each other at the wheel." Appreciate that being out of sync might allow you precious solitude, time to develop special friendships outside the relationship (one to do yoga with at 7 A.M., another to breakfast with in a diner at 3 A.M.), and, above all, increased tolerance and acceptance of your best beloved. *This tolerance will flow into all areas of your love life.*

One final note: Research has determined that body clock mismatched people who can work out their differences end up with the best relationships of all, because they develop special strategies to minimize their differences. Vive la différence!

A Reconnecting Ritual

When you've been spending little or no time together for too long, your relationship can quickly reach a stress point. Issues of abandonment might be touched on, as well as the ever-changing optimum amount of distance and closeness, not to mention the fact you just don't know what is happening with your partner. Here is an easy ritual that is very reassuring. Whoever is feeling most stressed out, unappreciated, or abandoned becomes the receiver. If both of you are feeling equally out of touch, repeat by exchanging roles directly afterward.

This can be done on a daily basis, to signal the beginning of a vacation or evening together, or before going to sleep.

Lie together in bed, spoon fashion. The partner on the inside is the receiver and is enfolded in the arms of the partner on the outside, who is the giver.

Close your eyes and **Relax.** Focus on your breathing. After a few moments, become aware of your partner's breathing. When the receiver is ready, he or she inhales deeply, holds the breath for a moment, then exhales. The giver matches this breathing pattern. Inhale, hold, and exhale together for several minutes. During this, the receiver concentrates on receiving the energy of his or her partner's breath and the giver concentrates on sending energy by emphasizing his or her exhalations.

When the receiver is ready, he or she begins to vary the breath so that as the giver breathes out, the receiver breathes in. One partner holds a breath in, while the other blows a breath out. Continue for several minutes.

When the receiver is ready, he or she turns to face the giver. Gaze into each other's faces. Bask in the connection silently.

This entire breathing meditation should last around ten minutes. To make it more special, light a candle, play some relaxing music very softly, fluff up the bed.

Life Decision Discord

Life decision rhythms are the hardest ones of all to accommodate. Whether it is the rhythm of a person wanting a child or a conflict over career oscillations (both partners want to shift careers at the same time but this won't work financially) or one person feeling ready for home ownership and the other not, these conflicts can etch painful crevices into the foundation of the relationship. Respect, heedfulness, and the ability to sacrifice is needed to traverse these transitions and give each partner her or his due. Some strategies:

RHYTHMS OF RAPPORT

See "Divine Sustenance: Sacrificing to the Marriage."

See "Recognizing Your Needs" for more.

Consider carefully if you are placing your *wants* before the *needs* of your partner.

Have as many soul-stroking sessions as needed to explore the issue, but between talks do not bring up the subject.

Affirm to each other as often as you can that things will work out, you are in this together. Put as much energy into strengthening your commitment to each other as you do into trying to get your way.

Gain perspective by helping people who have fewer choices than you do, by going away for a weekend and not talking about the issue, or by climbing to a place that offers a sweeping view of something besides your differences.

Chris and I faced a similar difference. I wanted desperately to move out of Los Angeles, and Chris felt a move was impossible for him because of his career dreams. We fought. I pushed. Chris tried to accommodate me, but his heart wasn't in it. I whined. Chris despaired. I had a realization on my birthday: he *needed* to stay, I *wanted* (granted, very much wanted) to move. His dream is to be a successful cinematographer. My dream of living in the wilderness could wait. We worked out a compromise to move outside the city, but close enough that Chris could commute. None of this has been easy—believe me, we tore our hearts over it—but the compromise just might work.

Accepting Your Differences

Accepting differences is the hardest part and the most rewarding. It can be frightening to accept the fact that your partner is not only different from you, but unwilling or unable to change. My sweetie will always do

See "Acceptance."

things more methodically and slowly than I do. I can continue to make snide remarks, sigh loudly and often, or I can try to see what is valuable about his way of doing things, about his point of view in a life cycle decision, about his need to immerse himself in his work right now.

We all have a choice. Get in the habit of questioning yourself when you are fighting about a rhythm issue. Ask, "Can I choose to react differently?" or "What is another possible reaction to this situation?" Treat each other with *at least* the same respect you accord your friends.

See "Romantic Illusions: Becoming Best Friends."

Resources:

Be Loved for Who You Really Are, by Judith Sherven, Ph.D., and James Snierchowski, Ph.D. (St. Martin's Press, 2003). How differences between partners can enhance rather than destroy a relationship.

Breathing Room: Creating Space to Be a Couple, by Elayne Savage, Ph.D. (New Harbinger Publications, 2001). Help recognizing what the balancing act between the need for closeness and the need for autonomy is really about.

Getting Real: Ten Truth Skills You Need to Live an Authentic Life, by Susan M. Campbell, Ph.D. (New World Library, 2001). Awareness practices for heart-centered communication.

The Conscious Heart: Seven Soul-Choices That Create Your Relationship Destiny, by Kathlyn Hendricks and Gay Hendricks (Bantam Books, 1997). On-target, practical help for living the power of "the conscious heart."

The Mastery of Love: A Practical Guide to the Art of Relationships, by Don Miguel Ruiz (Amber-Allen Publishing, 1999). Restore the spirit of playfulness that is vital to loving relationships.

Unmarried to Each Other: The Essential Guide to Living Together and Staying Together, by Dorian Solot (Marlowe and Company, 2002). For people who are unmarried now or forever, the book is filled with savvy information about the joys and the common challenges of love without wedding rings.

Winds of the Heavens

When to Do It:

- When you find yourself disagreeing about how much time you need to spend alone or together.

- When you have a hard time saying no to your lover.

- When you have a dream you can't or won't pursue because you believe having a mate or family prevents it.

What Is It?

To paraphrase oft-quoted philosopher Kahlil Gibran, it is imperative that you, as individuals in a relationship, maintain spaces in your togetherness, and allow "the winds of the heavens" to dance between you. Or as clinical psychologist John Welwood writes in his excellent book *Journey of the Heart*, a relationship "rather than being just a form of togetherness, is a ceaseless flowing back and forth between joining and separating." This is the most basic, and most complicated, issue in all relationships: how to be intimate without losing yourself.

Gay and Kathlyn Hendricks write in *Centering and the Art of Intimacy Handbook*, "Each relationship is a unique dance. . . . We have discovered that couples have a strong urge to impose order, or control, on what is inherently dynamic and asymmetrical. Each partner has different preferences for times and length of contact and separation. *Rarely do these rhythms match* [italics mine]." It is impossible to ever "solve" or settle this aspect of love. Love has cycles. These cycles are neither good nor bad. Trying to force yourself or your partner out of each other's natural cycle of intimacy "tends to flatten the effervescence that an appreciation of difference can bring to close relationships." However, before you can accept it, *you have to be aware of what your intimacy dance is*.

To find the right flow between separateness and togetherness, the yearning to mesh together and the longing for solitude and freedom, is to learn about and honor your relationship's asymmetry. There *is* a way to let the

You'll Need:

Pens.

A timer.

Enjoyable things you like to do alone.

Time required: From ten minutes to several hours.

winds of the heavens dance gently between you instead of forcing you apart or slamming you too close together.

What to Do:

Boundaries

Your boundaries make up the outline of who you are, the limits that define you as separate from others. You have physical boundaries—how close someone can stand to you, when and where they can touch you. You have limits on how others can treat you emotionally, what comments they can make to you. Your boundaries can be fluid or rigid, depending on the situation and person. Consider the checklist below to observe your boundaries in relationship to your mate. The goal of the checklist is to outline a picture of your personal boundaries. There are no right or wrong answers. Share your results with your partner if you like (that's a boundary decision).

YES NO

_____ _____ My lover can initiate sex anytime, and I'll go along.

_____ _____ My partner can hug me whenever she or he likes.

_____ _____ My mate can make comments about my dress or body size anytime and anyplace.

_____ _____ If my lover needs me to do a favor and I can't, I feel guilty.

_____ _____ When my partner is having a bad day, I get upset too, even if I was feeling great.

_____ _____ If I spend too much time away from her or him, I feel disoriented or otherwise impaired.

_____ _____ When preparing to be apart (say for a business trip), I usually feel fine.

_____ _____ If my partner says no to a request, I feel rejected.

_____ _____   I love spending time alone.

_____ _____   When I'm depressed, I turn to my partner. If he or she can't help, I take care of myself by calling a friend, going for a walk, or some other self-nurturing activity.

Do you see any places where you might need to strengthen your boundaries with each other? Or where differences in your individual limits might be creating problems? Write in your shared or personal journal about your findings, or have a soul-stroking talk about what you've discovered.

Boundaries (like almost everything in relationships) contain a wonderful paradox. The stronger yours are, the closer you can get to your partner. When you're not sure where you end and your lover begins, you hold back because *you are afraid you will be swallowed up and lost.* When you know who you are, you can become truly intimate without fear.

The Intimacy Two-Step

You will both need some kind of calendar. (Whatever you currently use is fine.) In addition to keeping track of appointments, events, and whatever else is going on in your life, every day for one month, jot down whether you feel close or distant to your lover and any reasons why you might feel this way.

Sample calendar:

ONE PARTNER   SECOND PARTNER

Monday, March 1

Big meeting at work   Hard day at work
Wanted to be alone when   Wanted to be close and play
   I came home   after work

Friday, March 10

One Partner	Second Partner
He returned after a week's trip	Returned after trip
Felt distant because it felt weird having him home	Tired, not sure what I wanted— just time to unpack and get
Felt closer by bedtime	organized

Saturday, March 12

One Partner	Second Partner
Went hiking, out to dinner	Day off in nature
Felt closer to him than he felt to me	Felt very close

Friday, March 27

One Partner	Second Partner
Mom and Dad arrived	In-laws arrived
Felt distant from him	Felt on edge, sort of distant
Felt closer at bedtime	

Do not use your words of observation as a way to judge your partner or mind-read how she or he feels. This is not "how do you rate me today?" but a tool to see your pattern of getting close and pulling apart.

At the end of the month (not before), sit down with your calendars. Read your partner's notes. Look for recurring events (monthly meetings, Sunday dinner at the in-laws', menstrual cycle) to see if these affect whether you feel close or distant. Look for times where you felt one way and he or she felt the opposite. Discuss, chew over, deliberate what you learn. No accusations: stay with "I" statements. For example:

"I noticed when you come home from a business trip, I feel like you are intruding on *my* house, like I have everything just so."

Your partner responds, "When I come home, I need time alone. What can we do about this?"

or

"I noticed that when we went hiking last month, I thought you felt distant but in fact you felt close to me. What was going on for you?"

Concentrate on conveying your insights and possible solutions in a *loving* manner. What this process does is make you conscious of your dance. No way is better than another, as long as it works for you.

Now, on your shared calendar, indicate in the upcoming month any days where you might be especially in sync or especially out of sync. For example, if another business trip is coming up, mark the day he gets home as a day to consciously be aware you both need space. Or if Friday nights have shown up as a time you both want to be close and play, mark those and take advantage of them.

Note: This is the same shared calendar you used in "Togetherness Time." Refer back for visual example.

Also, note on your shared calendar any information you want to know about each other: deadlines at work, deadlines for kids at school, anything that might affect the rhythm of the relationship.

Post your shared calendar where you can see it daily. Use it to remind yourself that by recognizing and compromising on the cycle of your intimacy, you will make life a bit more harmonious.

Saying No

It is okay to say no to the person you love, without feeling guilty. Just knowing that may help. In fact, it is more than okay; it is imperative for a balanced love life.

Saying no doesn't mean you have to be angry or closed off. Instead, *consciously work on keeping your heart open.* Stay focused on how much you love this person. Practice speaking clearly and calmly. It helps to design a ritual phrase together, something like "I love you but I need to say no because . . ." then fill in the blank. The person being refused needs to respond, something like, "I hear you and I understand."

After you've taken the plunge and refused each other a few times, talk about how it feels. What does it bring up? Is it scary sometimes and annoying others? Do you feel it could be misused? Keep open the lines of communication, as well as your heart, and see if saying no doesn't make it easier to say yes with greater honesty and enthusiasm.

The Need for Solitude

See "Self-Care in Relationships."

Time away from each other is a necessity in the ongoing adventure of keeping your love alive. Experiment with taking "conscious space" from each other. Designate a time frame, at least three hours and no more than a day, where you go off on your own simply to have fun. *Don't do anything productive*—no errand running, cleaning, or slipping back to the office to "tidy up a few things." When the time is up, meet back at your home and have a soul-stroking talk about how this felt. Did you have any urges—to work, to call your partner? How did you feel? What did you think about?

You may find this exercise works like a minivacation and helps you realize you don't spend enough time alone, doing fun things with yourself. If so, check out "Self-Care in Relationships" for help. And keep planning regular breaks away from each other. Make it conscious!

Resources:

Claim Your Inner Grown-up: Four Essential Steps to Authentic Adulthood, by Ashley Davis (Penguin Putnam, 2001). Develop a solid sense of self without giving up the positive childlike qualities that also distinguish us as individuals.

Dance of Intimacy, by Harriet Lerner (Perennial, 1997). Classic examination of intimacy issues.

Journey of the Heart, by John Welwood, Ph.D. (Perennial, 1996). A superb book about becoming a "warrior of the heart."

The Call of Solitude: Alonetime in a World of Attachment, by Ester Schaler Buchholz (Simon and Schuster, 1997). Carefully researched insight into how alone time and attachment are complementary, not exclusive.

The Marriage Sabbatical: The Journey That Brings You Home, by Cheryl Jarvis (Broadway Books, 2002). Although written from a woman's perspective, could inspire sabbaticals for men, too.

Empathy

When to Do It:

- When you're convinced you are living with an alien.

- When you are caught in a nagging fight with entrenched opposite views.

- When your mate is going through an especially stressful *or* rewarding time.

What Is It?

Do you remember the movie *Brainstorm*? (If not, rent it and watch it together as an empathy exercise.) The story is about a scientist who invents a machine that allows you to enter the mind, the understanding, of another person. The best scene occurs when his wife surreptitiously uses the invention to get inside *his* experience. She is flooded with understanding of his life, his side of their disagreements. Their marriage, which was close to ending, is renewed.

You struggle to know another person, to truly know them, yet this is essentially impossible. You can't know what it is like to be a man if you are a woman. You can't know what it is like to be a woman if you are a man. *We can never totally know another person.* It's an exhilarating and frightening fact. We will forever be separate beings unable to enter each other's minds, yet that's exactly what we need to try to do!

By using your imagination to get inside your partner's experience, you can see past your either-or thinking and grow into deeper communication, loosening crusty negative beliefs and misunderstandings while acknowledging and perhaps finding the ability to celebrate your differences.

You'll Need:

Relaxing music like *Santosh* by P. C. Davidoff.

Time required: Thirty or so minutes, uninterrupted.

What to Do:

Empathy Visualization

The person sitting in the back (the giver) reads the instructions for the person in the front (the receiver). Pause at the ellipses (. . .) and read *very* slowly. Take as long as you like. Feel free to improvise. This, like all the visualizations in the book, gets better the more you do it. This is great to do before bed. Doing this with your shirts off is also wonderful.

Decide who will be the receiver and who the giver. Sit spoon style, back to chest, close enough that you can touch your partner's shoulders. Get comfortable. Don't use being uncomfortable as an excuse to not participate fully. The giver reads the instructions, slowly and with feeling:

Close your eyes and (read **Relax** instructions or instruct your partner to center himself or herself any way that you like). . . .

Concentrate on your breath. . . . Feel yourself relaxing near the person you love. . . . Feel my loving energy traveling with you as we both begin to let go. (Pause and breathe deeply here.) . . . More and more you are able to feel safe and tranquil, your heart open to this moment.

Imagine that your breath is meeting and mingling with mine, and together our exhalations are forming a protective bubble that shields us from any outside distractions. (Pause and imagine together your exhalations mingling and creating this bubble.) . . . Imagine the walls of this bubble have the ability to absorb any discomfort or distraction, so that with each exhalation we are helping each other to become more relaxed and open, until we are each very still and quiet at our centers.

Concentrate on breathing easily and deeply. Allow yourself to simply be, relaxed and focused, feeling the warm energy around your heart. . . . Experiencing the endless supply of your delicious heart energy as it expands, filling your body. . . .

(Giver, read the next part silently to yourself.)

Focus your attention on your partner. Gently lay your hands on his or her neck. Feel your beloved's skin under yours. Sense what tension this neck carries, what a burden it can be to hold up this head. . . .

Move your hand to rest on the shoulders. . . . Feeling what these shoulders have carried and what they are carrying now. . . .

Move your hands to rest on your partner's back, focusing on what you consider to be a vulnerable spot. . . . Allow compassion to flow from your heart through your hands and into this vulnerable spot. . . . Moving your hands slowly, gently, lovingly to wherever else on your beloved's body you sense fear or tightness or tension. Allowing the warm energy from your heart to pour down your arms, through your hands, and into this body, nourishing and replenishing. . . .

Breathing deeply and feeling your heart coming alive with the energy of your own generosity, breaking wide open with compassion for what your partner has endured as you gently touch or massage his or her neck, shoulders, and back. . . . Slowly opening to an awareness of this other being. . . . Feeling the physical body. . . . Glimpsing your beloved's soul. . . . Allowing yourself to truly and honestly receive who this person really is.

(Now say the next paragraph aloud.)

Breathing slowly and deeply, follow your breath as it begins to slowly bring you back to the room you are in. Take all the time you need to open your eyes, softly seeing the room around you.

When you are both ready, and without speaking, switch places and repeat the visualization.

When you have both completed the visualization, share your experiences. Consider how it felt being the giver versus being the receiver. Which was more comfortable? What would you change next time to make the experience more enjoyable? What moved you the most?

See "A Couple's Journal."

What did you learn? You might makes notes in your shared journal to
remind you of this encounter.

Resources:

*Creating Harmonious Relationships: A Practical Guide to the Power of True
    Empathy*, by Andrew LeCompte (Atlantic Books, 2000). Twenty-five
    years of research backs up this author's ideas on how to practice true
    empathy.

Health Journeys: Meditations to Support Successful Relationships, by
    Belleruth Naparstek (Image Paths, 1992). If you can use imagery to
    heal the body, why not to heal and improve your relationship? Learn
    more at http://www.healthjourneys.com.

Is It You or Is It Me?, by Scott Wetzler, Ph.D. (HarperCollins, 1998). By
    understanding the ways each of you contributes to the problems in
    your relationship, you can find new possibilities for connection and
    change.

*Nonviolent Communication: A Language of Life: Create Your Life, Your
    Relationships, and Your World in Harmony with Your Values*, by
    Marshall B. Rosenberg (PuddleDancer Press, 2003). Simply the best!
    Guidance on identifying and articulating feelings and needs, express-
    ing anger fully, and exploring the power of empathy.

*The Power of Empathy: A Practical Guide to Creating Intimacy, Self-
    Understanding, and Lasting Love*, by Arthur P. Ciaramicoli and
    Katherine Ketcham (Plume, 2001). Learn and practice the eight
    expressions of empathy.

*The Sedona Method: Your Key to Lasting Happiness, Success, Peace, and
    Emotional Well-Being*, by Hale Dwoskin (Sedona Press, 2003). A
    Western approach to Buddhist philosophy for changing damaging
    thought patterns.

To Love and Be Loved, by Stephen and Ondrea Levine (Sounds True
    Audio). A life-changing workshop on what it means to be alive and
    in love. http://www.soundstrue.com

Women and Men
Nurturing Each Other
Understanding Gender

When to Do It:

- When you are so confused about gender roles you ignore the whole issue or rely on stereotypical responses because there are no alternatives.

- When one partner consistently nurtures more.

- When one partner feels incapable of giving or receiving any kind of nurturing that implies weakness or vulnerability.

What Is It?

As I wrote this book, I struggled with the belief that men not only would not, but honestly could not, nurture their relationships, their partner, their children, their friends, as well as women could. But my subsequent research exposed my belief for what it was: discriminatory, untrue, and even dangerous. And my belief poignantly illustrated to me what a serious crisis the split between the sexes is and also what a rich opportunity to nurture each other. When you apply love to the rupture between you and your partner, if you can heal the gender wound between you, you will meet each other's deepest needs in a way that will stun and thrill you. You will also move our culture that much closer to a much needed change in its attitude about gender.

Men don't show their feelings. Women do. Men are taught to be stoic and in control. Women are taught to be caretakers, emotionally and otherwise. Living out these generalizations creates an emotionally barren and imprisoning ghetto *for each sex*. We are trapped in the excruciating position of having most of our beliefs about each other blown to bits but not yet having created new beliefs to fill the void. Nurturing each other provides the best place to resolve this agonizing dilemma *because it is the way*

You'll Need:

Courage to look at deeply entrenched patterns.

Couple's journal or paper, and pens.

Time required: Who knows!

See "Introduction: Gender and Nurturing."

we are failing to nourish each other as men and women that is perpetuating the split between the sexes the most.

(Warning: Proceed with caution. This chapter uses generalizations about the sexes. I apologize in advance. Also, I do not imply one ounce of blame in any of this. Take what makes sense to you, pay attention to what makes you angry, and flip a bird to the rest.)

Think about it. What are women's most common complaints about men? "He doesn't show any emotions, he won't do his share of the housework, and we don't talk about our relationship enough." What are men's most common complaints about women? "She doesn't want to have sex as much as I do, she rarely initiates sex, and she wants to talk all the time." What do these complaints have in common? *Lack of nurturing!*— the inability to understand what would most pleasure, delight, and heal the other. It is as if we are standing on opposite sides of a thick, glass wall, screaming at each other but to no avail.

There is a way out. There are straightforward ways to nurture each other (not simple or instant, however). The first step is realizing *separate but equal* applies to the sexes. *Men and women are different.* I am not stating the obvious. One of the reasons we aren't nurturing each other in our places of greatest need is we won't recognize that we have different needs. Taking care of your partner does not mean you are going to create a man in a woman's body or a woman in a man's body. Throw that fantasy out now, or you won't be honestly and effectively working toward solving this quandary.

By taking on the responsibility of deeply nurturing each other *as who we are*, we can begin to bring about the larger social changes of equality and, with equality, a fuller, more expressive, more just life for all.

What to Do:

Explorations: Examining Your Gender Beliefs

Consider what you have learned and what beliefs you hold about men and women. These beliefs affect you and your partner and the whole fabric of society every day. Make conscious what you have internalized about being a man or a woman, because you can't change what you aren't aware of.

Answer these questions alone in writing. Write *whatever comes into your mind,* as quickly as possible, without self-criticism or censorship. Only honesty will bring about change. Trust at least yourself with the truth.

For men: How and when did you learn to be a man? Was there a specific moment or ceremony or symbolic activity that welcomed you into manhood?

What is the hardest thing about being a man? What do you resent? Hate? Wish you didn't have to do?

What is the best thing about being a man? What do you cherish? Love? Consider your right?

Name three things you do on a regular basis that are typically masculine.

Name three things you do on a regular basis that are not typical for your gender.

Are you relieved that you are not a woman?

Do you believe women should have equal rights? If so, what would you be willing to do in your relationship to make that happen?

When I think of being equal to a woman, I feel . . .

When I think of having power over a woman, I feel . . .

When I think of nurturing my lover, I feel . . .

For women: When did you first consider yourself a woman? Was there a specific moment or a ceremony or a symbolic activity that signaled your change?

What was your first period like?

What is the hardest thing about being a woman for you? What do you resent? Hate? Wish you didn't have to do?

What is the best thing about being a woman? What do you cherish? What do you consider your right?

Name three things you do on a regular basis that are typically feminine.

Name three things you do on a regular basis that are not typical for your gender.

Are you relieved that you are not a man?

Do you believe women should have equal rights? If so, what would you be willing to do in your relationship to make that happen?

When I think of being equal to a man, I feel . . .

When I think of having power over a man, I feel . . .

When I think of nurturing my mate, I feel . . .

Share your answers only if you want to. Do so with care. Don't ridicule your partner's answers or use them later in a fight to prove why your mate does or doesn't do something.

What Women Need

In terms of nurturing, one answer to Freud's century-old question, "What do women want?" (and need) is:

1. A man to verbalize his emotions.

2. A man to do his share of the housework and child care.

But here is the catch. For a man to meet these needs, women have to change *and* so do men. There is much paradox in love. To get what you need, you have to give your partner what he or she so desperately needs. And of course, what both sexes need are opposite sides of the same coin, interlocking pieces of the same jigsaw puzzle.

To get what you want, women, you could consider doing these things:

Step 1: Take responsibility for yourself. Women have to give up the idea that men are around to protect us. It makes me quake in my feminist boots to write this. I've tried to deny it, but I think many women still believe men should shoulder more of the financial burden, protect us from the world, or at least get up on a cold night and turn up the furnace.

Just like you want men to share the responsibility of housework and child care without your having to ask, your sweetheart might want you to shoulder more of the responsibility of providing and protecting. "Both men and women have revised what they are doing—women now work and men now change diapers—but we still haven't changed the way our collective social unconscious views our respective responsibilities. In our hearts, women are still the nurturers and men are still responsible for everything else," writes Daphne Rose Kingma in *The Men We Never Knew.* I strongly disagree with Kingma's use of *everything.* Women are already responsible in their hearts for much more than nurturing, but I do agree that men feel overly responsible and that one potent way to nurture them (which in turn allows them to nurture us the way we want to be nurtured) is to take on more responsibility.

Bull, you might be saying. The only reason women let men take on more financial responsibility is because men still control the power and make more money, and men are physically stronger than women and so they must protect us. Consider this: if we take full responsibility for our lives, if we stop entertaining the idea at the very back of our psyches that men are here to protect us, we remove one of the roadblocks and come one step closer to completing the revolution and gaining economic and political power, which in turn will lead to a safer world where being physically stronger is much less of an issue.

Start to take responsibility by observing how you perpetuate the myth of men as protectors who are incapable of feeling. *This is not about blame.* Be on the lookout for how often you let your mate do something because he is a man. For example, who kills bugs, fixes the plumbing, prowls the

See "Nurturing Your Relationship Through Money" for ideas on overcoming money fears.

house when there is a strange noise? Don't neglect the positives. Notice where you don't fall into stereotypical gender roles. You might want to make notes in your shared journal.

Step 2: Teach him about feelings. Do you say you want your man to talk more about his feelings? Are you willing to teach him how? You are fluent in the rhetoric of feeling. Your man might be still learning the alphabet. Help him out.

Practice patience. When your mate starts to talk, don't cut him off. Take a deep breath, wait till he pauses, and say, "Tell me more."

Focus on him when he shuts down. This is a good time to gently inquire, "What just happened?" If he says, "Nothing," be polite and say something like, "It feels to me like something is going on with you. What does it feel like to you?"

See "Soul Strokes;"
"Ease into Nurturing
Each Other: Give Each
Other Permission to Do
Nothing"; and
"Rhythms of Rapport:
A Reconnecting Ritual"
for nonverbal ways
to be together.

Set up regular soul-stroking sessions, at least twice a week. Try to make the date sacrosanct. This will help you feel less needy (you know he will at least try to talk during these times), and nothing teaches like regular practice.

Use the questions and sentence stems throughout the book to give him something to hook into.

Teach him to put feelings into words. When he is lost for words, you can say, "I think if you could say to me how you feel you would say, 'I am sick and tired of doing this stupid job and I want to quit, but I'm too afraid.' Does that feel right?" Don't use this technique to put words into his mouth, that is, what you want him to be feeling. Accept that you will be wrong. Make sure you ask, "Does that feel right?"

I am not advocating women leap back thirty years and greet men at the door naked and wrapped in cellophane, holding a dry martini. But if we can work together in the service of meeting our own deepest needs, *not* in the service of giving our deepest needs up for our partner, we might all be a lot happier.

Step 3: Accept his feelings. Many of the men I interviewed told me what they most want from a woman is to be listened to—to not be squelched. "Accept my fear, my rage. Don't try to fix it," said the leader of one men's group I talked to.

If you want your man to be more expressive and he agrees that he wants to be, when he actually is more caring and expressive, how do you react? Are you really comfortable when he cries at pictures of war on TV, rages at his job, gives a male friend a greeting card? Or do you want a sensitive, loving, talkative man who is also the Marlboro man?

See "Empathy" and "Acceptance."

When he does share his feelings with you, accept them. You might feel afraid, surprised, even disgusted. Fine. Don't show it. Now is not the time for honesty and emotional transparency; now is the time for courage. It takes courage to change thousands of years of patriarchal influence. It happens in small, daily ways, not just at peace marches.

When he does disclose a personal revelation or feeling, respond encouragingly and specifically. "I feel weird about going home this Christmas," he might say. "I'm glad you told me that. It must feel strange to know your father won't be there," you could respond.

Step 4: Tell him what you need. One night over dinner, my friend Naomi and I were talking about men's ways of nurturing us when we are sick. Naomi gave an impassioned speech. "I am an expert at nurturing him, but when it's my turn, he doesn't know what to do. I say *pay attention*, like I do. Read my psyche, be interested in my nuances, listen to the things I complain about. I do it for you."

As a woman, you were raised to silently anticipate and meet the needs of everyone around you. But most men weren't. So you may have to ask for what you need. You may have to stop believing (if you do) that things given without asking are better, more sexy, more fun. Spell it out—gently, often, and clearly. "I need you to care for me when I'm sick like my mom did. And this is what she did. . . ." "I need you to tell me everything will be okay this week." Simple, sure, but the resistance and resentment you feel around doing this are not. Men don't have to spell it out, why should you? Face the fact men and women have been raised very differently, stop

See "Recognizing Your Needs" for more; "Releasing Resentment" for help when you feel angry about doing this; and "Self-Care in Relationships" for taking care of your own needs.

seeing one way as better than the other (each way is just that, one way we invented to survive), and keep spelling out your needs.

See "Tea and Sympathy"
for help with this.

One special area: women complain because their men won't just listen to their complaints. "He always wants to take action, to solve my problem." If you want to talk to only vent your frustrations and you don't want any solutions, tell him that before you begin. Then be sure to thank him for listening and to assure him he helped a lot by doing so.

Step 5: Honor his nurturing actions. He does nurture, he does say, "I love you," every day. But he does this with actions, not words. Actions are men's loving vocabulary. Notice these actions. Appreciate them verbally.

See "Daily
Communication:
Nonverbal
Communication" for
additional ways to
communicate without
words.

"Thank you for fixing the garage door. It made me feel good." Or "I appreciate your mulching the roses. It makes me feel good to know they will survive the frost." Or "Thanks for dinner. I feel fab-u-lous!"

Special note: Appreciate him for listening, especially when he can't talk, can't open up. Men listen well but aren't acknowledged for it nearly as much as they are dunned for not talking. Listening *is* as important as talking.

See "Letting Go" for
more.

Step 6: Let go. If you want him to do more housework, child care, talking, emoting, caring, nurturing, try to stop being so perfect, so competent. If you don't *let go* and allow your partner to do things his way, allowing for different styles and a period of adjustment (maybe a long period) for learning new skills, then you must take responsibility for discouraging change and for how you subsequently may feel—lonely, frustrated, taken advantage of, and overworked.

What Men Need

What do men want?

1. A woman who wants to have sex more often.

2. Freedom to communicate the way they want and to be heard when they do.

To get what you want, men, consider these things:

Step 1: Take responsibility. Women are sick and tired of bitching about how men don't do their share of the housework and child care. The key here is the same as it is for women: take responsibility. *It isn't helping if you don't initiate the action yourself.* If one partner is always psychologically responsible for most of the child care and housework, then it is just as draining as doing it herself or himself. Initiate more housework and she just might initiate more sex. (I say "just" for good reason: sex is a very complex subject, just like nurturing, and there are no pat answers. Don't do more housework to get more sex. Do it because you love her.)

Step 2: Learn the language of emotions. Words are the most expedient way humans can communicate. They are definitely the most socially accept-able. Learn how to communicate verbally. Try these suggestions:

Read a book or listen to a tape of this subject. Try attending a men's group. Try some of the suggestions in "Community Context: Friendships Outside the Relationship."

Look for feelings, and try to identify what they are. Is your heart racing? Do you feel warm and relaxed? Does your back hurt? Men learn to hide their emotions in their bodies. Accept bodily sensations as indicators of emotions, then try to translate those sensations into metaphors or word pictures. For example, you have a great day at work, and afterward you notice your body feels strong and purposeful. Conjure up a metaphor for this feeling. "I feel like a bull running at Pamplona in Spain."

When you have even an inkling of a feeling, communicate it to your partner. Trust your mate to accept your feelings and honor them. Don't worry if you are not sure or your feelings don't make sense. Feelings just are—they are neither good nor bad. Only squelching them is harmful. Take a leap into the void and name a feeling.

Step 3: Stop trying to solve everything. Do you communicate your affection and love by trying to solve the problem at hand? This can cause a con-flict because a woman may want to talk just to talk, not to accomplish

See "Toilets" for more about this vast subject.

See "Resources" at the end of this chapter.

See "Recognizing Your Needs."

See "Empathy."

anything. This might make you feel powerless and useless in the face of her problem or complaint. She might want you to just listen and perhaps nod and say, "Yes, that is bad," not remedy, fix, smooth, or otherwise make better. Before you offer a solution, *gently* ask your mate if she wants one.

Step 4: Accept her assertiveness. Do you honestly want a woman who is clear and assertive about what she needs? Or are you going to respond with, "It takes the mystery out of it" or "What a bitch"? You might complain you don't know what your mate wants, but are you honestly willing to hear the answer?

See "Daily
Communication:
Catching the Inner
Dialogue in Action."

Examine your underlying beliefs. Bring this up with your sweetheart. Check in with your body when a woman is assertive. It doesn't have to be your mate. Listen to your internal dialogue. What are the voices in your head saying? No blame, just be conscious.

Step 5: Don't pull away silently. "Men are like rubber bands. When they pull away, they can stretch only so far before they come springing back. A rubber band is the perfect metaphor to understand the male intimacy cycle. This cycle involves getting close, pulling away, and then getting close again. . . . A man automatically alternates between needing intimacy and autonomy," John Gray notes in *Men Are from Mars, Women Are from Venus.* While this cycle is perfectly natural, it hits a snag if you don't tell your mate you are pulling away. She might think you are receding because of something she did wrong. Tune in to your cycle, your need for solitude. Tell your partner. Reassure her you love her, and make specific plans to reconnect. "I need time alone. When I come back, let's go to a movie." Realize that when you do come back, she may need time to warm up to you again. This too is perfectly natural.

See "Rhythms of
Rapport: A Reconnect-
ing Ritual" for one way
to get back into sync.

Step 6: Accept your terror and ambivalence. Very few humans can accept the full range of emotions that being alive subjects us to. We can't accept these emotions in ourselves, and we certainly don't know what to do when someone else has feelings that frighten us. We aren't schooled in how to deal with each other's rage, despair, anguish, as well as unbridled joy, boiling lust, even simple satisfaction. No one is empathetic all the time. The problem arises when men run away from women's feelings (and women squelch men's reactions).

If you can't handle the emotional heat, get out of the kitchen, but *tell your mate* why you are fleeing. "I can't handle your rage right now. I love you, but I have to get away for awhile" is acceptable. She might not like it, but it is fair. Of course, staying around sometimes, *not* handling it but just holding on, is even better.

See "Tea and Sympathy" for a way to hold on.

For Both Genders

Are you saying to yourself, "When does helping a man or accommodating a woman become too much? Haven't I spent too many years concentrating on nurturing or supporting others?" The answer lies in attitude and balance. Try thinking, "I want to help my mate because I love him or her and because I want a great relationship" instead of "I have to help him. Who else will?" or "Poor me. I wanted to be a stand-up comic but she relies on me so I have to be a banker for the rest of my life." If you can focus on the fact you are responsible for your own happiness, and only yours, you will maintain balance, at least part of the time.

Overcoming Prejudice

Stop relying on sweeping gender generalizations to overcome uncomfortable feelings or to explain situations you don't understand. Statements like "Men, they're just like that" or "Women, I'll never understand them" only further the confusion and inequality. When you feel yourself wanting to resort to a generalization, stop, take a deep breath, and ask yourself, "What can I learn from this situation?" or "What can I appreciate about my partner's way of doing things right now?"

One day I was in a bookstore looking at Robert Johnson's series of books, *He, She,* and *We.* I remember considering whether I should buy *He.* I thought, "Why do I want to learn about men?" My answer was slow in coming: because I live with and love one! It astonishes me how little we endeavor to learn about the other sex.

See "Resources" for
more.

Read books about what it is like to be a woman or a man. Try nonfiction like *Backlash* by Susan Faludi, *Women's Reality* by Anne Wilson Schaef, *Awakening from a Deep Sleep* by Robert Pasick, or *Finding Our Fathers* by Samuel Osherson. Or check into fiction like *Disappearing Acts* by Terry McMillan or *This Boy's Life* by Tobias Wolf.

And

We have a long way to go to gender equality. Don't believe this issue doesn't affect you every day. It does. By taking small steps to have a more equal relationship (by your definition), you change the world.

Resources:

Be Loved for Who You Really Are: How the Differences Between Men and Women Can Be Turned into the Source of the Very Best Romance You'll Ever Know, by Judith Sherven and James Sniechowski (Griffin, 2003). Clear help for boundaries.

Genderspeak: Men, Women, and the Gentle Art of Verbal Self-Defense, by Suzette Haden Elgin (John Wiley and Sons, 1993). A practical and useful guide for treading the minefield of communication between men and women.

How to Love a Woman: On Intimacy and the Erotic Life of Women, by Clarissa Pinkola Estés, Ph.D. Audiotape. Order from Sounds True Recording, 1–800–333–9185, or visit http://www.soundstrue.com. Through her incredible storytelling, Ms. Estés teaches about the cycles of relationship and what women really need from a relationship.

Love Between Equals: How Peer Marriage Really Works, by Pepper Schwartz (Touchstone, 1995). Is it possible to have a truly equal partnership?

Myths of Gender: Biological Theories About Women and Men, by Anne
   Fausto-Sterling (Basic Books, 1992). While not a quick or easy read,
   one of the more factual and well-researched books about the brain
   differences—and lack of differences—between men and women.

We Have to Talk: Healing Dialogues Between Men and Women, by Samuel
   Shem and Janet L. Surrey (Basic, 1999). Forget men are from Mars
   and women from Venus, and discover what you do have in common.

What Could He Be Thinking? How a Man's Mind Really Works, by Michael
   Gurian (St. Martin's Press, 2003). Following two decades of neuro-
   biological research, Gurian answers the questions women and the
   world are asking about the male psyche.

Toilets

You'll Need:

Your sense of humor.

Your sense of fairness.

Your couple's journal or paper, and pens.

Time required: Twenty minutes.

When to Do It:

- When you find yourself muttering murderous threats under your breath while doing the dishes or taking out the garbage.

- When you have recurring fights about which one of you is doing more housework or parenting.

- When housework is affecting your sex life.

- When you feel like you're caught in an "Ozzie and Harriet" episode and you don't know how to get out.

What Is It?

There is a part of me that is sure human beings are not supposed to mate for life, or at least not share a bathroom. Admittedly, this is the cynical aspect that emerges when my mate has left his dirty clothes puddled on the floor, hangers on the shower rod, and electric razor beard debris in the sink.

Doesn't sound like a reason for divorce, does it? Several long-term, nationwide studies show that in fact it is. Arlie Hochschild, Berkeley professor and author of *The Second Shift,* found in her ten-year study of parents who both work that husbands who helped at home had better marriages than those who didn't. Several other long-term studies have found the second most common reason for divorce was neglect of home or children. This is a downer, but the mundane yet essential tasks of house and child care must be attended to with a spirit of fairness or the resulting schism of bitterness will tear an intimate partnership apart. Ignoring it doesn't make it go away; it just increases the resentment.

What to Do:

Accept the Importance

If there is one piece of advice I feel qualified in giving partners who feel (or are being told) they aren't doing their share around the house it is this: *Listen. This issue is important. It wears down the relationship.* It causes *great* resentment.

Power and the Toilet

Why is who does the housework such a loaded issue? *Because it is an issue of power.* Who cleans the toilet can become a teeth-grinding microcosm of the power struggle going on throughout your relationship. Arlie Hochschild discovered that men in her study who earned less than their wives did no housework, while men who earned the same amount did the most, and men who earned more than their wives helped somewhat. She found couples develop a complicated "balancing" act to keep power equal between them. For example, in relationships where husbands earned less, their wives kept the balance of power equal by doing more of the "toilet" work.

The bottom line about housework is *it isn't who is doing what but how each partner feels about the arrangement.* To begin to see the underlying reasons behind housework conflicts, you must be willing to examine your beliefs about domestic tasks in relationship to balance of power.

Open a dialogue by exploring your beliefs with a quiz. Again, often a lot more than housework is at stake, so don't think this is silly.

1. In your estimation, who does the most housework and (if applicable) child care in your house?

   A. Me.
   B. My partner.
   C. Our housekeeper.
   D. We do equal amounts generally, but on occasion I or my partner does more.

2. If you do most of the housework and child care, how do you feel?

    A. Angry.
    B. Overwhelmed.
    C. Okay, but I would change _____.
    D. Good about the arrangement for now.

3. If you do less housework, why?

    A. "I work fourteen hours a day, and you don't."
    B. "My parents did it this way."
    C. "I don't know how, and you do it better than I do anyway."
    D. "A clean house is more important to you than to me."
    E. Fill in your own reason: _____.

4. How do you rate your partner's work in relationship to yours?

    A. More important than what I do.
    B. Less important.
    C. Equally important.

5. Why?

    A. My work is more important because I make more money.
    B. My work is less important because I work at home.
    C. My work is more important because I enjoy it more.
    D. My work is less important because I enjoy it more.
    E. Fill in your own reason: _____.

6. What, if anything, are you getting out of believing your work is more or less important than your partner's?

    A. Power over my partner.
    B. More time for myself.
    C. Less responsibility for our shared life.
    D. The ability to run the house the way I want without compromise.

7. What, if anything, are you willing to change to make things more equal?

    A. See a counselor and discuss this issue with outside help.
    B. Make a list together of who does what and keep my agreement to do my fair share.

C. Ask my partner to help and then step back and let him or her do it without criticizing or taking it over and doing it myself.

D. Fill in your own ideas: _____.

What did you learn from your responses? Decide together on *one* small change to try in the next week to make things more equal. Or have a talk about what you learned. Or have a nurturing fight.

Practical Ideas

Adjust your attitude. Keeping a house together can entail endless boring chores, while shaping a home together can mean partaking in the ongoing creation of a delightful sanctuary. Also, consider that caring for your home is a crackerjack way to nurture your partner.

See "Nesting" for more about creating a home together.

Decide who does what by matching the tasks to each person's ability and level of interest. Use these categories as guidelines.

1. Age (with children)

2. Time availability

3. Talent

4. Degree of distaste

5. Standards

For example, I have no talent for cooking, but Chris does and likes it. I get overwhelmed in grocery stores, but Chris loves to read labels. I don't mind doing the laundry (I work at home), and I actually like to clean (I know, how weird). We hire gardeners to do the front and side yards (high degree of distaste). Time availability is the big challenge, because we both travel for our work and Chris works long hours. So we decided I would do the laundry before I leave; he stocks up on food before he takes off. If I'm gone more than a couple of weeks, we pay for help to clean before I come home.

Don't always assume you can't afford to hire someone. Try giving something up to hired help. Or budget gardening help into your house payment.

Use hired help to solve dead-end crises about who does what. But don't fall into this trap: whoever feels put out by the chore hires and makes the arrangements for someone else to do the work. Hiring must also be a shared task. Hiring help does not work as a temporary cease-fire measure—it only postpones the battle.

Identify which tasks make you feel overwhelmed in your domestic life and see if a little well-spent money and time could help. For example, watering my garden is time consuming. Spending the money to put in a drip irrigation system saves time and money in the long run (less water wasted).

Attempt to never leave a mess for someone else to clean up.

Do chores together and talk about your day. Reward yourself with a fun activity directly after finishing. Trade chores occasionally. Don't leave stuff for the weekend or other prime time; do it in the evenings when you're tired or before work.

Children can help, even very young children, but involving kids means letting them know that what they are doing is needed, not just busywork to get them out of the way. Knowing that what they are doing is truly important will change their attitude, even teenagers (okay, maybe not teenagers).

Make chores into vivid memories for yourselves and your children by combining regular routines with sounds, smells, and tastes. Set the table every evening to Beethoven, bathe the kids each night with a certain scented soap, sit in a circle and rub each other's backs when no one is in the mood to pick up the house.

Making chores into a game works well with kids, but it also works to motivate each other. When my sister and I were little and didn't want to do the dishes, we would see how fast we could clean the kitchen. It made a huge difference in our attitude. Set a timer for ten minutes, have each person pick a room to clean, and see who can get done first. Fold the laundry together while watching TV and wearing each other's underwear on your head. Mop the floor by covering your feet with moist rags and doing the twist across the room to the beat of the Talking Heads or Smetana's *The Moldau.*

If you have a baby-sitter or someone who comes in to clean house, find out what else they are willing to do for extra money. Peel potatoes, mending, ironing, or folding laundry?

See "Music: Music and What to Do on Friday Night."

Buy in bulk. At one of my workshops, a woman told me she takes her calendar to the card store (already marked with everyone's birthdays) and buys cards for the entire year.

Simplify! Use a comforter and duvet instead of sheets and blankets. Store knickknacks and display only one or two at a time. Group houseplants together for easy watering. Make a list together of everything you hate to do, and eliminate as many of these hated tasks as you can.

Planning meals can be grueling. Start a jar in which each family member contributes dish and menu ideas. Take turns after family dinners drawing the menu for the next day. Handle "But I hate zucchini" with "Then put more of your own ideas in the pot and your favorite meals will get drawn more often." Note: this method requires prior ground rules. If the kids put in macaroni and cheese with Vienna sausages, are you going to eat it? Decide ahead of time on guidelines for menu suggestions, and prepare to be gastronomically flexible.

Additional Ideas

Work on your life vision together by doing the meditation in "Cocreators."

Work on your empathy by doing the visualization in "Empathy."

Consider the consequences to your partnership if you don't do your fair share.

Consider the consequences if you don't allow your partner to do his or her fair share.

Resources:

Co-Housing: A Contemporary Approach to Housing Ourselves, by Kathryn McCamant and Charles Durrett (Ten Speed Press, 1993). Co-housing is a grass-roots movement to address the time, cost, and community crunch many people feel today. If you live in co-housing, you have less housework to do!

How One of You Can Bring the Two of You Together: Breakthrough Strategies to Resolve Your Conflicts and Reignite Your Love, by Sue Ellen Page (Broadway Books, 1998). In a power struggle? Hear yourself saying, "If only she/he would?" Then buy this book!

How to Clean (and Care for) Practically Anything, by the editors of Consumer Reports (Consumer Reports, 2002). Hundreds of timesaving solutions.

Lifescripts for Family and Friends: What to Say in 101 of Life's Most Troubling and Uncomfortable Situations, by Erik Kolbell and Stephen M. Pollan (Pocket Books, 2002). Offers you five tools for "scripting" difficult topics. Includes "Debating Household Chores with a Spouse."

Lillian Too's 168 Feng Shui Ways to Declutter Your Home, by Lillian Too (Sterling, 2003). Surefire strategies for eliminating excess baggage, renewing energy, and generating new pathways within your house and mind.

Perfect Husbands: Demystifying Marriage, Men, and Romance (and Other Fairy Tales), by Regina Barreca (Anchor, 1994). Bitingly honest look at power in marriage.

The Second Shift, by Arlie Hochschild with Anne Machung (Penguin, 1989). For help understanding how important and complicated the issue of housework is.

Couple Customs

When to Do It:

- When you feel like roommates keeping house together instead of lovers sharing your lives.

- When you've been neglecting your private world because of work or children. (Who doesn't?)

- When you are lonely.

- When the holidays are approaching and you want to create new rituals for your family.

What Is It?

Successful couples share many things in common, one of which is their ability to create their own world, their own rituals, their own sense of family. It may sound ridiculously simple, but to be in a relationship together, you must do things together that you *both* enjoy.

This aspect of love develops naturally up to a point and then often deteriorates under the pressures of daily life and the familiarity of the relationship. You lose sight of the importance of pet names or of taking classes together in a subject you both want to explore or of collecting tree ornaments for the holidays. And yet these simple acts make up the heart of your relationship; they are the lifeblood of intimacy, what helps hold your relationship together during tough times. To create your own customs, your own set of celebrations, behaviors, and ways of living, is to give form to your love.

What to Do:

Too Independent? A Personal Note

This chapter is a very personal one for me because it speaks directly to the struggle Chris and I have had in creating a world of our own. Over

You'll Need:

Things you enjoy doing together, like solving the *New York Times* crossword puzzle, strolling through wildflowers, tennis at dawn, or baking rosemary whole wheat bread.

Time required: Varies from a few minutes to however long you can delight in each other.

our years together, we have both grappled with a fear of commitment. One of the ways we have addressed this fear is to work hard at defining our marriage for ourselves, a definition that includes a lot of trust and autonomy. That part has worked great. But we concentrated so hard on maintaining our individuality, we began to feel we weren't in it *together*.

Observe your relationship for balance: Are you in it together? No blame. Things can change only if you want them to.

Reconnecting

See "Rhythms of Rapport: Battle Over Body Clocks."

Go to sleep and get up together when at all possible. If your cycles are "dyssynchronous" (you are a morning person, your sweetie is a night owl), then agree to cuddle when the night owl comes to bed.

Once a week do something *simple* together you both enjoy. Try browsing in a cozy bookstore and sipping hot chocolate afterward, sauntering down a tree-lined street on a crisp, fall night, or cooking a Thai meal together.

See "But There's Nothing to Do" and "Everyday Rituals" for ideas.

Create a standing date once a month to make new memories together. Take turns being responsible for scheduling the day or evening (or both). The focus should be on unique, silly, wild, one-of-a-kind, *memorable* activities. Fill up your reservoir of experiences particular to your relationship.

Pick a class to attend together. The only rule is you must both be *equally* interested. Keep searching until you find something that appeals to you both. Or become independent scholars on a mutual subject—pottery, sailing, dog breeding, photography, or one I saw recently in an adult education catalog: "The Art of Goat Farming."

Find a joint passion. Bob and Sue, a couple in Arlington, Virginia, share such a passion for Henry Miller, they traveled to Big Sur together to purchase his watercolors. Another couple share a love for Matisse and have spent many a Saturday at museums looking at his paintings and collecting framed posters. The options are endless. Hitchcock movies, chess, first-edition books, baseball, quilts: you can dabble *or* obsess together.

Finish a project that has been lying around for ages that will benefit both of you when it is completed. Iron out a budget, put gravel in the driveway, buy an overdue wedding gift. If you can't agree on a project that is equally important to both of you, then each of you pick a pet "to-do" and help each other complete it with no complaining.

Pick an activity you usually do alone or with someone else and invite your partner to join you instead.

Next time you are making a personal decision that you would usually make without any input from your partner, take a moment to ask his or her opinion.

A World of Your Own

Bedouins are reported to have seven hundred words for camel. The English language has only one word for love. In a small, blank notebook (or at the back of your shared journal) begin a dictionary of expressive names and secret words. Create a private language. Start by stating to each other your intention to enrich your love language. See what comes out. Write love notes using your language. One man told me he writes a story for his wife each year on Valentine's Day, using mostly their secret language, with the story line evolving out of the silly, personal, and touching moments they shared in the last year.

See "Gratify and Delight: Notes" for more ideas.

Fantasize about the future. When you first met and began to get serious, one of the ways you probably created a feeling of closeness was discussing long-range plans and goals. Talk about where you want to be in five years, where you want to go on a vacation, how you would like to fix up the garden.

See "Cocreators" for help.

Pick a microgoal to work on together: eating more broccoli, running a mile in so many minutes, counting to ten when you are angry. Set a date for review of your progress. Be sure to celebrate.

Create a dream box. Clip pictures and articles about things you both love and are working toward or just contemplating: vacations, new careers, children, any images that inspire you.

Designate a shelf, curio cabinet, or box as an exhibit of your relationship. Go beyond pictures (although these are great). On an especially romantic moonlit beach, John and Anita found a shell with an *l* on it (for love). They kept it to remind them of that special night. Experiment with framed love letters, champagne corks, all manner of souvenirs to give expression to your love. Regularly add, rearrange, or store items.

See "Community Context: Mentor Couple."

Make a pact to observe relationships around you to notice how other couples create a feeling of togetherness. Share your ideas over dinner. Decide which ones you would like to pursue. Again, be sure both partners are equally curious.

Raising children together is a familiar place to create shared memories. Together, make a scrapbook of your child's life. Schedule regular sessions to talk about the kids, where they are going, what they need more or less of. Read a book about child rearing together, like *Whole Child, Whole Parent* by Polly Berrien Berends.

Take a picture a month for one year. Arrange them in one frame.

See "The Art of Gift Giving."

Look through old photographs. Pick out a few that depict your relationship, your "coupleness," your special world. Make or buy a lovely box or album to arrange them in. Add to it when appropriate. (It also makes a great gift.)

See "Holidays: Anniversaries"; "Moving into Your Bodies"; "Everyday Rituals"; "Nurturing Merriment"; "But There's Nothing to Do"; "Natural Nurture"; "Erotic Delights"; "Shared Sanctuary"; "Writing Your Own Comfort Book"; and "Cocreators" for more ideas on creating your own world.

Renew your commitment or wedding vows. Sounds like a cliché, but it has the possibility of being an incredibly powerful ritual. It doesn't have to be elaborate. My fantasy: reading our vows to each other in the wilderness, with the dog as our witness.

Becoming a Family

Becoming a family, creating a feeling of belonging, of roots, is a crucial part of any serious relationship. Often unconsciously and long after you've become a couple, you may rely on your parents for a sense of home. This can block you from being completely committed and present in your relationship. Focusing on the primary importance of *your* family is the key. Whether a family is you, your partner, and your pet turtle, or you, your partner, two kids, and grandma, try these ideas:

Originate holiday rituals unique to your home and separate from your family's observances. For example, even if you travel across the country to spend Christmas, you can still decorate your home, send cards together, or set up a tree. John and Julie collect a new tree ornament each year and share a ritual of buying and decorating their tree together, while playing carols and sipping eggnog. Steve and Julie buy a live Christmas tree each year, then plant it in their side yard. Ned and Raffi make a big deal over Halloween, carving pumpkins, having friends over to help give out candy. Susan and Miriam plan a winter solstice celebration that includes a plunge in the freezing Atlantic Ocean.

See "Holidays."

Eileen McMahon, a writer and mother of three, wrote a story about finding her own tradition for Sundays, a day when she and her husband particularly missed New York and their large families. "I suppose the problem about Sundays for us is that, back home, Sunday was always family visiting day, and that as children, we came to associate Sundays with seeing people who loved us unconditionally, who found us wonderful and worthwhile and fascinating: our aunts and uncles, grandparents, our cousins." Think of the family traditions you miss, and consider starting your own version of them. Or there might be customs you always wished your family practiced. Fulfill your fantasy.

See "Nesting" for ideas on creating a home together.

Resources:

A *Book for Couples,* by Hugh Prather and Gayle Prather (MJF Books, 2001). Encourages letting go of your ego to serve the relationship.

Connect: Twelve Vital Ties That Open Your Heart, Lengthen Your Life, and Deepen Your Soul, by Edward M. Hallowell, M.D. (Pantheon Books, 1999). Learn the steps to deeply connect.

Into the Garden: A Wedding Anthology, by Robert Haas and Stephen Mitchell (HarperSanFrancisco, 1993). Love poetry and inspiration.

Love Poems from God: Twelve Sacred Voices from the East and West, edited by Daniel James Ladinsky (Penguin, 2002). Ladinsky is a profoundly talented translator, and this selection of sacred love poetry will inspire you to open your hearts and maybe even write your own.

The Book of New Family Traditions: How to Create Great Rituals for Holidays and Everydays, by Meg Cox (Running Press, 2003).

The Enlightened Heart: An Anthology of Sacred Poetry, edited by Stephen Mitchell (Perennial, 1999). Inspiration for creating your own language of love.

The More We Find in Each Other: Meditations for Couples, by Mavis and Merle Fossom (Hazelden Foundation, 1992). Over one hundred meditations to help couples find balance one day at a time.

Weddings from the Heart, by Daphne Rose Kingma (Conari Press, 1989). Five complete ceremonies.

Nurturing Your Relationship Through Money

When to Do It:

- When you fight about money often.

- When when you were starting out you believed things would get easier once you had more money, but nothing has changed even though your salaries have grown.

- When you want to unhook your relationship from the consumer machine.

What Is It?

Nurturing your love through money entails more than buying each other gifts. It entails nurturing your life vision, creating what you both need to function at your optimum, without overpowering yourself with obsessions and useless desires. It means you are willing to give enough time and energy to your money life, neither ignoring it nor making it the center of your life. It means you are willing to explore together the childhood messages you received about power and money and see how these messages are surfacing in your relationship. It means becoming present—knowing what enough is, knowing what your goals are, and becoming aware if they are hurting or helping your love.

Nothing has more symbolic meaning than money. Money is power, control, self-worth, identity, and *love*—proof of what one partner can do for the other. Perhaps no other issue in a relationship, besides sex, has the ability to foster greater growth and understanding (or wreak havoc and cause heartbreak). At the core, nurturing your relationship through money, finding true prosperity, means you are willing to cultivate a conscious relationship with money *together*.

You'll Need:

Two pocket-sized notebooks.

An inventory of your biggest wishes.

Your couple's journal or paper, and pens.

Time required: A few minutes a day to an hour or more.

What to Do:

Explorations: The Connection Between Love and Money

To untangle your relationship with money, to understand how money is affecting your love, you first have to understand your beliefs about money. Our resistance to learning about money is in direct proportion to our fear.

Finish the sentences either by writing as many completions to each sentence stem as you can think of (try for five for each question) or by facing each other and verbally giving your answers. Say or write *whatever comes into your mind,* as quickly as possible, without self-criticism or censorship. Be courageous. You will feel you have nothing more to say. Keep going, the truth lies ahead.

Money is . . .

When I was a child, money was . . .

As a child, did I think I was rich, middle class, or poor?

How does that affect my feelings about money now?

What are some additional messages my parents gave me about money?

I think money means to you . . .

When I fight with you about money, what I am really trying to say is . . .

We would get along great around money issues if only you would . . .

If I were to respect your attitude about spending as much as I do my own, I would . . .

If I were to respect your attitude about saving as much as I do my own, I would . . .

I define economic power as . . .

In our relationship, _____ has the most economic power.

What financial setbacks have I experienced?

What financial successes have I experienced?

Have these experiences altered the way I deal with money now?

What is my greatest fear about money?

If I had all the money I needed, how would my life be different?

What would the loss of a job or a chunk of our savings do to our relationship?

To improve our relationship with money, I would like to . . .

Discuss what you learned. Be gentle and supportive. Quit if these questions seem too intense, and go back to them later. The information you gain can illuminate many of your conflicts about money, because our basic conflict is almost always about style and fear—what we learned as children and what negative experiences we have had as adults. If you want to profoundly nurture your beloved, *listen to her or his answers* and then strive in the future to not push these buttons, to compromise and honor your beloved's early beliefs and the fears he or she learned later in life.

Finding Balance

We create a painful schism when we deny the importance of money in our relationships. As an example, consider two couples under financial stress, say through the loss of a job. The couple that has adequate savings, adequate knowledge about loans and other financial help, is much more likely to survive the tough time than the couple that has been putting no time and energy into their financial life. A healthy relationship with love and money comes from a balance (there's that word again) between respectfully and consciously handling money, giving it enough importance in your life, while spending enough time and effort nurturing the inner life of the relationship too. Try these suggestions:

Transform financial drudgery into relationship nurturing by changing your attitude. Instead of grumbling while you pay the bills, reframe your thinking. Paying your mortgage can become an act of love; you are creating a physical haven for your relationship. Take a financial seminar together with an attitude of caring for each other by learning what you can to enhance your financial well-being. Take your negative, resistive beliefs about this work and reframe them into caring actions. When you are feeling stuck or bored about learning how to budget or invest your IRA savings, stop and ask your partner to help you reframe your feelings into an act of love and safekeeping.

See "Resources."
Read about the history or philosophy of money. Pick up a book from the library, and spend some time leafing through and reading just a bit for a larger cultural perspective.

Nurture your inner life in tandem with your financial life. For example, if you spend half an hour working on your budget, then spend the next half hour nurturing your relationship, whether through playing racquetball, meditating together, or telling each other your current dreams for moving to Montana and opening a dude ranch or expanding your business or retiring early.

Getting Unstuck

Work toward trusting each other enough to experience both your fears and your joys around money more vividly. Study your relationship *in the throes* of your money debates, problems, and triumphs. During these moments you have a golden opportunity to become much more intimate because your fears and beliefs about money cut right to your core self. What you run away from in the realm of financial matters is directly related to what you run away from in your relationship. Use your times of conflicts *and* happiness to draw closer together by stopping *in the moment* and proposing one or all of these questions to yourself and your partner:

What are we afraid of?

How does this make us feel about each other right now?

What are we avoiding?

Give Each Other Permission to Spend on Yourselves

There is no right way to deal with money in a relationship. Some couples pool everything. Some keep their money separate and give proportionally to a common account. Whatever works for you is great. However, to help foster a nurturing attitude with money, it helps if each partner controls a weekly or monthly amount of money to use at her or his discretion, without feeling guilty. Decide on an amount each person will set aside for himself or herself. If one partner works at home taking care of the children or is out of work, it can be even more important to use this system, to help give each person a feeling of autonomy and personal control.

Would You Know Enough if You Met It on the Street?

One day when Chris and I were wrangling yet one more time about how to make a budget, I was struck silent (a true event for anyone who knows me) by the question *"Will there ever be enough?"* I realized we lived our lives always pointed toward the future. We believed our happiness would increase when we made more money. But when we thought about it, we realized what an impossibility this was. *Enough, like tomorrow, never arrives.* It was then we realized we had to decide exactly what we needed and wanted financially if we were ever to be at peace with money in our marriage. Because, if you are always pointed toward the future, how will you ever be *here* enough to enjoy the present? Nothing is more destructive and tragic for your love, your beloved, and yourself than to miss this life because your eye is on the horizon and not on the people and love that surround you.

Three steps to deciding what is enough:

1. Tracking every penny you spend and rating how much you enjoyed what you spent your money on.

2. Exploring your fantasies to see what you honestly need and want.

3. Finding other experiences to satisfy your cravings for material objects.

Step 1: Keep track of every cent *that goes in and out of your life for one month.* This is not a budget! This is a simple, wonderful thing to do. I promise it is worth the effort. Don't do it in a parsimonious manner but in a spirit of knowledge. By knowing how much you spend and where it goes, you can dispel fears and illuminate any differences in your spending habits. Get two pocket-sized spiral notebooks, carry them with you, and write down how much you spend and on what for one month. Keep your receipts for "mixed" purchases, like supermarkets and drug stores.

(This part of our process was improved after reading *Your Money or Your Life*.)

At the end of the month, sit down with your notebooks, receipts, and a legal-sized piece of paper. Across the top, write categories like Groceries, Dining Out, Mortgage or Rent, Household Items, Utilities, Clothing, Medical Care, Insurance, Movies, Travel, Car Repairs, Gas, and any other categories you like. Avoid blanket categories like Food or Entertainment. Be specific enough that you get an overview but not so specific you end up with an unwieldy number of categories.

Once you have your categories set up (you might need to tape two pieces of paper together), fill in each with the amounts spent over the last month, using the information you've gathered. (This exercise brings up all kinds of resistance and fear. Stop in the moment of fear and ask each other, "What are we afraid of? What uncomfortable memories or feelings does this exercise bring up?" No, this is not fun in the strictest sense of the word, but it is nurturing and very important.)

Now go through each category and ask yourself, "Did I receive satisfaction in proportion to how much money I spent?" or in other words, "Was it worth it?"

If the answer is no, then ask yourself, "How can I change my spending habits in this category to receive more satisfaction?" or "How can I work with my partner to change these spending habits?" or "What can I do instead of spending money that will make me feel as good?" (See Step 3 for help on this one.)

If the answer is yes or neutral, keep spending the same amount of money in that category. And enjoy it!

The results will give you a complete picture of how much satisfaction you are getting out of what you are buying. If you can, repeat this process for several months.

Step 2: Decide exactly what you want out of life in terms of material goods. There are no limitations except "Do I really, *honestly*, TRULY want this?" Refer back to your monthly expense/pleasure breakdown to check with reality: was a similar experience or item worth it? Investigate your dreams and cravings. Peer into that seemingly bottomless well of "I wants." This step takes a few weeks or even months. Help each other by pointing out wishes and daydreams. Compose a list of everything you want. Be thorough and have fun. It might help to imagine you've won a billion-dollar lottery.

When your list feels pretty complete, share it. Focus at first on how it feels to have put some conscious time into examining what *enough* is for you. Is it liberating? Is it frightening? Is it impossible? And how, if at all, will you live your life differently now that you know what enough is?

This exercise can open the door to considering life plan changes. If it does, my advice is to take it very slowly. Have lots of soul-stroking talks about your new thoughts and possible plans. See where your ideas fit in your life plan. Do the visualization in "Cocreators" and see where that information fits.

Step 3: Find ways of nourishing yourself that are not related to money. You cannot spend your money in a manner that meets your deepest needs unless you have other ways to nurture yourself besides spending. To find alternatives, compose a list of things you like to do, together and alone, that give your lives meaning *that have as little as possible to do with money.* When you have the urge to spend your money on something that you now realize doesn't give you satisfaction, you can turn to your list of meaningful pleasures and enjoy one of those instead.

See "Writing Your Own Comfort Book" for ideas on how to compile a list.

And

Putting some attention into the role money plays in your relationship allows money to take its proper place in your shared lives: as a powerful force that can be controlled and used to foster your love, not wear away at it like the Colorado River does the Grand Canyon. Take it slow and easy, see if you can make it fun, and realize dealing with money creatively is a wonderful way to say "I love you."

Resources:

Conscious Spending for Couples: Seven Skills for Financial Harmony, by Deborah Knuckey (John Wiley and Sons, 2002). Highly recommended advice on working as a team.

Couples and Money, by Victoria Felton-Collins (Gabriel Books, 1998). Ideas about budgets, hidden agendas, and power plays from a psychologist and financial planner.

Seven Stages of Money Maturity: Understanding the Spirit and Value of Money in Your Life, by George Kinder (Dell, 2000). The only book I have found that combines perennial spiritual wisdom with modern fiscal how-to.

The Couple's Guide to Love and Money, by Jonathan Rich (New Harbinger, 2003). Learn each other's money style and how to avoid finance-based conflicts.

The Energy of Money: A Spiritual Guide to Financial and Personal Fulfillment, by Maria Nemeth, Ph.D. (Ballantine Books, 2000). An excellent blend of the metaphysics and psychology of money. More grounded than many of the other new-thought money books.

The Soul of Money: Transforming Your Relationship with Money and Life, by Lynne Twist (Norton, 2003). Lynne Twist is a global activist who has raised more than $150 million for charitable causes. She demonstrates how we can replace feelings of scarcity, guilt, and burden with experiences of sufficiency, freedom, and purpose.

Self-Care in Relationships

When to Do It:

- When your partner says no to your request and you become depressed and don't know what to do with yourself.

- When you feel that without you, the house, kids, car, or social life would fall apart.

- When you resent your partner for taking time for himself or herself.

- When you believe that in a *real* relationship with your true soul mate, you wouldn't have to take care of yourself.

What Is It?

As I've written, said, sung, and shouted elsewhere (okay, maybe not sung), we cannot honestly nurture someone else until we nurture ourselves. It is perfectly okay to ask someone else to meet our needs, but if they can't we have to be able to meet those needs ourselves. And we have to be able to do this without being secretly angry and distrustful of our partners.

Unhealthy dependency is believing it is someone else's *responsibility* to make you happy. Healthy interdependency is celebrating how you and your partner complement each other while maintaining separate identities, and recognizing that you are ultimately responsible for your own well-being. An integral part of your well-being is your ability to nurture yourself because self-nurturing helps you find and stay in touch with your authentic self, and knowing your authentic self is a central requirement to relating intimately with your mate.

I hope this doesn't sound grim, because it isn't. Self-care can be a real hoot: lying in the sun eating strawberries, reading a Philip Marlowe mystery, tiptoeing through a museum on a quiet afternoon. If you both explore self-nurturing, you can infuse your love with new energy and respect because when you see your partner celebrating himself or herself,

You'll Need:

Paper and pens.

A timer.

Various things that make you feel good, like flannel sheets, a green and quiet golf course on Sunday morning, a fascinating exhibit at a gallery, your running shoes.

The belief you deserve self-care (which comes with practice).

An understanding with your partner (which comes with time).

Time required: Twenty to thirty minutes.

doing what she or he needs to do to live life fully, you gain a new appreciation for your lover's beauty, and your interest and respect is renewed. Also, self-care reduces stress and resentment because you don't feel responsible for aspects of your lover's life that you neither want nor should have to worry about. And in the same way, self-care can clarify boundaries. A partner who knows you can take care of yourself feels much freer to take care of you because she or he knows you are not a bottomless well of need.

What to Do:

Explorations: How Do You Really Feel About Self-Care?

Over the last six years, I've learned that men have less guilt about taking care of themselves but a hard time coming up with creative things to do. Women, on the other hand, can sometimes dream up inventive things to do, but they often feel guilty or conflicted about actually taking the time. Vivian, an artist and mother of two, talks about what happens in her relationship: "He takes care of himself, and I resent it because I don't. So I feel even more put upon and pressured while he's lounging on the couch reading the paper. The result is I blow up." You must acknowledge to each other you each have an equal, *critical* need for self-care.

Explore negative beliefs and guilt surrounding self-care using the sentence stems below. Either write or verbally come up with as many responses as you can (try for five for each question). Say or write *whatever comes into your mind*, as quickly as possible, without self-criticism or censorship. Push yourself past the obvious.

I deserve more time for myself because . . .

When I take time for just me I feel . . .

When I take time for just me I think *you* feel . . .

When I spend money on myself, I feel . . .

When I was a child, I learned others came first when . . .

Your answers will point out conflicts and childhood messages that are influencing you now. Talk about what changes you would like to make based on what you learned. One change you can make is to become each other's permission buddy. Convince your lover that he or she deserves self-care. An example: Diana wanted to take the day off from work to go canoeing. The night before, she was struck with an attack of guilt. She went to her mate, Herb, and told him all about it. He gently, honestly, and with great support told her why she deserved a canoe trip down the St. Croix on a fine April day and how the project she was working on couldn't fall apart in one day. Do more than tolerate self-nurturing; advocate, entreat, assist each other to recharge.

Responsibility

Down deep, do you believe your partner is there to take care of you, to read your mind, second-guess your wishes? It can be very difficult to truly believe it is your responsibility to make yourself happy. You might believe it intellectually, but somewhere inside a hurt child or sulking teenager might lurk, saying, "No way, they're supposed to make me happy, and they sure better do it!" Taking responsibility for your own well-being isn't easy, but it may be one of the most important things you can do for your relationship.

Here are four steps toward taking responsibility for your own happiness.

Step 1: Stop blaming your partner for your problems and frustrations. If you are trying to avoid fat and your partner eats Ben and Jerry's Heath Bar ice cream in front of you and you give in and pig out, I'll bet you ten bucks you'll blame your partner. Instead, try biting your tongue (gently) and silently answer the question: "I'm blaming you because I didn't. . . ." The second part is *Don't blame yourself either.* This is not about self-punishment! Imagine yourself as a kindly old aunt observing your behavior lovingly so you can change, *not* so you can blame.

Step 2: Make a self-nurture list. Set a timer for ten minutes. Sit down with paper and pen. Write down every response to the sentence stem "If you really loved me, you would. . . ." Don't censor yourself; be totally honest (your partner does not have to see this). Keep your hand moving, and write whatever nonsense or complaints appear in your mind *until the timer goes off*. Reread your list, then if necessary put it away for a few days to allow the emotional intensity to smooth out.

Sit down with your list. Starting with your first response and working your way down, ask yourself how you can transform each expectation into a *self*-nurturing action. A few examples from my list:

If you really loved me, you would . . .

> fix up the house
>
> make more money
>
> plan things on the weekends
>
> move to the country with me

I transformed these into *specific, small* actions I could initiate or do alone.

Fix up the house became, I can buy plants for the front yard on Sunday and plant them slowly over the next week. I can paint the baseboards in the bedroom. I can ask you to do two equal projects. (Notice self-nurturing can involve asking for help but not demanding, manipulating, or whining.)

Make more money became, *I* can make more money. I can be more responsible for how much I spend. I can spend a day learning about investing. I can ask you to work with me on a budget.

See "Nurturing Your
Relationship Through
Money" for money
ideas.

Move to the country became, Have soul-stroking sessions about our life plans and don't talk about moving any other time. I can spend a month every summer in the wilderness. I can make hikes in the mountains a part of my regular life.

See "Recognizing Your
Needs" for another way
to view complaints;
"Winds of the Heavens"
for taking responsibility;
"Negotiating" for getting
unstuck; and "Accept-
ance" for how to change
the way you perceive
your sweetie.

Some things on your list will be easy to transform. Others will be more difficult. Maybe one item on your list is "have sex with me whenever I want to" or "agree with me always." These are impossible, right? What about pleasuring yourself, asking your mate to visit a therapist with you, or reading a book about how to get more pleasure out of sex? You want your lover to always agree with you? What about agreeing with yourself by working on a positive inner voice? What about agreeing with your lover? What about discussing some ground rules for making decisions? *Nothing is impossible if you take responsibility!* This process makes you realize, concretely and directly, that *you* are in control of how you feel.

Step 3: Release the resentment you feel for all the times you've sacrificed your needs for your partner.

See "Releasing
Resentment" for
techniques to release
anger and dissolve
bitterness.

Step 4: Work on your independence. Think of places you go and activities you do only with your partner. Go to one of these places or do one of these activities alone.

Do something you usually have your partner do for you. Say no to a pushy phone salesperson, fix a leaky faucet, say no to your child.

If you always rely on your partner for advice about certain issues, make a decision or take action without her or his input. (This doesn't mean buy a Jaguar with your life savings. It does mean you can take the car to the mechanic or go to the grocery store without being told what to buy.)

Overcoming Guilt

In my workshops and conversations with women around the country, what I often hear is, "But if I take care of myself, how is my family/husband/boyfriend/girlfriend/dog going to react?" The same question is true for men. The answer (from the audience) is always, "You are *still* worrying about other people." If you've been doing everything for your partner, family, boss, or coworkers and you suddenly stop, they *are* going to be upset, and they *are* going to push your guilt buttons. The best way to instigate change is to *start small*. Don't start taking care of yourself by announcing you're leaving for a month's retreat. Build up to that by announcing that Saturday afternoon or Thursday night is your time.

Be consistent. If you are going to take Saturday afternoon, take it. Don't give in to demands. If your lover suddenly needs her car serviced and you *have* to pick her up, or the *only* time your mate can play racquetball is Thursday and you *have* to watch the kids, what are you going to do? You always have a choice.

Ideas for Self-Care

Define self-care for yourself. Get some paper and a pen or your personal journal. Sit or lie down alone, close your eyes, and **Relax.** Spend a few minutes simply paying attention to your breath. Settle into yourself. Concentrate on *you.* When you are centered, ask yourself, "What can I do that makes me feel more me, centered, and pleased with myself?" Whatever occurs to you, jot it down. Then close your eyes and focus back on your breathing for a few minutes, then query yourself, "What choices am I making in my life now that don't nurture me?" Let ideas float to the surface, and write them down. Go back to breathing, taking lots of time, and finally ask yourself, "What have I always wanted to do just for me?" Record your ideas. Each day, indulge yourself in one of these items or choose to use your time in a more nurturing manner or work toward part of a dream. (It can be as simple as making a phone call to find out how much flying lessons cost or as superb as wrapping yourself in a soft blanket and watching the sun come up.)

Each day on your appointment calendar or in your personal journal, do what Robert Pasick, author of *Awakening from the Deep Sleep,* does. He jots down TGCOY (Take Good Care of Yourself) and then records what he is going to do that day to nurture himself.

Sit down with your lover, and have a brainstorming session for each of you, naming everything you can think of that your partner might enjoy doing for self-nurture. Make two lists, and refer to them when you need new ideas.

Resources:

Comfort Secrets for Busy Women, by Jennifer Louden (Source Books, 2003).
    A reflection on self-care for women but of interest to men as well.

Meditations for Men Who Do Too Much, by Jonathan Lazear (Fireside, 1992). This book might help a man in your life recognize that over-doing has become a genderless problem.

Self-Nurture: Learning to Care for Yourself as Effectively as You Care for Everyone Else, by Alice Domar, Ph.D (Penguin, 2001). A truly wise book.

The Gift of the Year: How to Give Yourself the Most Meaningful, Satisfying, and Pleasurable Year of Your Life, by Mira Kirshenbaum (Plume, 2001). Carve out a year within your current life to follow a dream. Why not do it together?

The Great Sex Weekend: A Forty-eight-Hour Guide to Rekindling Sparks for Bold, Busy, or Bored Lovers: Includes a Twenty-four-Hour Plan for the Really Busy, by Pepper Schwartz and Janet Lever (Perigee, 2000). If you still love each other but can't make the time to have sex.

Twenty-Minute Retreats: Revive Your Spirit in Just Minutes a Day with Simple Self-Led Practices, by Rachel Harris (Owl Books, 2000). Short, inventive retreats.

Well Being: Rejuvenating Recipes for Body and Soul, by Barbara Close (Chronicle Books, 2000). A gorgeous and useful book with recipes for all kinds of luxurious botanical body potions and treats.)

Music:

Ocean Surf by Dan Gibson, *Essential Recordings* by Stan Getz, *Talk to Her* [soundtrack], *Enchanted: The Best of Robert Gass* and *On Wings of Song, Breath of the Heart* by Krisna Das, *Shiva Stations* by Jai Uttal, *Baroque at Bedtime*.

Websites:

Comfort Queen
  http://www.comfortqueen.com

Self-Nurture
  http://www.selfnurture.com

Self-Growth
  http://www.selfgrowth.com

Nurturing Merriment

You'll Need:

Your sense of humor.

Inexpensive toys, like Silly String, squirt guns, and animal noses.

Jokes, gags, and weird bumper stickers.

Comedy videos or tapes.

Time required: Depends on how hard it is to get you to relax and have fun.

When to Do It:

- When your partner never laughs at your jokes anymore. (Or maybe never did.)

- When everything is "just fine," day in and day out.

- When play was once a part of your relationship but has been pushed aside in the name of getting ahead, raising the kids, and just plain surviving.

- When you are bored in your relationship.

What Is It?

Nurturing merriment is tickling each other until you collapse in a heap on the floor; laughing your way out of a stale fight; playing hide-and-seek without the kids; commuting together and making up extravagant stories about the people around you. This all constitutes couple play, "a great way to forget the tyranny of everyday life, and become like a set of angels playing hide and seek behind the clouds," writes Dan Sutherland, a Chicago playwright.

You may not always recognize your couple playtime because it is so personal and spontaneous. You may quickly forget you called your partner at work, made animal noises, said "I worship your hairy toes," and hung up. There is a close relationship between couple play and dreams, and, like dreams, memories of spontaneous moments of playtime can slip away. The game is impossible to hold in your hands but crucial for restoring your vision and faith in love.

But recognized or not, shared play contributes to your relationship by providing an enjoyable way of relating. Play allows tenderness and animosity to exist side by side, and frolics relieve the tedium of life. Which sounds like more fun: screaming uncontrollably because your partner is eating with his or her mouth open *yet again* or putting on a plastic pig nose and continuing to eat your dinner?

In case you don't believe me, ask Dr. William Fry of Stanford University, who has found laughter not only increases muscular activity, heart rate, and oxygen exchange, but also indirectly stimulates the production of endorphins, giving you a "laughter high." It is even conjectured that laughter might increase life expectancy.

What to Do:

Self-consciousness squelches couple play. Therefore, it works best to read the suggestions below, then forget about them. Your creative unconscious will push ideas and images to the surface when you need them, and you'll find yourself gamboling and cavorting all over the place without feeling self-conscious.

Also, for those of you who think playing is stupid and only for kids, Dr. Steve Allen, Jr., has a definition of *stupid* and *silly*, as told in C. W. Metcalf's book, *Lighten Up*. "'Stupid means ignorant and uneducated. You do stupid things because you don't know any better. Having fun and playing is not stupid—it is silly.' Silly, Allen points out, derives originally from the Old English *(ge)saelig*, which meant completely happy, blessed. *Silly* was a blessing you wished upon those you loved. It meant to be happy, prosperous, and healthy."

Getting Started

Bring home a joke a week to share over Friday night dinner. Create a penalty for forgetting to have a joke ready, say jumping on one foot while barking like a seal.

Start a humor library in a corner of your bedroom, shared sanctuary, or library. Visit a bookstore together, and check out the humor section. Collect cartoons lampooning subjects dear to your heart (for us, those subjects would be fights about fixing up the house, men talking less than women, and anything about chocolate). Whimsical letters, absurd

See "Shared Sanctuary."

postcards, facetious articles, jocular videos, audacious audiotapes—
indulge yourself whenever you or your lover needs some humor
replenishment.

Crack Each Other Up

Declare a weekend laughfest. Prepare by collecting jokes, harmless gags,
and witticisms. Declare the laughfest opened on Friday night. Crack each
other up all weekend. Give prizes on Sunday for:

1. Who laughed the loudest.

2. Who made whom laugh at the oddest time.

3. Who laughed until they cried. (You can, of course, add prize
   categories of your own.)

Award prizes: a whoopee cushion, a comedy tape for the morning commute, tickets to a comedy show. (If this seems too complex or requires too
much planning, adapt to your circumstances. Surprise each other with
one joke a weekend, or involve children, friends, or parents and use this
as the basis for livening up a holiday weekend.)

The Workday

Imagine you are doing everything for the first time. Imagine you are suddenly a five-year-old in an adult's body. Imagine a bothersome coworker
wearing a mohawk or your boss on the toilet. Share your humorous observations with your mate after work.

Dealing with Conflicts

Shoot Silly String at your mate when he or she is taking life too seriously
or not laughing at your jokes. Shoot Silly String at yourself when you nag
about your partner's faults.

Buy two squirt guns, and squirt each other when you discover you are
arguing about a stale issue.

Visit a video store together. Pick one or two of your favorite comedy films featuring an actor who deals with life using humor. At home, make a cozy nest for yourselves with blankets, popcorn, and hot chocolate. Watch your tapes. In the future, when a tense or tedious moment presents itself and neither of you knows what to do, pretend you are your comedy role model. Wail like Lucy ("Rickkkkkkyyyyy"), or make a face like Martin Short. Or say to your partner, "How would Steve Martin in *Roxanne* deal with this?"

Use your pets. Once, when playing with my dog in the "dog park" (a park where dogs can roam free), I overheard a couple sniping at each other. The woman covered her dog's ears and said, "Shhh. Sasha might hear us."

Turn a problem into a game. If a salesman is being rude, whisper to your partner what kind of animal he reminds you of. If you are late for a movie and can't find a parking place, instead of getting into a fight imagine your car is a spaceship and you are searching for the space station to dock at.

Keep a humor scrapbook to refer to when you are stuck at an impasse of conflicting desires or when both of you are blue. Items for humor book: snapshots of goofy times, cartoons that depict in startlingly accurate ways some of your common problems or differences (the *New Yorker* and *Utne Reader* are great sources), truly funny jokes that might crack you up when you are tense or down—anything that will remind you of the larger picture and your loving connection to each other. Add to this little book whenever you can. It works well to add items without telling the other person so there is an element of surprise next time he or she looks at the book. (Variation: One couple I interviewed suffered from Sunday night blues. They developed a ritual of making popcorn and looking over their photo albums. "It gives us a warm feeling of being connected to our whole lives.")

See "Writing Your Own Comfort Book" for ideas on keeping a book of fun things to do together. You could combine the two.

Childhood Revisited

Declare an afternoon or evening with your mate and perhaps several close friends for being a child again. Decide what age you'll be. Bring playthings. Mess around with clay, read to each other, watch an animated video. (For those of you who are horrified and embarrassed by this idea, incorporate several young children as a cover. You can call it "quality time.")

Visit a playground in the moonlight. Swing on the swings, and swish down the slide.

Write a note to your partner using your nondominant hand (the hand you don't usually write with). Hide it someplace funny like inside the refrigerator or wrapped around his or her razor.

See "Nesting: The Inviting Bedroom."

Lie under the covers with a flashlight, and read a book together while eating Oreos. Choose something fun like a ghost story, fairy tale, or for the very silly or very tired, Dr. Suess (*Horton Hears a Who* is the best).

Together, do something you never got to do as a child. Buy that train set you always wanted, visit Disneyland and go on every ride you want, have a slumber party and stay up all night.

Physical Play

Next time life is overwhelming one or both of you with petty details and monumental crises, climb a tree and sit on a branch. Or ride bikes in the summer twilight. Rake leaves and jump in the piles. Lie outside and watch for falling stars, or make pictures from clouds as they go by. Go fishing and read poetry to each other while you wait. Bake bread and take turns beating your frustrations out on the sticky dough. Walk in the wet grass barefoot holding hands. Jump on your bed and yell. Jump rope with your kids. Play Smashball in the living room.

See "Moving into Your Bodies: Inner Calm."

Outrageous Acts

When buying something big together, like a house, car, or major appliance, bring your sense of play along. Bring Groucho glasses and slip them on when the salesperson drives you crazy. Pretend to be extremely clumsy to communicate to your partner how much you hate a house you're being shown. Walk in silly walks around the appliance store. (Silly walks are from a Monty Python sketch. Essentially, you take ridiculously long steps, then hop, skip, jump, perhaps pirouette. Be creative.)

Play "I can top that," a game created by author and therapist Dr. Harville Hendrix for his workshops. Stand facing each other. One partner goes first, doing something slightly crazy like jumping up and down on one foot. The second person jumps up and down on one foot *plus* pats himself on the head. Back to the first partner, who jumps up and down on one foot, pats herself on the head, *and* makes a bellowing noise. Keep taking turns adding elements until it is either physically impossible or you are laughing too hard to continue.

See "Moving into Your Bodies: Release" for a related, silly idea.

Several couples I interviewed talked about the characters they have created—alter egos that allow them an opportunity to be someone else for a little while. For Halloween four years ago, Christina and Steve created Gary and Vivian. Gary and Vivian are farm people from the Midwest (and the exact opposite of Christina and Steve). Christina explains, "They have become so much to us. We learn from our characters. They are such good, innocent people." They revisit Gary and Vivian every Halloween, and it has become an important ritual. Another couple (inspired by an *I Love Lucy* episode) separated for a day while each created a new persona, which they unveiled to each other when they met later at a restaurant. They slowly picked each other up, taking their time to learn all about this "new person" before going home together. No, this isn't kinky; it is an opportunity to explore different ways of seeing the world and each other, as well as giving a voice to parts of yourself that may not see the light of day very often.

Collect absurd pictures, bumper stickers, and *National Enquirer* headlines. Pop one out when your partner is feeling stressed. Or hide them around the house to be discovered at odd times (imagine taping an *Enquirer* headline to the inside of the toilet lid).

Imagine things you wanted to do as a child but couldn't because you would have gotten in trouble. Do one of these things with or to your beloved. (Turning the kitchen sink hose on my husband is one of my favorites. I was a mean child.)

Honor a Mosio (my husband's) family tradition like his brother-in-law did: greet family members at airports wearing an animal nose or with spoons balanced on your proboscis. (The spoon thing requires a special nose.) Also works as a way to greet your partner after you know she or he has had a long day.

Feeling Stupid

If you feel stupid playing at any point, ask yourself, "Would a three-year-old feel stupid?" Become a child, not an adult playing a child, and the feeling of being stupid might fade away.

Resources:

To get you in the mood to play, watch funny films like *Big, Benny and Joon*, anything made by Monty Python, and *Mary Poppins*, to name just a few.

For comic role models, consider any Three Stooges movie, early Woody Allen films, Hepburn and Tracy combos (especially *Adam's Rib*), Carole Lombard in *To Be or Not to Be*, Buster Keaton, Charlie Chaplin, Audrey Hepburn in *My Fair Lady*, and *Murphy Brown* reruns.

For funny movies about love, check out *Groundhog Day, Housesitter, The Object of Beauty, When Harry Met Sally, Bringing Up Baby, Pillow Talk, High Society, Lady and the Tramp, Singin' in the Rain*, and *An American in Paris*, to just skim the top.

Or how about *The Full Monty, The Man Who Loved Women, A Fish Called Wanda, Meet the Parents, Bull Durham*, or *All of Me*?

Lighten Up, by C. W. Metcalf and Roma Felible (Perseus Publishing, 1993). Humaerobic exercises and lots of scientific reasons why laughter, especially under stress, is crucial to our survival.

Love and Marriage, by Bill Cosby (Bantam Books, 1990). A tender, funny celebration of commitment.

Ten Fun Things to Do Before You Die, by Karol Jackowski (Hyperion, 2000). A gentle, funny reminder to loosen up—written by a nun. Use it to make your own shared list of ten things to do together before you die.

The Healing Power of Humor, by Allen Klein (Jeremy Tarcher, 1989). Funny, practical ways to use humor to ease your path in life. Excellent.

They Shoot Canoes, Don't They, by Patrick F. McManus (Henry Holt, 1982). He has written many hilarious books with a hunting and fishing theme. Great to read aloud.

Websites:

Funny Times
http://www.funnytimes.com

The Onion
http://www.onion.com

World Laughter
http://www.worldlaughter.com

But There's
Nothing to Do

You'll Need:

Considerable strength to resist the deadly pull of entropy.

A sense of humor.

Various fun items, like secluded pools, blindfolds, champagne, and pennies for flipping.

Time required: A few minutes to hours of fun.

When to Do It:

- When you are bored, depressed, in a rut, tense, or overworked or haven't laughed in a long time.

- When it is Friday night and you get that itchy feeling of wanting to drive in the summer twilight in a convertible with your sweetie, drive until you find some fun (or get into a little trouble . . .).

- When it is Saturday night, you've been a good mother/father/employee/employer all week, but if you don't get out of the house and go a little wild, you may hurt someone.

What Is It?

A lack of creative, fun, different ideas of things to do together plagues every relationship I know. I call it "almost anywhere in August" syndrome. You know, those dog days of summer when the humidity is 98 percent, there's nothing good to eat in the refrigerator, you've seen all the new movies and rented all the decent videos, your conversations consist solely of "How was your day?" "Fine." And boredom coats everything like wet sap. . . .

What to Do:

Drives

Drive to a neighborhood you have never visited, park, and go for a stroll. Visit a ritzy area and admire the architecture and gardens; walk through an ethnic district and let the new smells, languages, and colors wash over you; hike a route you drive regularly; look for walking guidebooks for your area for more inspiration.

Drive out to the country or beach on a night with a full moon, and have a lunar picnic. Bring a Frisbee that glows in the dark.

Rent a "dream" car for a day, dress up, and play "rich" together.

Rent a horse and buggy, and go for a ride in the moonlight, the snow, or a soft, spring rain.

Get Wet

Go skinny-dipping in a pool, ocean, pond, or quarry. Feel the balance between holding yourself up and the water supporting you. Swim as close to each other as you can without touching.

Imagination

Listen to radio dramas in bed, in front of a fire, out in the yard under the stars, or on the roof. Call your local public radio station for programming information. Also experiment with books on tape or love poetry on tape.

See "Music" and "What to Do on Friday Night."

Rent a video with a favorite love scene. Watch it, then reenact it together. (This may take some preparation. Don't be afraid to decorate a set, gather a few props, even costumes. . . .)

Have you ever taken your partner someplace blindfolded?

Drag out old love letters and cards to reread while sitting in front of a crackling fire or on the porch while a sweet breeze ruffles your hair.

Shopping

Go to a bookstore, record store, or clothes store. Select one item you know your partner will like and one you would like your partner to try on, read, or listen to. Then go for coffee and dessert to talk about why you picked what you did.

See "Nurturing Merriment: Physical Play."

Dancing

Sample big band dancing. No place near you? Dig out old albums, borrow
from friends or the library, and make a couple of long-play tapes. Then
push the furniture out of the way, invite friends, dress in cocktail attire,
and dance the night away! Do the same for Cajun music, waltzes, line
dancing. Chip in for an hour's instruction by a dance teacher, or rent a
dance instruction video to watch.

Learn to tango. Naked.

Fantasize

Recline over champagne, around a fire in your backyard, or under the
covers. Take turns answering:

You win $100,000. How will you spend the money?

Now you win a free trip, a dream vacation for two weeks. Where would
you go, and with whom? How about a dream weekend trip?

If you could be a famous person, whom would you be?

*See "Getting to Know
You: A Few of My
Favorite Things" for a
related exercise.*

If you could have free, unlimited service for one year from a chauffeur,
maid, cook, personal dresser, or accountant, whom would you choose, if
anyone? Why?

If you could have anyone in the world to dinner, whom would you
invite? How about anyone from history?

If you could travel back in time, what date would you choose? How
about traveling into the future? Why?

If you could "borrow" brains from any person in history, whom would
you choose? Why?

Relationship Growth

*See "Resources" and
also "Ruts: Long-Term
Changes."*

Research and attend a couple's workshop or lecture together. Check your
local college for classes, scan the announcement section in your paper, or
call a national organization for a workshop being given near you.

Games

Play a favorite game. Naked.

Play strip gin rummy.

Go on a lucky toss hike. At each corner or fork, or wherever you like, flip a coin. Heads, you go right. Tails, left.

Or use a toss of a coin to determine who is "it," then play tag. Naked.

Play hide-and-seek around your neighborhood at night. Not naked.

Together, pick a small object that has meaning for both of you (a piece of lingerie, a "white elephant" wedding gift, a button with a funny slogan), and take turns giving it to each other in silly, touching, weird, surprising ways. Examples would be mailing the object to the hotel where your honey is staying on business and having the concierge place it in her room before she gets there or placing it (with chocolate) in the refrigerator for Valentine's Day or mailing it to him during a stressful week or baking it in a birthday cake.

Get Wacky

Visit a mall, arcade, or airport that has a photo machine. Take some snapshots together. Make wild faces. Post these photos where you can see them often.

Write a poem to each other.

Dress up in each other's clothes—even underwear!

Trade with a friend: while you're out with your partner doing something boring, like buying new underwear at Kmart, your friend sneaks into the house and arranges a romantic dinner in front of the fireplace; a bottle of champagne and a bubble bath with a trail of Hershey kisses leading the way from the front door to the bathroom; or flowers, dancing music, and a table full of delectable desserts, all of which can be smeared on one or more parts of the body. . . . Reciprocate when the time comes!

*See "Holidays:
Birthdays" for
variations.*

THE COUPLE'S COMFORT BOOK

Kidnap your mate. Timing is everything: you want your sweetie caught off-guard but not covered with mud from the garden. Blindfolds are essential, big money is not. For example, it is Thursday night, your partner is in a funk; blindfold and take out for a cheap, healthy dinner. Kids can be kidnapped too. (They love to be blindfolded.)

Find or recreate your wedding clothes, and wear them out to dinner. Or rent a dream outfit and wear that out to dinner.

Variety

Go through the weekend paper together. Cut out five or so things you want to do. Put them in a hat. Each of you draws one. Do each activity without one word of protest or grousing. You can also dream up five activities on your own or use ones from the book.

If you live in an urban area, buy a restaurant guide and keep it in your car or carry it with you as prevention against the restaurant black hole. "Where do you want to eat?" "I don't know, I can't think of anyplace." "Me neither." "How about pizza?" "No, I had pizza for lunch. . . ."

Resources:

Workshop Sources

The Association for Couples in Marriage Enrichment—an international, nonprofit, nonsectarian organization whose purpose is to promote better marriages by providing enrichment opportunities and resources that strengthen couple relationships, increase intimacy, and enhance personal growth, mutual fulfillment, and family wellness. Visit http://www.bettermarriages.org, or phone 800–634–8325 or 336–724–1526.

PREP (Prevention and Relationship Enhancement Program)—based on over twenty years of research, the PREP approach is for *all couples*, from the newly involved to long-time partners, who want to learn the specific skills essential to a lasting love. You will not be asked to share personal concerns with other members of the class. PREP is a

straightforward educational approach, quick paced and often humorous. Visit http://www.prepinc.com, or phone 303–759–9931 or
800–366–0166.

Please Understand Me: Character and Temperament Types, by David Keirsey
(Prometheus, 1984). Bored? Figure out what type your mate is—and
yourself.

Websites:

Gratefulness
http://www.gratefulness.org

Love Games
http://www.lovingyou.com/content/lovegames

Getting to Know You

You'll Need:

A sense of adventure.

Personal objects with special meaning.

Photographs and/or home movies of your childhood.

Time required: Fifteen minutes to an hour.

When to Do It:

- On vacation when you've run out of things to talk about.

- When you are bored with your partner.

- When you want to get closer but you're not sure how to go about doing this.

What Is It?

One of the mistakes I make in my relationship is thinking I know my husband. I know that he likes squash (the vegetable), his favorite author is Steinbeck, and he wants to win an Academy Award for cinematography. But there are so many other things I don't know. Like what he felt like the day his fifth-grade picture was taken. Or what his favorite flavor of ice cream is. Does he have a role model? What is his favorite memory of his father? What would he do with three wishes?

In the deepest sense, knowing someone is impossible. We can never fully share our separate worlds. But there is an infinite amount of pleasure and knowledge in trying! Getting to know your partner allows you the chance to meet him or her all over again, to gain a fresh perspective on your loved one's opinions, her vast personal history, his fierce likes and dislikes. We want to be known. We crave our partners to know these details about us because it helps us feel loved and less alone.

What to Do:

Pictures of Childhood

Have you ever said, "I wish I had known you as a child?" Very few of us had the opportunity to grow up with our mates, but you can glimpse what your partner was like as a child and gain insight into his or her present struggles and triumphs.

Select several pictures or one home movie of when you were a child. Don't use your rational mind to pick these pictures. Instead take a few deep breaths and shuffle through the photo pile or album, or pick a movie at random.

Snuggle where you won't be disturbed. Silently view the images. Then look at them again, this time talking about what it felt like to be that child in the pictures. Start with specifics and stick to feelings, then expand from there. For example, Patty showed Brenda a picture of her sitting on a stone bench. She started with her memories and feelings about that bench, what she was wearing, what it felt like to be six. Then she expanded to the bigger picture: the garden, the house, the neighborhood. She didn't limit herself to reality but combined memories with what she knows now.

The point is not to recount a dry history but to use the images to inspire you to tell a story about your childhood. Use the pictures as a jumping-off point. Talk about what you were doing and feeling on the day the picture was taken. Study your body language and that of anyone else in the photo. If you can't remember, extrapolate from the picture. How did you feel about yourself? What were your fears at the time? What did you enjoy doing? Are there friends or siblings in the pictures? What was your relationship with them like? What about your parents? Consider the historical times you were living in when the picture was taken. What events were influencing your life?

Note: If you have been sexually abused or otherwise are trying to heal from your childhood, use this exercise with caution or under the guidance of a therapist.

If you experienced a childhood trauma such as your house burning down or a parent dying, choose a date before that occurred, or describe your childhood bedroom or tree fort to your mate. Do not do this if you find it too depressing.

What Did Mommy or Daddy Do?

This exercise was given to me by Robin Siegal, a clinical social worker in private practice in Beverly Hills. Proceed cautiously or under the guidance of a therapist if your childhood was abusive.

Relax together, perhaps lying side by side on your bed. Silently and each at your own pace, think back to when you were young, back to a time when your opposite-gender parent (your father if you are a woman, your mother if you are a man, and for same sex couples, choose the parent who was most nurturing to you) made you feel loved . . . comforted you . . . nurtured you. Allow your mind to drift through whatever images and feelings float up. Remember to breathe deeply. Take plenty of time.

When you are ready, share what you discovered with your partner. Be sure to listen to each other fully and to not interrupt. You might want to make notes of what your partner says.

Siegal says, "We internalize in a very primal way what our parents did to nurture us. We expect our partners to do the same." *It is these childhood experiences of being comforted that form the expectations you have of how you should be cared for today.* If your mother made you soup and waited on you hand and foot when you were sick, you can see why you may overreact when your partner doesn't do the same. If your father marched down to the principal's office and stood up for his little girl, you might understand why it hurts you so if your partner doesn't defend your honor in even minor episodes.

What do you do with this knowledge? Make it conscious. Talk about it. When you comfort your partner, especially when he or she is hurt, tired, or vulnerable, try to be conscious of how his or her parents acted.

See "Self-Care in Relationships."

Realize your expectations about how to be comforted can't always be met. Find ways to comfort *yourself* that meet these deepest needs. As always, be kindhearted with each other.

A Few of My Favorite Things

All relationships get into conversational ruts, a condition I call "Temporary Boredom Caused by Too Much Familiarity." You want to have a meaningful discussion, but you can't think of anything to talk about. A good antidote is the exercise below. These questions might help you rediscover your partner. At the very least, you won't be bored.

If you were stranded on a desert island and you could bring only five foods, what would you choose?

Same desert island, but now pick five books.

How about five movies? (A generator and VCR are available.)

What five pieces of music could you listen to over and over again?

If you could make one telephone call a month from this island, who would you call?

When you were a child, what was your favorite book?

When you were a child, what was your favorite fairy tale?

When you were a child, what was your biggest fear?

When you were a child, what would you never, ever eat?

When you were a child, who was your hero/heroine?

What is your favorite thing to do on your birthday?

What is your favorite thing to do on _____ (fill in a holiday)?

What is your favorite thing to do on Saturday?

What is your favorite thing to do on Sunday?

What is your favorite childhood memory?

What is one of the best vacations you ever had?

What is one of the most memorable meals you ever ate?

What is one of the most perfect days you ever experienced?

What did you learn from your mother?

What did you learn from your father?

What teacher in your life influenced you the most?

How do you want to be remembered?

What have you always wanted the two of us to do together?

What have you always wanted to do by yourself?

What place or person have you always wanted to visit?

Object Lessons

Remember the opening sequence from the film *To Kill a Mockingbird*? Scout caresses the treasures in her cigar box: a collection of marbles, Atticus's watch, the gifts Boo Radley had left her in the tree hole. We all have such prizes. Heirloom candlesticks, a childhood doll, a scarf woven by a grandfather—gifts of numinous value that preserve precious memories that can help your mate know you better.

Go in search of a special object, one with an exceptional meaning or story attached. Meet back in a comfy spot, maybe your shared sanctuary. Take turns telling your lover why this object is important to you. To get your imagination going, start by completing the sentence "This object symbolizes _____ to me."

When you are finished, give your partner a moment to respond, then switch places. This is a great game to play with children (they can participate or just listen to Mom and Dad).

Resources:

A Natural History of Love, by Diane Ackerman (Vintage Books, 1995). A lovely series of essays on love.

Romantic Rendezvous Game—Card and board game combining sex with romantic communication. Available on the Web. Search for the best price.

To Know You Better Game—Board game with dice and cards with questions such as "What household chore would you most likely want to avoid?" The winner receives a prize (chosen beforehand from the "prize" list) from their partner. Available from http://www.time-fortwo.com.

What's My Type, by Kathleen V. Hurley and Theodore E. Dobson (HarperSanFrancisco, 1991). A guide to figuring your strengths and weaknesses using the Enneagram. Another way to get to know each other.

Would You? Questions to Challenge Your Beliefs, by Evelyn McFarlane and James Saywell (Villard Books, 2000). My favorite in the best-selling series. Be prepared for deep conversation!

Zen and the Art of Falling in Love, by Brenda Shoshanna Lukeman (Simon and Schuster, 2003). Open your life to love, fall in love . . . and stay in love.

Websites:

Questions for Couples
http://questionsforcouples.com

Time for Two Games
http://www.timefortwo.com

Reminisce and Rekindle

You'll Need:

Relaxing music like Kay Gardner's *Garden of Ecstasy*.

Your couple's journal or paper, and pens.

Creative materials—paints, instruments, your imagination.

Time required: Thirty minutes to an hour or more.

When to Do It:

- When you find yourself complaining about things he or she does that you once found charming, beautiful, or magnetic.

- When you catch your partner picking his teeth, smelling her socks to see if she can wear them again, or prying his underwear straight.

- On vacation, before making love, before a soul-strokes talk.

- When mired in a long, drawn-out dispute.

What Is It?

We've all said it or at least thought it once, usually during a disagreement or an especially dry period. "Why did I commit to this person?" (Or why did I marry them, love them, put up with them?)

Because of our unconscious agenda, over time we begin to detest the very things that first attracted us to our mates. Regularly reaching back into our emotional memory banks to refresh and stoke the original passion is one way to keep our unconscious selves from destroying our relationship. Recalling why you fell in love, recapturing the vivid emotions you felt during your courtship, brings the focus back to the invaluable aspects of your relationship.

What to Do:

Rekindle

Start by playing some peaceful music. We like to use two pieces with a brief pause between because this helps you know when to open your eyes. Read on for clarification. Either record the meditation and play it back while you both follow, or read it over several times and play it back in your mind.

Sit facing each other in a comfortable position. Close your eyes and
Relax. . . . Continue to breathe slowly and deeply. In your own time and
in your own way, imagine your heart. Visualize a flame or ball of light in
your heart. It may be clear or it may be a color. Spend a moment enjoying
the warmth, the power of the light. . . . Now imagine you are breathing
into this light. With each of your powerful breaths, the light grows
brighter and brighter, gradually filling your chest. . . . With another deep
breath, the light begins to radiate up into your neck and face and head,
filling your mind with a wonderful sense of balance and peace. . . . Continue to breathe deeply as you visualize this glowing illumination spreading along each of your arms. . . . The light now moves down, warming
your stomach and genitals. . . . Another breath sends the warmth shoot-
ing down into your legs, all the way to your toes. . . . Take several more
breaths to send this tingling, wonderful light throughout your body. . . .
Bask in the sense of aliveness and well-being you've created. (This is
where the pause in the music comes in.)

And now, open your eyes and *without speaking,* hold hands and look into
your partner's eyes. Keep taking deep breaths, focusing on the warm,
beautiful light that is filling your body. Feel the light beginning to expand
beyond you . . . out through your eyes and into the eyes of your beloved.
With each breath you take together, the light grows stronger, connecting
your hearts. Stay with this for a moment or two. Don't worry if you feel
embarrassed or overwhelmed. Just keep breathing.

Maintaining eye contact and heart contact, let your mind drift back, back
to when you and your lover first fell in love, a time when passion and fas-
cination filled your life. Reach back into your memory and allow these
beautiful memories to flow through you. Keep taking deep breaths. Keep
feeling the love that fills you and fills your partner while you spend a few
moments reliving the details of your shared past. What did your lover
smell like? Do you remember a particular smile or gesture that captivated
you? How did you feel? Where were you? Allow these powerful desires
to arise.

Slowly, realize this isn't a memory but the present. This is actually happening. The person facing you is still the person you fell in love with.

Allow this thought to break your defenses down just a little bit. Allow more of your love and admiration to flow. If you feel afraid or anxious, breathe into that fear, and remember your partner is supporting you with her light, his love. Surrender to your feelings little by little. Trust your partner to stay with you. Breathe away your fears, breathe away your blocks, breathe away your anger. Allow yourself to open to your feelings. If you feel sexually aroused, let these feelings fill your heart and body too.

When you are ready, embrace your partner.

In the next day or so, find a way to express your experience to your partner—through words (a soul-strokes talk is one way), by touch (making love right after this meditation can be great), or in writing (a love letter).

Remember When We Used To . . .

*See "Togetherness Time:
What Do We Want to
Do?" and "Writing Your
Own Comfort Book" for
help remembering what
fun is.*

Relax and daydream back to when you were wooing each other. What did you do? There was probably a period of several years when you couldn't get enough of each other. Staying relaxed and in the spirit of fun, make a list of activities you used to enjoy that you may or may not have done for a while. You may want to do this together, with one person recording ideas. You don't have to limit yourself to things you actually did; you can also include almosts, wish we would haves, and if we had had the moneys. In the next week, schedule one thing from your list to do.

Resources:

Authentic Happiness, by Martin E. P. Seligman (Free Press, 2004).
Seligman has dedicated his life to helping people find happiness. An important and practical guide.

Keeping the Love You Find, by Harville Hendrix (Atria Books, 1992).
Although marketed for singles, this book has plenty of stuff to help couples, especially with unconscious agendas. If you want to go deeper and are willing to spend a little time, this is a great book to do it with.

Living Happily Ever After: Couples Talk About Lasting Love, by Laurie
Wagner with photographs by Stephanie Rausser (Chronicle Books,
1996). Eighty photos revealing how couples express their love.

Simple Loving: A Path to Deeper, More Sustainable Relationships, by Janet
Luhrs (Penguin, 2000). A vast sourcebook for creating lasting intimate relationships built on values.

Acceptance

You'll Need:

Your best self.

Time required: A few minutes in the moment.

When to Do It:

- When you are obsessed with trying to change your partner.

- When you are more comfortable being negative than positive.

- When you are being ruled by expectations, beliefs, or complaints from your past.

What Is It?

Acceptance is the heart of exultant love. It is what every human being craves. It is the turning point in the never-ending search for wholeness through relationship.

But we all know the hard truth: acceptance doesn't come cheap. It is very rarely easy. No one ever achieves total acceptance forever. (I shouldn't say no one. Perhaps saints and religious figures have attained total acceptance of humanity for extended periods of time. But every minute of every hour of every day? Hmmm. . . .)

Acceptance as a concept has become very muddied. Blame it on the seventies (along with disco music and shag haircuts), but somewhere we learned unconditional love should be our ultimate goal. This is impossible and wrong, and it causes disaster. Adults cannot love other adults without conditions, at least not for very long. Unconditional love is only possible for pets and children. The dictionary defines *unconditional* as absolute, unqualified, categorical. But we all have conditions, also known as human needs. Acceptance is a profound, healing process. It means you are continually trying to embrace the whole person you love, including his or her limitations. On the other hand, loving unconditionally is a dead-end. It means you throw your needs out the window and try for sainthood.

The person we choose to be intimate and committed with is a mirror image of ourselves, the missing parts of our own psyche. Our mates represent many things to us, but primarily they represent everything we love and hate about ourselves but are unwilling to lay claim to. Hence if we accept our partners, it means we are accepting ourselves, and perhaps nothing is more difficult for most humans beings to do.

There is no easy recipe for accepting your sweetheart, with all his or her beauty marks. Perhaps the following suggestions will improve the frequency with which you are able *to be with* instead of try to change your beloved.

What to Do:

Stop Trying to Change Your Partner

"It is our job to state our thoughts and feelings clearly and to make responsible decisions that are congruent with our values and beliefs. It is not our job to make another person think and feel the way we do or the way we want them to," writes psychotherapist Harriet Goldhor Lerner in *The Dance of Anger.* If only it were this clear and easy in everyday life!

Acceptance begins when we take responsibility for our lives, when we stop thinking our lover must do things our way or that he or she is wrong, flawed, less than we are. Each of us perceives the world in a different way. Each perception is just as valid. None is more right than another. We must absorb this fact into our blood, into our essence, and not just our heads. We can repeat to ourselves, "This is my lover's reality. It is neither better nor worse than mine. He or she doesn't have to do everything my way." If we can truly believe this, we become able to honestly see and appreciate who we are in relationship with.

The next time you find yourself saying or thinking, "If only my partner would do this . . ." or "My mate makes me so angry when he . . ." or "My lover makes me so crazy when she . . . ," *stop!* Take a deep breath. Ask yourself, "What can I do in this situation to change my own perception or behavior?" Wrest your attention away from what your partner is doing wrong and realize the liberating truth: no one makes you do or feel anything. *You always have a choice*. Never is that more heart-wrenchingly annoying than when you have to choose between spending your energy trying to change your lover or spending your energy trying to change yourself. It is much more tempting to try to change your partner, but you will never, ever succeed.

Busting Negative Thinking

We all have a constant inner dialogue running in our heads. Unfortunately, much of that inner dialogue is made up of negative, judgmental voices whose sole purpose is to erode our self-esteem and tempt us to judge, railroad, and denounce our sweetheart. By helping each other to recognize and stop this negative chatter *in the moment* you can break the cycle of negativity and constant judgment.

Next time you notice your partner's mood shift abruptly for the worse, or if your lover overreacts to a situation or a comment made by you or someone else, ask him or her:

> What are you telling yourself?
>
> Is it making you feel good or bad?
>
> Is there a different way to talk to yourself in this situation?

This is a powerful but tricky tool. *Never use it with an attitude of psychological superiority*. Always take a deep breath and put yourself in your partner's shoes *before* you ask the questions. Example: You've been manipulating your lover all day to do something *you* want to do. He or she finally blows up at you. You smugly say, "What are you telling yourself? How is it making you feel?" This is a misuse of the technique, and I promise it will only make things worse.

A better scenario: You are driving and your lover is directing from the passenger seat. "Why don't you change lanes? We're going to be late." You take a deep breath and ask, "What are you telling yourself?" Several things might happen. Your partner might tense up and be silent yet underneath be thinking through his or her self-talk. Or your partner might laugh and share what's going on inside ("If we are late, then I'm a bad person"). Or your mate might snap and say, "I don't want to talk about this right now." Whatever happens, instead of being trapped in your anger, you will have reframed the situation and introduced the possibility of change.

Talk about this technique before using it. Get each partner's approval. Use it with an attitude of empathy. Do acknowledge to each other that there will be times when you won't be open to your partner's help. Communicate now how you will tell your partner this. "I don't feel comfortable examining the voices in my head right now" or some such comment will suffice.

See "Divine Sustenance: Love and Fear" for another take on positive thinking and "Daily Communication: Catching the Inner Dialogue in Action" for another "inner talk" technique.

Acceptance Meditation

You can record this meditation and do it together, or take turns reading it to each other, or read it to yourself a few times and then play it back in your head. If you do this alone, simply omit the very beginning and ending. Soft music might help you relax.

Find a few moments to be together, without interruptions. Sit or lie down and **Relax.**

See "About Relaxing."

Feel your body letting go, settling in. There is no place else to be but here, nothing else to do but accept your beloved.

Face your partner. Take a moment to smile into your lover's eyes, behold the unique beauty of your beloved. Spend a few moments with this, then separate and close your eyes.

Take a deep breath, and send your mind down, down into the place in yourself where you feel only love for your partner, only mercy and compassion and loving-kindness. Take a moment and settle into this place. Now imagine that this place of great love and acceptance in you begins to emit a beam of light. Visualize this beam any way you choose.

See this beam wrapping itself around your lover, bathing her or him in its softness, its high-definition beauty. As you breathe in, feel the light in you, and say to yourself silently, "I accept you as you are." As you slowly breathe out, say to your beloved, "May you be at peace."

Breathe into your judgments, your pain, the part of you that finds fault with this divine and perfect being. Feel the light working its magic, setting its peaceful mantle over your heart, opening you more and more to acceptance. And breathe out, send out the peace and lovingkindness you always feel deep in your soul for this wonderful person who stands before you.

Breathing in, "I accept you as you are." Breathing out, "May you be at peace." There is nothing else to do but accept your beloved. Feel your heart breaking open with devotion, with grace, with love. Keep breathing in acceptance and breathing out peace as long as you need to. Then slowly come back to your beloved, open your eyes, and conclude by smiling into each other's eyes.

Resources:

An Unfinished Marriage, by Joan Anderson (Broadway, 2002). After a year away from her marriage (recounted in *A Year by the Sea*), Anderson wrote this insightful, honest, moving memoir of the new journey that she and her husband undertook, seasoned by their years of marriage but newly awakened to the possibilities of their future together.

Embracing Your Inner Critic, by Hal Stone and Sidra Stone (HarperSan-Francisco, 1993). How to turn self-criticism into healthy growth. Some discussion of the critic's role in relationships.

Love Is Never Enough, by Aaron T. Beck (Perennial, 1989). Cognitive therapy applied to relationships. Excellent.

The Highly Sensitive Person in Love: How Your Relationships Can Thrive When the World Overwhelms You, by Elaine N. Aron (Broadway Books, 2001). Fifty percent of what determines divorce is genetic temperament. If you are in the 20 percent of people who are highly sensitive, the risk of an unhappy relationship is especially high. Work with your sensitivity and grow closer.

Gratify and Delight

When to Do It:

- When your love expression muscles have atrophied.

- When you think surprises are foolish.

- When your partner is going through a rough time.

- When you feel incapable of coming up with innovative ideas.

- Anytime you want to say, "I treasure you."

What Is It?

Picture this: You want to declare your devotion, ardor, and zeal for this majestic person you share your life with, but you can't think of any good way to do that. Candy? He's cutting down on fat. Flowers? I did that last time. Shoe shine? Hmm. . . .

A mainstay of nurturing the relationship is finding small, *frequent,* remarkable, and discriminating ways to acknowledge your sweetheart. While there is nothing wrong with flowers (I got some while writing this chapter, and I loved them) or other dear stand-bys (every woman I interviewed mentioned how much she likes to be waited on), you have so many feelings to express, so many shades of gratitude to give form to, that you need a kaleidoscope of delicious choices to choose from.

What to Do:

Notes

The questionnaires I sent to couples almost all came back with suggestions for love notes. Try:

A full-blown love letter. Check out *Love Letters* by Lady Antonia Frazer for inspiration. You could start your letter by completing the sentence:

You'll Need:

Greeting cards, notepaper, cartoons and jokes cut from newspapers and books.

Inexpensive gifts such as a stuffed Piglet, a hand-crafted mug for his morning tea, a bottle of body lotion that she loves but won't spend the extra three bucks for.

Time required: A few minutes a day.

How do I love thee . . .

I would marry you again because . . .

I appreciate you for . . .

See "Couple Customs: A World of Your Own" for a related idea.

Mail it to work or home. Another nice touch: when going on vacation, mail a love letter ahead of time to the hotel or bed-and-breakfast where you'll be staying.

Funny greeting cards can be a giant relationship help. Visit a card shop when you are down, read and laugh at the silly cards, then stock up. Keep some cards at work.

Write a note on an unusual surface: the bathroom mirror, toilet paper roll, the inside of a candy wrapper, your body, the honey jar. Relate your note to the form, for example, "You're the honey in my hive."

Hide notes, cards, or cartoons in your partner's suitcase when he or she travels. A *New Yorker* cartoon a day in an envelope is one idea. Debra includes love poems, gum, and snapshots of fun times along with notes about how much she'll miss her mate. She packs him one envelope for each day (less on long trips), puts the first one in his carry-on bag, and writes, "Open at 30,000 feet." (If this idea overwhelms you, consider a single envelope.)

Perhaps a cartoon or love note placed on your mate's pillow at night with a chocolate kiss would be appreciated. Or tuck enigmatic clues around the house. "Meet me in our love nest at 9:00" or "You bring the whipped cream, I'll bring the hot fudge." Obviously, if you have children, put these rendezvous notes where they won't be seen.

If You Hate to Write

If you hate to write, find an image that depicts your feelings. Look in photography and art books (you could use high-quality color photocopies), visit student art exhibits, check out museum gift shops and catalogs for art postcards or posters.

Record a sexy message on a cassette, and leave it in your lover's car stereo. Add suggestive music and perhaps an invitation to meet for a "snack" during your lunch hours at a nearby motel.

GRATIFY AND DELIGHT

See "Music."

Call the radio station your spouse listens to on his or her commute and dedicate a song.

Do Something

Most couples I interviewed also suggested: Do a chore for your mate, without being asked. The more out of character it is for you (you never wash the dog), the more appreciated. Filling the car up with gas is always a great delight. Another is feeding the kids and getting them ready for bed before your spouse comes home from what you already know has been a day from hell.

Plan a Friday night out. Instead of coming home, flopping on the couch, and asking her what she wants to do, come home and suggest a plan. Let the evening reveal how much thought you put into it. Little extras like cleaning the interior of the car, buying him a flower, and refraining from starting any usual nit-picking ("Why did you drive this way? You know it takes twice as long") go a long way.

See "Acceptance."

Make a list together of things that need to be done around your home. Next to each item, make an initial of who will do it: you, your partner, or H for hiring someone. When you have extra time, do one of your tasks (or take the steps to hire someone), and cross it off.

See "Couple Customs: Reconnecting."

Phones

Message machines shouldn't be substitutes for love notes, but it sure is nice to come home to a loving message.

Jennifer of Durham, North Carolina, loves it when her husband calls and says, "I just want to tell you I'm madly in love with you."

For those of you who love technology, fax love notes or other items of interest. Or use your beeper to send a special code of love. Robin, a therapist who teaches workshops in making marriage work, developed a code with her husband to beep to each other "I love you."

Buy Something

Designate a day a month as dollar day (you could decide on a higher amount, but keeping it low is more challenging). During the day, each person spends one dollar *only* on a gift. In the evening, exchange and talk about your choices.

Or give a gift that leads to more giving. A bottle of massage oil, romantic music for slow dancing, scented soap. . . .

Or think of small gifts that save the other person time or hassle. Stop to buy a roll of stamps or a bottle of favorite body lotion, or buy your sweetie something you've noticed she or he has been doing without.

Treat Your Mate like a Customer

In their book *Search for Excellence*, Thomas Peters and Robert Waterman write that winning companies have several things in common, one of which is fawning on their customers. Find ways to delight your partner as if your business future depended on it. Fawning is always appreciated.

Ask her specific questions about her day that indicate you remember (and care) what her plans were.

Restore manners. Offer to unlock the car door on the passenger side first, use cloth napkins and perhaps forgotten table manners, clean the bathroom up after yourself.

Would you be late for an important business meeting? Would you make your boss or a big client late? Enough said.

Use more formal language. A culture is kept alive by its language. Help yours to thrive by calling each other by your full first names or by memorizing a poem to recite while you make love, or take time to make complete sentences or to look up a new word every week and see who can use it the most.

Agree

Is there something your mate does that drives you crazy? (Isn't that a loaded question?) Something you always discourage, like eating chocolate, hogging the bed, leaving dirty socks in the bathroom, or not putting the newspaper away? Give in for one day. Give your mate a little chocolate. Let him sleep in the middle. Put the newspaper away without a dramatic sigh. Don't announce your gift; just do it.

Tattoo

Mary's husband likes tattoos. So Mary, a very staid innkeeper and writer of profound essays, purchased some rub-on tattoos, rubbed one on her tush, didn't tell him, but conveniently rolled over in bed one night. . . . Tattoos might not be your style, but giving your lover a sample of something he or she likes but is positive *you* would never do is highly nurturing.

Water

Initiate a shower together. Wash your lover. All over.

Serve your partner a surprise snack in the shower or tub. Sections of orange to suck on while she showers, cookies and coffee while he soaks, a glass of champagne for both of you and after a sip you jump in the tub with your lover, fully dressed. . . . (Okay, maybe not fully dressed.)

Salute

Deliver a toast to your mate at a family dinner or in front of close friends. Practice ahead of time. Don't wait until a special occasion to deliver.

Find and carry a picture of your beloved in your wallet. Don't announce it, but make sure he or she spies it one day.

Praise

See "Ease into Nurturing Each Other: Express Your Love."

Along with love notes, praise ranks right up there as a great way to show affection. The basic rule for giving praise is *pay attention* to your partner and then speak from your heart about what you see that you like, admire, or find sexy. Details like "I love the curve of your jaw" or "That perfume is fantastic" are most appreciated. The basic principle for accepting a compliment is to do just that: open your heart and take it in. Believe it. *Never make a disparaging remark that cancels out the compliment.* If every time your mate says something nice to you, you respond with, "Oh no, not *me*. I'm a worthless dog, a toothless moron. I'm lower than a snake's belly," he or she might not be as enthusiastic about complimenting you in the future.

More praise hints: Melinda always tries to say thank you and take nothing for granted. Her mate, Vince, likes to brag to friends or whomever will listen about how great she is.

Unrequested public displays of affection can be priceless for pumping up the relationship. Take his hand as you grocery shop, kiss her gently as you wait in line at the movie, show the world you love this person and find him or her desirable.

See "Everyday Rituals: Evening."

Compliments can be a daily occurrence. They don't wear out.

Pay Attention

Learn about each other, and surprise each other with the knowledge. Guess what he will order when you go out, suggest several of her favorite drinks when she can't think of what to order, buy a shirt in his favorite color, take her to a little restaurant she remarked on.

When your mate talks to you, put down what you are doing and give him or her your full attention.

Outrageous

Cover the bed with flower petals. (You can buy them in bags at flower shops. Cover the bed first with an old sheet.)

Give a flower a day for a month.

Write a love note in colored chalk on the sidewalk outside your home or your partner's office.

Mark and Nancy of Long Beach, California, give each other facials. Check out a natural beauty book for recipes that can then be eaten off.

In York, Pennsylvania, Iris and her husband dedicate and sing songs to each other. (If you have a horrible voice, you could lip-synch.) Or visit a Karaoke bar (a Japanese bar where you can sing popular songs to recorded accompaniment) and serenade your lover.

Can you imagine walking into where your soul mate works, grabbing her in a big hug, kissing her long and hard, then turning around and walking out without saying a word? Perhaps handing your sweetie a single flower, a ticket to a concert or ball game, or a greeting card on your way out would also be effective.

Resources:

How to Write a Love Letter: Putting What's in Your Heart on Paper, by Barrie Dolnick and Donald Baack (Harmony Books, 2000). Practical advice for writing all kinds of love letters, including e-mails, for every reason.

Love Notes: Intimate Expressions and Lyrical Verses Which Inspire Romance, Emotional Healing, and Inner Strength, by Jeff Samuels (Xlibris, 2002). Tons of inspiring ideas and examples.

1001 Ways to Be Romantic, by Gregory J. P. Godeck (Casablanca Press, 1991). A slightly sexist book (the subtitle: *A Handbook for Men, A Godsend to Women*), but some of his ideas are clever.

Comfort at a Glance

	INTRODUCTION	BRINGING THE BOOK HOME	ABOUT RELAXING	WHEN I THINK OF NURTURING THE RELATIONSHIP . . .	EASE INTO NURTURING EACH OTHER	A COUPLE'S JOURNAL	SOUL STROKES	DAILY COMMUNICATION	RECOGNIZING YOUR NEEDS	WHEN LIFE IS TOO CRAZY	TOGETHERNESS TIME	EVERYDAY RITUALS	RHYTHMS OF RAPPORT	WINDS OF THE HEAVENS	EMPATHY	WOMEN AND MEN NURTURING EACH OTHER	TOILETS	COUPLE CUSTOMS	NURTURING YOUR RELATIONSHIP THROUGH MONEY	SELF-CARE IN RELATIONSHIPS	NURTURING MERRIMENT	BUT THERE'S NOTHING TO DO	GETTING TO KNOW YOU	REMINISCE AND REKINDLE	ACCEPTANCE
Afraid to Grab Life	4	7	12		21				47										121	125	132				
Angry						31		44	49	54					87	91		105	120		134				156
Anxious			12		21	30		45	49	53	57	68	75						120	125	132				
Big fight		7				31		44	50	54					87				120					152	159
Birthdays		7			23		34							83				114	121	125	132	140	146		
Blaming					23			41	49	53					87			105	117	126	134			152	156
Bored with each other	2				22		34		49			65	75	86				111		125	132	140	146	154	
Bored with yourself								42	49			65		86						125					
Both sexually bored							34	45	49								104	111							
Both too serious			18	16	24				49	53								113		125	132	140		154	
Boundary problems					24	31	34	44	47		63			82	87					125					
Broke					22					53		71							117						
Burned out	4				22				49	53	57	65	74							125	132	141		152	159
Can't accept your partner					23			41	49				75	82	87	91							146	152	156
Can't agree					24	31		41	50	54			76		87	91		105	121		134			152	159
Can't come up with pleasurable ideas	3	7		15	22	30	30				59	65						111	123	130	132	140	148	154	
Can't forgive					23	31		41	50						87		104							152	159
Can't say no to your partner							34	44	49					85						125					
Children	5									54	63	69						107			135	144	150		
Couch potato				15	22	26	34					68						112		125	132	140	146	152	
Crowded									49					81											
Despair	4				21				47									109	121		132				156
Different spending styles					24	31		44	50										118						
Disconnected from body									49																
Don't know what nurturing is	2			15	21	29	34					65				91				126			148	152	
Exhausted			12		24	30				55		72	74							125					

THE COUPLE'S COMFORT BOOK

Comfort at a Glance

GRATIFY AND DELIGHT	TEA AND SYMPATHY	THE ART OF GIFT GIVING	HOLIDAYS	NATURAL NURTURE	A SENSORY BANQUET	EROTIC DELIGHTS	MASSAGE	MOVING INTO YOUR BODIES	MUSIC	NESTING	SHARED SANCTUARY	ROMANTIC ILLUSIONS: WHAT DID YOU EXPECT?	DIVINE SUSTENANCE	CREATIVE CONNECTION	NURTURING DURING CRISIS AND LOSS	LETTING GO	RELEASING RESENTMENT	HOW TO HAVE A NURTURING FIGHT	FORGIVENESS	NEGOTIATING	RUTS	COMMUNITY CONTEXT	COCREATORS	WRITING YOUR OWN COMFORT BOOK	
				198				226					254	262		273					304	311	317	322	Afraid to grab life
								227	230		245		256	263			276	280	289						Angry
	176			192	200		218	224	230		242		258		268	272				295					Anxious
									230			251	256	263			276	286	289	295					Big fight
161	176	180	187	196	200	209	218			238				264										324	Birthdays
											245	251	256			271	276		289	295					Blaming
161		180	184	192	200	208	218	227	232	237		250	254	264		272	276				302	311	317	324	Bored with each other
				192				228				250	254						293		308	311	317		Bored with yourself
161					205	206			233	240				264							307				Both sexually bored
			184	192				227						261		272					304		317	322	Both too serious
						211					244	252				274				300		313			Boundary problems
																	276							334	Broke
161	176			192	202		218	228	231	240	242	250	256	263		273			289		303	310			Burned out
											246	250	254		269	271	276		290						Can't accept your partner
								227		239			254	262		271	276	280		300	307				Can't agree
161		182	184	192	200	209	218														302			322	Can't come up with pleasurable ideas
			188	198								250			269	271	276		289		307				Can't forgive
												252					276		293	295	307				Can't say no to your partner
	178	182	186		204				231	240	245			262			276				304	311		323	Children
				192		210	218	226	232					261							303	311		322	Couch potato
										239	244														Crowded
	176		188										255	263	268	273	276		289		307	311	317		Despair
	181									239							276		289	295	307				Different spending styles
				192	204	210	218	226																	Disconnected from body
																								322	Don't know what nurturing is
					204		218		230		242				269		276				303				Exhausted

Comfort at a Glance

	INTRODUCTION	BRINGING THE BOOK HOME	ABOUT RELAXING	WHEN I THINK OF NURTURING THE RELATIONSHIP…	EASE INTO NURTURING EACH OTHER	A COUPLE'S JOURNAL	SOUL STROKES	DAILY COMMUNICATION	RECOGNIZING YOUR NEEDS	WHEN LIFE IS TOO CRAZY	TOGETHERNESS TIME	EVERYDAY RITUALS	RHYTHMS OF RAPPORT	WINDS OF THE HEAVENS	EMPATHY	WOMEN AND MEN NURTURING EACH OTHER	TOILETS	COUPLE CUSTOMS	NURTURING YOUR RELATIONSHIP THROUGH MONEY	SELF-CARE IN RELATIONSHIPS	NURTURING MERRIMENT	BUT THERE'S NOTHING TO DO	GETTING TO KNOW YOU	REMINISCE AND REKINDLE	ACCEPTANCE
Guilt about time with kids							34		48					82											159
Guilt about time without kids	5						34		48			63	71	82						129					159
Feel like you'll never get enough			12		21		34		47		57								121	127					159
Feel unappreciated					21	30	34	44	49				71				104	112		127				152	
Frazzled			12			30		43		55		67					104	112		125	132	140			156
Frustrated	2		12			31		41	50		57		74	83	87	91	104		117	125	134				
Gender conflicts	4					31		41	49	54				83	87	91	104			126	134		148		156
Grieving						29	34			53					87										
Heartache						29	34								87					125					159
Holiday blues									49									114	121	125	134				
Housework conflicts				16	23	31	34	40	50	54					87	91	104				134				
Ignored					21	30	34	40	49		57		76	83						127			146		
Introducing the idea of nurturing	2	7		15	21	29	34			53					87	91		112		125			148		
Joyless					23	30			49										120	127	132	140		152	
Kids preventing sex									49				71					112			132				
Lack of community						31			49	55															
Lack of empathy				16	22			40	49						87									152	156
Lonely						31	34	40	49	55	57							111		127					
Mired in past mistakes					23	29	34	41							87				117		132			152	159
Money conflicts					23	31	34	40	50	54					87				117		134				156
Morning person mated to night person					23		34	41	50	55			74	83	87			112			132				159
Need more nurturing		7		15	21	26	34		47	53			77			91		111		127	132	140	146	152	159
Need more ways to communicate		7		16	22	29	34	40	47	53		65	77	83	87	92	105	113	118	126		142	149	152	159
Need new friends						31														125		142			

Comfort at a Glance

GRATIFY AND DELIGHT	TEA AND SYMPATHY	THE ART OF GIFT GIVING	HOLIDAYS	NATURAL NURTURE	A SENSORY BANQUET	EROTIC DELIGHTS	MASSAGE	MOVING INTO YOUR BODIES	MUSIC	NESTING	SHARED SANCTUARY	ROMANTIC ILLUSIONS: WHAT DID YOU EXPECT?	DIVINE SUSTENANCE	CREATIVE CONNECTION	NURTURING DURING CRISIS AND LOSS	LETTING GO	RELEASING RESENTMENT	HOW TO HAVE A NURTURING FIGHT	FORGIVENESS	NEGOTIATING	RUTS	COMMUNITY CONTEXT	COCREATORS	WRITING YOUR OWN COMFORT BOOK	
													258				276		289	300		311			Guilt about time with kids
											245		258				276		289	300	303	311		324	Guilt about time without kids
						211				238			258			273	276			300		311			Feel like you'll never get enough
161						211	218						257				276			296					Feel unappreciated
			184	193	202	210	218		231	238	242										302				Frazzled
	176			194				227	233	237	245	248	256	262	268	271	276	280		295			317		Frustrated
				195		214			233	238		250	256			271	276	280	293	295	305				Gender conflicts
	176								230				255	263	266	273			290						Grieving
	176	180					218	227	230				255		268		276	280	289			310			Heartache
161	176	180	184												266	273	276				303	310			Holiday blues
										236		250	256			273	276	280	289	295					Housework conflicts
161		180			206							250		262			276								Ignored
161					206																			322	Introducing the idea of nurturing
161		180	184	193	200							248	255	262	266		276		289		304	311		322	Joyless
						210			233	240							276	280		300	305				Kids preventing sex
			185												267		276				308	315			Lack of community
												250	256		269	273	276					310			Lack of empathy
	176												258								308	312			Lonely
													258			271	276		289			311	317		Mired in past mistakes
									233	239			256			271	276	280	289	295			320		Money conflicts
									230			250	256				276			300	309				Morning person mated to night person
161		180	184	198	204	211	218	223			242	251		263	268									322	Need more nurturing
	181		186	198	204	207	218	223	229	237	243	248	255	263	268	273			290			312	317		Need more ways to communicate
			185												267						306	312		324	Need new friends

Comfort at a Glance

	INTRODUCTION	BRINGING THE BOOK HOME	ABOUT RELAXING	WHEN I THINK OF NURTURING THE RELATIONSHIP…	EASE INTO NURTURING EACH OTHER	A COUPLE'S JOURNAL	SOUL STROKES	DAILY COMMUNICATION	RECOGNIZING YOUR NEEDS	WHEN LIFE IS TOO CRAZY	TOGETHERNESS TIME	EVERYDAY RITUALS	RHYTHMS OF RAPPORT	WINDS OF THE HEAVENS	EMPATHY	WOMEN AND MEN NURTURING EACH OTHER	TOILETS	COUPLE CUSTOMS	NURTURING YOUR RELATIONSHIP THROUGH MONEY	SELF-CARE IN RELATIONSHIPS	NURTURING MERRIMENT	BUT THERE'S NOTHING TO DO	GETTING TO KNOW YOU	REMINISCE AND REKINDLE	ACCEPTANCE
Need solitude			12		24			41	49			68	76	86		100				125					
Need sympathy							34		49	55													148		159
Needy					21	31	34		47				77	83	87				121	125			148		
New baby	5				24				47	55	71			83			104	114			132				
No feeling of home								41	49								104	114							
No relationship goals				16	22	26	34		49		57							113	123						
No time for each other	5	7		16	21	26	34	41	49	54	57	65	79		87			112	117						
Not enough fun together				15	21			42	49		59	65						111	123			140	146	154	
Not enough sex		7		15		31			49			72				98	104					140		152	
Out of touch with nature									49	54												141			
Overworked				16	24	30			49	55	57						105			125	132	140			
Partner doesn't initiate sex					24			45	49							98				127				152	
Partner doesn't listen			7		24	26	34	43	49							91				127			146		159
Partner interrupts you					24	26	34	43	49							91				127					
Partner is exhausted					24				49	55		72			87					125					
Partner never initiates nurturing	4	7		15	21	29		45	47							91				125			148	152	
Partner is too serious								42	49											125	132			154	
Pessimistic about relationship				15				41	49		57						109			125					156
Relationship stuck in a rut	2	7		15	21	26	34	44	47			68	74	86	87			111	120	127	132	142	149	154	159
Repetitive arguments							34	44	49					86	87	91	105		120	125	134			152	156
Resentful								44	48					86			104		117	125				152	
Sad							34		49						87			112		127	132				159
Sensory deprived									49									112			132	143		152	

Comfort at a Glance

GRATIFY AND DELIGHT	TEA AND SYMPATHY	THE ART OF GIFT GIVING	HOLIDAYS	NATURAL NURTURE	A SENSORY BANQUET	EROTIC DELIGHTS	MASSAGE	MOVING INTO YOUR BODIES	MUSIC	NESTING	SHARED SANCTUARY	ROMANTIC ILLUSIONS: WHAT DID YOU EXPECT?	DIVINE SUSTENANCE	CREATIVE CONNECTION	NURTURING DURING CRISIS AND LOSS	LETTING GO	RELEASING RESENTMENT	HOW TO HAVE A NURTURING FIGHT	FORGIVENESS	NEGOTIATING	RUTS	COMMUNITY CONTEXT	COCREATORS	WRITING YOUR OWN COMFORT BOOK	
									237	242											308				Need solitude
161							218								266										Need sympathy
							218					248	256		263							312			Needy
	176					211	218			239	245			262	267	273						312	317	324	New baby
				203						236	242						276					315	317		No feeling of home
				196									256		263		276			295	303	310	317		No relationship goals
			184							239	242						276		289	295	303		317		No time for each other
161				192	200	206	218		232						264		276		289		303		317	322	Not enough fun together
				198	205		218		233	240					264		276		289	295	307				Not enough sex
				192											269						308				Out of touch with nature
				194	202		218			238	242					272					308			322	Overworked
						213									264	273	276	280	289	300	307				Partner doesn't initiate sex
											242		257			274	276	280	289	300	307				Partner doesn't listen
											242		257			274	276	280	289	300	307				Partner interrupts you
					202		218	224	230	240	242				269						305				Partner is exhausted
161											242		257	262	267		276		289	300	307			322	Partner never initiates nurturing
								227					257	261		272	276				304				Partner is too serious
													256		263		276	280	293	295		311			Pessimistic about relationship
161		180	184	194	200	208	218	227	232	240	242	248	256	261		272	276		293		302	310	317	324	Relationship stuck in a rut
				194				227	232	237	245		256	262	263	271	276	280	289	295	307				Repetitive arguments
			188	194		213		227		237			257				276		289						Resentful
163	176			192			218		230		245				266	272	276		289		304	310			Sad
165				192	200	211	218	223	229					262											Sensory deprived

Comfort at a Glance

	INTRODUCTION	BRINGING THE BOOK HOME	ABOUT RELAXING	WHEN I THINK OF NURTURING THE RELATIONSHIP...	EASE INTO NURTURING EACH OTHER	A COUPLE'S JOURNAL	SOUL STROKES	DAILY COMMUNICATION	RECOGNIZING YOUR NEEDS	WHEN LIFE IS TOO CRAZY	TOGETHERNESS TIME	EVERYDAY RITUALS	RHYTHMS OF RAPPORT	WINDS OF THE HEAVENS	EMPATHY	WOMEN AND MEN NURTURING EACH OTHER	TOILETS	COUPLE CUSTOMS	NURTURING YOUR RELATIONSHIP THROUGH MONEY	SELF-CARE IN RELATIONSHIPS	NURTURING MERRIMENT	BUT THERE'S NOTHING TO DO	GETTING TO KNOW YOU	REMINISCE AND REKINDLE	ACCEPTANCE
Sex talk					22	29	34	40	48							92									
Sharing your dreams				16	22	29	34		48			70	78		87			113	123			142	149		
Sharing your past						29	34		48						87	92							149	152	
Shy sexually						31	34	40																152	
Skin hungry																						141			
Smothered								44	49	54			78	83						125					
Spiritually disconnected from each other			12				34	43			58	67			87		112		123	127	132		146	152	159
Spouse less committed than you		7					34	44	49		57			81		95	104								
Stinky									49								104								
Tense with each other	1		12		22			40		53		68	74	86	87	91	104		120	125	134	143		152	156
Tired of initiating all the fun	3				23		34	44	49						87					125		142			
Too dependent		7		16	24	29		44	50					81	87	91			121	128		142			
Too independent		7		16	24	29			50					81	87	91	111					142			
Transition conflicts					24			45	50	53		68	77				112			125	134				157
Understanding your love cycles				16	24								74	81									148		157
Unemployed			12					45	49	53			77		87				121		132				156
Uninspired	2	7			23		34					65						113	117	125	132	140		152	159
Unloved						30		45	49			67	77						117	127					
Unsupportive during rough times					21		34		49	55			77		87					127					159
Want to show appreciation		7		15	21	30	34	43	50			71					107	114	117			140	148		159
Want to appreciate your lover's magnificence	1											71												152	159
Worried												72							120	125	132				

Comfort at a Glance

GRATIFY AND DELIGHT	TEA AND SYMPATHY	THE ART OF GIFT GIVING	HOLIDAYS	NATURAL NURTURE	A SENSORY BANQUET	EROTIC DELIGHTS	MASSAGE	MOVING INTO YOUR BODIES	MUSIC	NESTING	SHARED SANCTUARY	ROMANTIC ILLUSIONS: WHAT DID YOU EXPECT?	DIVINE SUSTENANCE	CREATIVE CONNECTION	NURTURING DURING CRISIS AND LOSS	LETTING GO	RELEASING RESENTMENT	HOW TO HAVE A NURTURING FIGHT	FORGIVENESS	NEGOTIATING	RUTS	COMMUNITY CONTEXT	COCREATORS	WRITING YOUR OWN COMFORT BOOK	
						207																			Sex talk
										237		248	255	263									317		Sharing your dreams
						207						248	255		267		276								Sharing your past
						206			233	240				264											Shy sexually
				198	204	206	218	223						264											Skin hungry
																									Smothered
	176		184	194	204	213	218	224	232	238	242	247	254	263	269	273			290		304	311	317		Spiritually disconnected from each other
																	276			295					Spouse less committed than you
				201						240															Stinky
161		180		194	202	210	218	227	232	238	242			262		274	276	280	289	295	303				Tense with each other
																	276	280		295	308		317	322	Tired of initiating all the fun
													257	266							308	313			Too dependent
													257	266							307	315			Too independent
						210	218	227	230	237	242						276	280	289	295	304				Transition conflicts
				197									256								309	311			Understanding your love cycles
	176													266								315			Unemployed
161			184	201	208					238	242		254	261					289				317	322	Uninspired
				193		214	218	226	232								276								Unloved
161	176										242			262	266	273	276			295					Unsupportive during rough times
161		180	184		200	209	218				251			264										325	Want to show appreciation
		180				206	218				250		256	264											Want to appreciate your lover's magnificence
	176			193			218						258	262	268	273									Worried

Tea and Sympathy

You'll Need:

Hot beverages or cool drinks.

Hugs.

A private, comforting space. (Your shared sanctuary or comfy bed works great.)

Time required: Ten to fifteen minutes.

When to Do It:

- To state the obvious: after a bad day, an upsetting event, or when you've been rejected.

- When you have trouble taking help from your loved ones.

- When you want to be cuddled and accepted.

- When you want your partner to simply hear your anger and hurt and not do anything about it.

What Is It?

Life is difficult. We sometimes need our relationship to act as a shelter, a place where we can lick our wounds, unburden ourselves of the day's hardships, and get some commiseration, cuddling, and "It'll be okay." Sometimes that's easy, but other times we are hurting and, for whatever reason, we can't ask for understanding and love. How many fights start after one person has had a bad day but doesn't know how or can't ask for solace so miscommunication and unmet needs lead to disaster? Or how much comfort is lost because one person is afraid of being overwhelmed by the other's problems or can't handle hearing a lover's pain and hurt? Perhaps there is a solution.

What to Do:

Guidelines

The most important part of tea and sympathy is defining it clearly. It *is* asking for a warm hug and a listening ear. It is *not* offering solutions, trying to fix the problem, or giving any comments or advice. It is a time to get things off your chest, no matter how petty or personal. It is a time to let go of responsibilities and worries. It is not a time to harangue or complain about things your partner did or didn't do. *Tea and sympathy is strictly for venting about events and people outside the relationship.*

The trick to *giving* tea and sympathy is listening and honoring whatever your partner says. What each of us wants and craves is to be heard. The trick to *accepting* sympathy is to not minimize your problems and to allow the other person to parent you.

Providing a structure or ritual is helpful because it keeps the person giving from being overwhelmed while providing a sense of closure and helping to prevent miscommunication.

Decide together on a phrase that will communicate your need for attention. "I need tea and sympathy" is an obvious choice. Be clear. Perhaps record the phrase on the inside cover of your couple's journal.

See "A Couple's Journal."

How It Works for Us

A recent day in my life: The accountant calls with bad, bad tax news. I drive across town on the wrong day for my doctor's appointment then lose the parking garage ticket and have to repark and go hunting for the ticket or pay the maximum charge. My back goes out exercising that afternoon. Our dog gets attacked by another dog. My friend cancels our dinner plans. Chris works late.

What do I do when he comes in the door? I alert him by saying, "I need tea and sympathy as soon as you can give it to me" (our ritual phrase). He says, "I hear you, and I'll be there as soon as I can." I can relax while he does whatever he needs to do (brush his teeth, put away the car, change clothes).

Chris gets me something to drink, hugs me before *anything* is said, and then gives me his full attention without interruptions except to ask a question to clarify a point. Then, lots of encouragement and taking my side is essential. The person asking for sympathy picks the place to be comforted. I sometimes choose the hammock outside or curl up in bed.

Other times, I might want to go for a walk. We always end with a hug, and I like to be patted on my back. When it is Chris's turn, I lay his head on my chest and hug him.

Involving Children

Children are incredibly sensitive to mood shifts in their parents. If it feels okay and they want to, allow your children to participate in giving comfort. Surrounding the hurting person with loving bodies in a group hug is wonderful. Older children might participate; it can help them understand why Mom or Dad is so tense and make them feel important enough to be trusted with the full picture.

Resistance

See "Letting Go" for more.

It can be hard for some people to accept sympathy. Men may think asking means they are weak; women may be too used to giving to accept support. Start small by asking for a hug, then graduate to uttering one sentence about what went wrong.

Have a soul-strokes talk about your resistance. Start by completing the sentence "Accepting understanding and empathy makes me feel . . ."

Variations

Follow the directions in the section "Moving Energy" in the chapter "Moving into Your Bodies," but instead of the emphasis being on enlivening different parts of the body, shift the emphasis to sending healing energy into your partner to make her or him feel better. For the partner receiving, concentrate only on relaxing and taking the healing in. (This is a good exercise for nonverbal communicators.)

Tea and sympathy can be different for each partner. One of you might like talking; another might like a quiet walk. Just specify clearly ahead of time. It doesn't work if when you need comforting you have to spend time deciding what to do. The whole idea is setting it up ahead of time so you can easily slip into it and you can count on it. "First aid for the soul," as a friend said.

Resources:

Healing Words for the Body, Mind, and Spirit: 101 Words to Inspire and Affirm, by Caren Goldman (Marlowe and Company, 2001). Whatever the occasion, Goldman offers gentle support.

See "Nurturing During Crisis and Loss" for help coping with more lasting problems.

Romantic Intelligence: How to Be as Smart in Love as You Are in Life, by Mary Valentis (New Harbinger Publications, 2003). Enhance emotional self-awareness, practice emotional honesty, and deal with toxic emotions such as jealousy, competition, and dependency.

Solved by Sunset: The Right Brain Way to Resolve Whatever's Bothering You in One Day or Less, by Carol Osborn (Harmony Books, 1995). A step-by-step one-day process to find a breakthrough to any problem.

The Dance of Connection: How to Talk to Someone When You're Mad, Hurt, Scared, Frustrated, Insulted, Betrayed, or Desperate, by Harriet Learner (HarperCollins, 2002). How to be vulnerable, voice concerns, set limits, and more.

The Art of Gift Giving

You'll Need:

Your calendars.

Detective abilities: observation, note taking, perceptive questions.

Paper and pen.

Imagination (not essential but helpful).

Catalogs.

Time required: From twenty minutes to whatever it takes to find a good gift.

When to Do It:

- Anytime.

- If, when your lover asks you what you want for your birthday, you always say, "I dunno."

- When you dread gift giving or gift getting with your beloved.

What Is It?

Gift giving is a potential relationship quagmire, a marshy pit where best intentions can be lost, childhood disappointments poignantly recalled, past gift disasters rudely reawakened, especially if it is overlooked or downplayed as an insignificant act. Gift giving can be dangerous for the relationship. But it can also be an act that fundamentally enriches your intimacy, if it includes the most important ingredient: the investment of your self. A loving gift enlivens your bond. But how to overcome the pitfalls of disappointing your partner, the pressure of gift giving, and perhaps the belief one partner may have that presents are unnecessary, frivolous, or wasteful?

What to Do:

Explorations: Acquiring the Gift-Giving Attitude

Come up with as many responses as you can for each question, either verbally or in writing. If you do this verbally, either make notes for each other or tape-record your responses.

I am a person who believes gifts are . . .

When I was small, getting a gift meant . . .

Birthdays are . . .

Holidays are . . .

Anniversaries are . . .

If I could ask you for anything, I would ask for . . .

If I dared to give you a gift that would make you feel totally loved and appreciated, I would give you . . .

When you give me a gift I love, I feel . . .

For me, the best gifts are . . .

Let what your partner writes or says sink in. Let what you've learned about yourself sink in. Discuss any surprises. Discuss past gift disappointments not as a way to rake your lover through the coals again but in light of your new information. What consistent gift conflicts do you have, and how can you better meet each other's needs? Alone, decide on five ways you can act on the knowledge you have gained.

Avoiding Gift Pitfalls

Ask yourself these questions before picking a gift (yes, even in the store):

Do I honestly want to spend time and energy finding a gift? If not, why not?

What's my motivation for buying this particular gift?

How do I want this gift to make my partner feel?

Run through these questions in your head, briefly. Perhaps you want your gift to express how angry you are about some incident two weeks ago. If you don't figure this out, you may end up mistakenly giving your mate an outfit three sizes too big. Or you may discover how grateful you are for the support he or she has been giving you, and you really feel like spending a little more money on an outrageous gift.

Don't give something you think your partner *should* have. A glaring example might be a certificate to a weight-loss program. A more subtle example might be giving a book on mathematics you think he should find fascinating (but he hates to balance the checkbook) or a miniskirt you wish she would wear (but in fact she wouldn't be caught dead in).

Don't give a gift intended to change your partner. When a former boyfriend gave me a check with instructions I was to give the money to the charity of my choice, I almost exploded with anger. It felt like he was telling me I wasn't generous enough, that I didn't care about those less fortunate and had to be reminded.

Use your personal calendar to keep yourself from being caught unaware. Have a brainstorming session with yourself or your children for five minutes at least three (even six) months before a big event (like a fortieth birthday). If you give yourself a few minutes early on, you'll feel less pressured, more creative, and you'll have more options.

Even with preparation, you may still give or receive a not-so-great gift. React with an honest but gentle comment. Start with a positive ("this is so thoughtful"). Then gently but clearly state why this isn't the gift for you, and make a firm date to exchange the present together for something you would enjoy more. Use this excursion to window-shop together (see below), to learn more about what you each like.

Gathering Ideas

Start a gift book—a file folder, pocket notebook, or wrinkled sheet of paper in your wallet. Collect information on a *regular* basis.

Spend an afternoon window-shopping together, without buying. Make notes. Fantasize by mentioning everything from Jaguar cars to Jockey underwear to each other. My mate and I did this, and months later he surprised me with a marbled paper desk set I had wanted for years. I still get warm inside when I think of him remembering my desire, *taking it seriously,* and honoring me by honoring what I like.

Post a wish list on the refrigerator. Every time someone in the family utters "I want this . . ." or "I've got to have that . . ." they jot down their idea on the refrigerator (especially effective with teenagers). It feels good to write it down, and it makes a great ongoing gift list. Scan the list occasionally, and cross off items that no longer appeal to you or that you've bought for yourself.

Become a gift detective. Decide on a number together, say fifteen or, if you want to be audacious, fifty. You have to deduce that many ideas for gifts by simply observing your partner. You cannot cheat by checking the wish list (see above). Clue: your partner is writing a speech and needs a good quote. Deduction: a book of notable quotes.

There is at least one benefit to the endless stream of junk mail: catalogs make great inspirational sources for gifts. Keep catalogs and a pen in the bathroom. During that reflective time, circle items you are interested in. A couple in Lexington, Kentucky, cuts out pictures of items they desire and places them in file folders. They soon forget what they've selected, but when their partner wants to buy a gift, he or she has a thick file of assorted ideas supplied by the other. (If picking your own gifts from catalogs seems to lack the all-important element of surprise, then let the catalog suggestions inspire related ideas.)

Finally

Keep in mind that time and effort spent are usually more appreciated than money.

Best rule of gift giving: recognize who the person receiving the gift really is.

Never use gift giving to express anger or get even.

Resources:

The Gift, by Lewis Hyde (Vintage Books, 1983). The history and philosophy of gift giving.

2001 A Romantic Odyssey: A Thousand More Ways to Be Romantic, by Gregory Godeck (Casablanca Press, 1992). A good source book of numbers, companies, and ideas for romantic gifts.

Websites:

For Romance
   http://www.forromance.com

Imegamall.com
   http://www.imegamall.com

Holidays

You'll Need:

Couple's journal or paper, and pens.

Various seasonal items, like fall apples, spring bulbs, winter moonlight, and summer straw-berries.

Nurturing friends and family.

Blank cards.

Time required: Varies widely.

When to Do It:

- When your holiday traditions need sprucing up.

- When pressure, high expectations, or bad memories regularly ruin your special days.

- When you yearn for a more conscious, loving way to celebrate your life.

What Is It?

Is a holiday a time to overeat and overspend? Or is it a time to show your affection and gratitude for your mate and cement your sense of togetherness as a family? Is it a time to fight and be depressed because you aren't a perfect TV family? Or a time to revel in how unique and wonderful your family is?

Whether you are restoring, revitalizing, or creating celebratory traditions for the first time, looking at each one as an opportunity to reinforce your intimacy puts a new angle on your planning and your expectations. Whether it be the grandeur of Christmas or Hanukkah, the bittersweet quality of birthdays, or the tender deepening of an anniversary, it takes planning and an occasional influx of fresh ideas to create holidays that nurture you and yours. Stop accepting other people's definitions for what your holidays should be like. Take a minute to think about what you want the celebrations of your life to be, because these rituals allow us to feel gratitude for all the days that pass between.

What to Do:

Anniversaries

Anniversaries can be a time of great stress and failed expectations. Have a soul-stroking talk about what your anniversary means to you and what your expectations are.

Contemplate writing a vow to express acknowledgment of the relationship over the last year, and make a pledge to each other for the coming year. Take turns being responsible for the arrangements around reading your vows. One anniversary, one partner might plan a picnic and pick a spot for the ritual high on a hill fragrant with wildflowers. Another might gather children and close friends for a potluck supper and read the vows surrounded by loving faces and candles. Embellishments like drinking from one goblet to symbolize your connection, giving each other symbols of your hopes for the coming year, or dancing to the same song each time can round out the celebration.

See "Everyday Rituals: Dinner."

Time travel. Recreate the year you met or a year you were especially happy. Start by reminiscing together about what you each enjoyed about that time in your lives while each of you makes notes. Separately, plan for your time travel day. You could divide up the day, one recreating the morning, the other the evening. Or decide where you will go, say the restaurant where you went on your first date, and then each recreates a certain moment for the other. Items from the past can add depth and humor: wearing the same clothes (which can be very humorous if you have gained a few pounds or met wearing platform shoes and leisure suits), playing the same music, a gift of pictures from that time arranged in a special photo album, ordering the same food or bottle of wine. If a certain aspect of your memory day didn't go perfectly, you now have the power to change it to a more pleasant experience.

Being in a committed relationship is hard work. If you've had a rough year, either because of relationship growth pains or because life has been testing you, consider having an anniversary support party. Invite trusted friends and family. Provide a ritual format for each person to express personal support and appreciation for your marriage. One idea is to have everyone sit in a circle with eyes closed, breathing deeply for a few moments, then have each guest name a strength or quality they wish to bestow on you as a couple. Write these down, then read them aloud in unison, adding your own wishes for each other at the end. The guests then hold hands and dance in a circle around the couple. End with big hugs.

Remarriage when children are involved calls for special attention to anniversaries. Consider including your children in your anniversary plans or creating an anniversary day to recognize the creation of your family. A family in Oregon puts on a play that spoofs the events of the last year, then goes out for ice cream. Another family plans a camping trip, and on returning home the children from the first marriage are dropped off for dinner with their birth father. Another idea for second families is to have a soul-stroking talk on this day. Spend lots of energy reassuring your children and listening to their concerns without judging. Soul-stroking questions:

When I think back to when we all met, I feel . . .

When I think back to when we became a family, I remember . . .

What I love about our being a family is . . .

What I dislike about our being a family is . . .

One couple I know has two anniversaries: one the actual date they were married on, and the other the day they had a wedding in her hometown in Germany. They decided to celebrate both. The original date became his, and she showers him with appreciation and attention. The second day is her anniversary, and he gives her acknowledgment and accolades. Any couple can do this: the day you got engaged and the day you married; the day you first said "I love you" and the day you moved in together; your first date and the day of your partnership ceremony. (Faith and Danny celebrate the first day they walked home from school together twenty years ago.)

Whitney and Glenn celebrate the full moon every month. They first realized they were in love on the set of a film they were working on. As Glenn filmed a huge, glowing moon, Whitney stood behind him. "It was a balmy summer night, and huge clouds raced across the moon's face," Whitney told me. Afterward, they rode his motorcycle over country roads and talked until the sun came up. Fourteen years and two kids later, they have a huge box filled with cards bearing pictures of the moon and have never missed the full moon as a night to celebrate and recognize their lasting connection. (If you are feeling sorry for yourself because you and your sweetie don't share such a romantic moment, it is never too late to begin one!)

Do you ever honor your parents' anniversary or that of good friends or a couple you admire? Their committed relationship deserves your validation and support. Additionally, your relationship might get a boost from reaching out and supporting others.

See "Community Context" for more ideas about nurturing others.

Birthdays

A great way to start a birthday: the family surrounds the bed and awakens the birthday person by singing "Happy Birthday," then serves coffee or tea in bed.

Buy lots of small gifts for your lover and hide them all over the house. Devise a treasure hunt to find the presents.

Most of us experienced at least one painful or disappointing childhood birthday. A parent who was too depressed to do much, a stressful time in the family when you were forgotten, a recent move so you had no friends to celebrate with—whatever your history, you can now redo that birthday, turning it into whatever you wanted. Plan a party appropriate for the age you want to recelebrate. Send childlike invitations, ask friends to bring symbolic items appropriate for your age, play games you always wanted to play, eat foods you loved or never got to have. (If you are too grown-up to do this with friends, recreate part of it with just your mate.)

See "Nurturing Merriment: Childhood Revisited."

Plan a birthday ritual to be done with your partner. Buy a large candle and carve a few words on it to express a goal you would like to accomplish in the coming year. Talk about your goal and your hopes and expectations for your new year. Then take a piece of natural material—a rock, leaf, or piece of paper—and write down your main regret for the past twelve months. Together, visit a spot in nature and bury the object, burn it, or float it down a stream (use a small amount of paper and shred it so that it biodegrades easily). After you get rid of it, light your candle and imagine your wish coming true.

End with a hug. Together, once a month for the coming year, light your candle and review what you've done and what your partner has done to help your goal come true. Show appreciation to yourself for your hard work and to your partner for his or her support.

See "Forgiveness."

A variation is to do this together for your anniversary, writing on the candle a wish for your relationship in the coming year and forgiving each other for a past mistake.

Holidays

Sit down as a couple (before you talk to older children, parents, or other family members) in mid-November, and discuss how you want the holidays to be this year. To enrich the discussion, try completing the sentences below:

> This year, the most nurturing way to celebrate the holidays would be . . .
>
> The true meaning of the holidays to me is . . .
>
> When I was a child, we celebrated by . . .
>
> As the holidays approach, I feel . . .
>
> On past holidays, I have been disappointed when . . .
>
> To nurture the relationship during the holidays, I would like to . . .

See what concrete suggestions you can draw from your answers to these questions. Decide in advance what you will and won't do, whom you will and won't see. Commit to doing at least two activities from your fantasy list and to *not* doing at least two things that disappointed you in the past or that you would like to change. You can use these questions with older children, housemates, and parents.

A common complaint couples have about holidays is they don't allow time to connect with each other. Take an early morning walk together, *sans* others, on Christmas morning. Make one night of Hanukkah about celebrating your relationship. Sneak ten minutes together on

Thanksgiving to talk about how the holiday is going for each of you. Make a commitment to connect even during the holiday crunch.

Slow down during the holidays. Take time off from work if you can. Cancel regular commitments and meetings. Before you accept a commitment, ask yourself if you really want to do this. If being close with your family is what you crave, you first have to reserve the time in which to see each other!

Simplify. Make a list of everything you love to do at the holidays, then pick one or two of these to do each year, alternating between the years. One year you send holiday cards and make some of your gifts, the next year you bake, decorate the house, and have a party, but no cards or gift making. Decide what you honestly enjoy about the holidays and what you do only out of habit. Eliminate the habitual aspects that no longer satisfy you.

Overspending can be a seasonal strain you impose on your relationship. Unplug yourselves from the consumer machine, and decide how much you and your partner will spend on each other and on whomever else you are buying gifts for *before* you go shopping. Take only that amount with you. Be realistic with your children. If they ask for something you can't afford, tell them and ask them to suggest something they want as much in a lower price range.

Disappointment after Christmas is only natural. Weeks spent building up to a two-hour frenzy of gift opening—what a letdown, especially for kids. Pace your holiday activities over several weeks. On December 1, listen to carols and write cards together (children can add a short note or sign their names). On December 15, go for a walk in the woods to collect pine bows and cones, then decorate the house with them. On December 20, have a story-telling party with a few close friends and children. The day after Christmas could be an open house for friends to drop by or an annual early morning shopping trip for returns and bargains, followed by lunch. New Year's Day is the perfect time for a ritual of new beginnings. A couple in Oak Park, Illinois, writes down everything they regret, resent, or would like to be forgiven for from the past year, then burns their papers and scatters the ashes. Then they write love letters to themselves (or each other), filled with good thoughts, hopes, and wishes for the coming year. They seal the letters in envelopes and exchange with each other. They mail the letter to their partner much later in the year, whenever he or she needs a lift.

To deepen the meaning of Thanksgiving, try this ritual. Before dinner, circulate blank cards with *Thanks* written on one side. Each person writes on one side what he or she is thankful for in his or her own life, and then on the other side what he or she appreciates about the others present. If you have guests who don't know everyone at the table, ask them to write their appreciation for the important people in their lives who aren't present. Read your cards before dinner.

See "Natural Nurture: Discovering Your Local Landscape."

Celebrating lesser-known holidays offers an opportunity to create rituals that are unique to your partnership and family. On Arbor Day, April 24, take a walk in the woods and adopt a tree to visit together throughout the year. Native American Day (end of September) could be a day for learning about native culture in your area and perhaps finding a local custom you can celebrate together, in honor of the first people. A midnight walk or slide down a snowy hill on the winter solstice, planting spring bulbs and visiting newborn animals on the spring equinox, apple picking or leaf raking on the first day of fall, and making strawberry pie or going for a skinny-dip on the first day of summer are nature-based ideas. Designate a few days a year to create your own unique celebrations. This is especially important if holidays and birthdays are complicated because of family difficulties or past disappointments. And by celebrating throughout the year, you can become more in touch with what you want to celebrate about life, what matters to *you*, not to advertisers.

Resources:

New Traditions: Redefining Celebrations for Today's Family, by Susan Abel Lieberman (Noonday Press, 1991). More ideas for celebrating the significant moments of your shared life.

Simplify Your Christmas: One Hundred Ways to Reduce the Stress and Recapture the Joy of the Holidays, by Elaine St. James (Andrews McMeel, 1998). Ideas galore.

The Book of New Family Traditions: How to Create Great Rituals for Holidays and Everydays, by Meg Cox (Running Press Books, 2003). Fresh ways to celebrate established holidays like Christmas, Passover, and Fourth of July, as well as create original observances for other occasions.

Unplug the Christmas Machine, by Jo Robinson and Jean Coppock Staeheli (Quill, 1991). How to have a more meaningful Christmas. Comprehensive and very helpful.

Natural Nurture

You'll Need:

Access to several types of outdoor areas.

An open mind.

Blankets or sleeping bags.

Time required: Ten minutes to a weekend or even a week.

When to Do It:

- When you spend most of your day surrounded by concrete, car fumes, and four walls.

- When you are intrigued with the idea of nature as a relationship role model.

- When you love being outdoors and would like to share the experience in a meaningful way.

- When you hate the outdoors and can't imagine what I'm going on about.

What Is It?

Allow your love to be renewed by encountering the divine beauty of the natural world. Being out-of-doors together can deeply nurture your relationship by putting you in touch with different parts of yourself, freeing you from habitual patterns of defense, breaking you out of ruts. Venturing into nature can allow you to see the growth of your relationship reflected in the cycles of the seasons. Connecting with the environment as a couple allows you to experience viscerally that you and your love are not separate from the Earth but are supported and enriched by loving this world.

Consider for a moment the outdoors not as a place for competition, being bitten by bugs, or forcing yourself into an activity for your mate's sake, but as a sacred place to experience love and intimacy.

What to Do:

Renewal

Yes, it might seem a cliché, but a picnic out-of-doors can be incredibly serene. Forget about making it a big production; just grab a simple lunch and go to a local park. Imagine yourself in a French impressionist painting. Feel the Earth under your body.

Walk barefoot in an ocean, lake, fountain, or puddle together. Breathe together, or describe the sensations you are experiencing, or simply be in silence.

Run in a spring rain together. Jump in puddles. Squish mud between your fingers.

Locate a "you-pick-'em" field of strawberries or an apple orchard, pick a peck, and then make a pie together, or feed each other. Naked.

Together, make a list of all the important people in your life. Decide what flower each reminds you of, then go to the florist (or a field of wildflowers or your own garden), and construct a bouquet of these flowers. Over the next few days, let this bouquet inspire you to reach out and nurture those around you, together.

Discovering Your Local Landscape

Exploring and connecting with the place where you live can help assuage the sense of rootlessness that affects many of us, even though we may be unaware of it. Many people have lost a sense of place. We have learned in the last sixty years to move away from what doesn't work, to throw away what insists on upkeep, and to rely too heavily on our relationships for our sole sense of community and rootedness. When malls are carved out of farms overnight, when one American family in five moves every year, when rain forests are disappearing at the rate of one hundred acres per minute (statistic from the Rainforest Action Network), how can this restless, relentless change not affect us? We are being assaulted by impermanence!

Together try learning the natural history of the land directly under and around you. Walk around your home and office. Imagine what the land looked like before it was built on, farmed, or subdivided. Find out what native plants grew, what native people lived where your house or apartment building now stands. Visit local libraries, historical societies, and elderly people for stories and pictures. You could try to each learn or observe a new landscape impression each month and share them over an outdoor picnic.

What features of your landscape bring you the most pleasure? What part of your daily surroundings cause you the most hassle: the weather, a big hill you bike over on your way to work, water that must be crossed via a drawbridge? Discuss your perceptions.

How often do you see undomesticated animals and birds? What natural sounds do you hear? Spend a minute or two to listen quietly on a regular basis.

Schedule an outing together to climb the highest point in your region. What do you see? What do you imagine it looked liked twenty years ago? Two hundred? Two thousand?

Don't let considering yourself "temporary" stop you from connecting with your region. You may live in an apartment you hate, you may be transferred in two years, you may upgrade to a new neighborhood soon, but that only makes connecting to the landscape that much more important.

Better Living Through Hiking

Imagine this: You have a fight. You work it out, but you still feel prickly. You decide to spend the afternoon hiking together. The renewed understanding and love you experience for your partner on this hike blows you away. The wind tousles your hair, the vistas swell around you, you banish your petty differences and are full of appreciation and perspective all week.

How is this possible? Has the ghost of Euell Gibbons taken over this book? No, I'm talking about the healing power of nature. Fred Kahane, a therapist who leads couples into the wilderness for self-exploration and healing, believes that when you are in nature "it puts you in touch with a different part of yourself, and then you are able to relate to someone else from this place. There is something very freeing about being in nature. Breathing the fresh air and going through the hike itself creates biological and physical changes that open you up. Simply getting into a more deep breathing pattern helps you become more clear about what is going on for you. In addition, if you live in a city, *you tend to become defined by what you see as well as what you think.* For example, in cities it is difficult to see a clear horizon. This affects your thought processes. Clarity of sight leads to clarity of thought, and vice versa." Nature offers perspective from vistas at higher elevations. Nature offers a big sky and wide horizon to help you out of "rutted" thinking about your relationship. Struggling up a trail gets you breathing deeply, which physiologically is known to help release stress and tension.

To enhance your time out-of-doors, consider these ideas:

Pay attention to how you feel. Check in with each other periodically, perhaps asking, "Do you feel any different? Does being out here make you feel any different about us?"

As you hike, point things out to each other that you find beautiful or that interest you. Pay attention to how your surroundings make you feel—peaceful, full of well-being, or fearful. Do these emotions make you feel close to or distant from your mate? Try to express these observations to each other.

Your needs when you are out-of-doors are very clear. You need water. You need to eat. You need warmth. You need to find the trail. Notice how much simpler it is to work together. You don't tend to get into fights about who is the most tired (as you might after a day of work). You have both hiked the same number of miles and you both need to eat, and so you work together to meet your needs. Try to absorb this and remember it at home when you are fighting over who should run to the grocery store.

Rubbing each other's feet after a long hike, keeping each other warm, working together to get the tasks done that must be done: all of these present wonderful opportunities to increase your trust and respect for each other. To make this process conscious, stop and talk about how you feel. "I am feeling wonderful and safe sitting by this fire with you" and "I resent doing all the 'manly' work. I would like you to help me chop wood" are examples.

Finally, realize that hiking together (or biking, canoeing, whatever activity) in the wilderness almost always conjures up control problems. Our lifestyles offer us multiple illusions of control: over our environment, over each other, over ourselves. A wilderness experience strips the illusion of control away, and this is exhilarating and frightening. Support each other in this test of letting go. Breathe deeply when you feel frustrated or find yourself still using the white-knuckle approach to life that you do in the city. Have a soul-strokes talk when you feel you are losing control. You could use the sentence stem "If I let go, I'm afraid . . ." or "Being out here makes me feel . . ." Give yourself up to the love you have for each other, and let the wild places nurture your soul.

Going Farther—A Retreat

Retreats have been used since the beginning of civilization as a way to go beyond day-to-day reality to see the greater truth. Try going into nature with the intent of deepening your relationship. Decide together on the purpose of your retreat. What will you be seeking? An answer to an important question, healing of a disagreement, forgiveness, renewal of lust?

See "Negotiating" for help.

Choose a wilderness area that appeals to both of you and is feasible for your needs. For example, if one person has never camped out, you might start by renting a simple cabin, without electricity or phones, in a national forest or park. The more adventuresome might hire a float plane to drop them on the shore of a remote Canadian lake. Negotiate a destination.

See "Everyday Rituals: What Makes It a Ritual?"

Create an opening and ending ritual for your retreat. Perhaps hold hands and state your intentions for your time together, then end by leaving a "give-away" (a gift to the place).

Things to do during your retreat: Discuss fears and previous experiences in the wilderness, especially if one person is more comfortable out-of-doors than the other; maintain silence; don't use any artificial light—rely on candles or the sun only; read nature-inspired poetry to each other;

have lots of long talks; take note of how the rhythms of your relationship change when attuned to the rhythms of nature.

Service Work

Can you nurture your relationship while restoring balance to the earth? Could time together be spent dropping off recycling? Rebuilding a washed-out hiking trail? Planting a garden in an empty city lot? Work like this offers you the chance to experience yourselves and your partnership as a part of the "big" picture. You get free of your petty differences for a while, and the time and energy you give comes back to you and your relationship threefold.

See "Community Context" for more service ideas.

Gardening

Plant a garden to symbolize your relationship. It can be as simple as a few spring bulbs in a planter or as elaborate as the careful selection of plants whose names conjure up connections to your relationship or whose fragrances remind you of cherished memories. Tend your garden together to experience how nurturing your relationship connects you with life.

Surprise your partner by planting a few bulbs in a corner of a public park in honor of your love. Visit them daily while they bloom.

Use outdoor chores as a time for relationship growth. Sweep the deck or porch together, and let the soft swish of the straw settle your worrying minds. Prune plants and trees, and talk about ways you can release built-up resentments to clear the way for "new growth" in your relationship. Take a moment each week to pay attention to the microseasonal changes in your garden or front yard, and be reminded of the microchanges constantly going on in your relationship and how "this too shall pass."

Find a peaceful garden or terrace spot outside your home to retreat to. Spend time here in silence, and try to carry that silence with you, to refer back to when you are angry with each other.

See "Shared Sanctuary" for more.

Wild Love

Find a very private spot in nature where you can make love without being disturbed or feeling self-conscious. It can be your own backyard or a hillside covered with wildflowers. The place must reassure the shiest person. Create a bed on which you can recline naked and be comfortable. The instructions below are intended as general guidelines, not a step-by-step visualization. Improvise!

Lie down next to each other on your backs and spend a few moments breathing deeply. Experience the air on your skin. Work on just being. What does it feel like to be outdoors and naked? Explore, silently, how the Earth feels under you. Imagine the ground supporting you, cradling you.

Visualize a golden cord running from the bottom of your heels deep into the Earth. Take a moment to feel the energy running up from the Earth, along this cord, and into your body. This is healing, dynamic energy you are receiving through your golden cord. After a moment, hold hands. Now feel the energy running between you. Breathe deeply. Focus on creating a live connection with your partner. Taking lots of time, caress each other, imagining you are spreading this wonderful Earth energy all over your lover's body. When you begin to make love, concentrate on feeling the energy moving back and forth between you, and up and down between each of you and the Earth, connecting the rhythm of nature with the rhythm of your love. Imagine as you climax that you are sending healing, loving energy back into the Earth, the flowers, the trees, and also showering it around you, into the air, covering everything with a soft, shining coating of love.

Resources:

Creating Eden, by Marilyn Barrett (HarperSanFrancisco, 1992). Wonderful meditations on the healing power of gardening and nature.

Drawing Closer to Nature: Making Art in Dialogue with the Natural World, by Peter London (Shambhala, 2003). Stories, poetic meditations, and guided exercises to show you how making art in nature can enhance your self-knowledge and creativity. Amazing to do together.

Rainforest Action Network, 221 Pine St., Suite 500, San Francisco, CA 94104, or call 415–398–4404 for info about how to help the rain forest and join their grassroots group. Web: http://www.ran.org.

Rowing to Latitude: Journeys Across the Arctic's Edge, by Jill Fredston (North Point Press, 2002). Fredston and her husband spend summers making their way around the edges of the Arctic by rowboat and kayak.

Sisters of the Earth, edited by Lorraine Anderson (Vintage Books, 1991). Poems, essays, stories, and journal entries about women and the natural world.

The Experience of Place, by Tony Hiss (Vintage, 1990). An exploration of the importance of place and ideas for changes.

The Magnificent Universe, by Ken Croswell (Simon and Schuster, 1999). Keep these pictures of the universe—many taken from the Hubble telescope—to restore awe and keep marital tugs-of-war in perspective.

The Practice of the Wild, by Gary Snyder (North Point Press, 1990). A brilliant book about understanding our relationship to the wilderness. Read it outdoors.

The Wilderness Family: At Home with Africa's Wildlife, by Kobie Kruger (Ballantine Books, 2001). Read and dream together of a very different life.

Retreats

Northwaters Wilderness Programs, Rt. 22, Westport, NY 12993. Phone 518–962–4869, or visit http://www.northwaters.com or http://www.temagamivisionquest.com or http://www.texperience.com. A phenomenal list of programs for adults, children, and young adults. Located north of Toronto, Canada.

A Sensory Banquet

You'll Need:

Essential oils.

Vegetable oil (sunflower, safflower, almond, *not* peanut) to use as a base.

Your fingers. Your whole body.

Finger paints or Play-Doh.

Any sensual toys that appeal to you, like feathers, silk scarves, flannel sheets, heated towels, flower petals.

Time required: Totally up to you. (Hint: the longer, the better.)

When to Do It:

• When you feel dull, lifeless, drained.

• When you feel overwhelmed, overloaded, tense.

• When you want to heighten sexual excitement.

• When you need a little soul refreshment.

• When you feel like getting naked and rolling around in the mud.

What Is It?

Consider all of your senses. Each is a channel of exquisite awareness linking you to your partner, a path to renewal of your enjoyment of each other, and a delightful way to learn about and stimulate your sensual selves. (Not to mention all the new ways you can stir and pleasure your sexual self as well!)

What to Do:

Shampoo

Shampoo each other's hair, slowly and deliberately. Enjoy the feel of the hair between your fingers, the feel of the fingers in your hair, the tactile rubbing, the smell of the shampoo. Pause frequently and breathe deeply to give both of you time to enjoy all the sensations.

Close Your Eyes

Separately, select some objects with different textures: a peeled orange, silk shirt, feathers, ice cubes, eggs. Decide who will go first. Blindfold your partner, and take turns putting items into hands or under feet, against elbows or behind knees. You can get as involved (and messy) as you wish.

Each item should be thoroughly explored! Have your partner guess what he or she is feeling. You can write down answers and compare notes later. If you wish, make it into a game, where the person with the most correct guesses wins. (The prize is up to you.)

You can do the same exercise with your nose, consciously smelling fresh flowers, herbs, peeled and cut fruit, soap, perfume, bath gel, earth, new books. The sensorial options are endless.

Eat a meal blindfolded, using only your hands. Don't eat the way you usually do. Chew longer, roll each morsel along the roof of your mouth, allow the essence of the food to flow into you. Stop often and breathe deeply. Stop and give each other a hand massage. Feed each other.

Try sampling different wines blindfolded. Or chocolates. Or ice creams. Or breads. Or . . .

Visit a sculpture garden. Take turns blindfolding each other and running your hands over different works of art. (Make sure this is okay with the guards; it usually isn't a problem with outdoor gardens.)

Creative Eyes Closed

Finger paint together, blindfolded. Put down plastic, or do it outside. Or do it blindfolded, outside, and naked! Watercolor together on the same piece of paper. Mold Play-Doh or clay together. Feel your fingers slipping over one another, your creative minds working together, without purpose, delighting in the sensations.

See "Creative Connection: Sex and Painting" for another creative way to connect.

"Scentual" Searches

Note: All essential oils recipes are approximations. The best way is to experiment with what strengths feel and smell best to you. Increase slowly to avoid any skin reactions. Essential oils have become very widely available. Check natural food stores, herb shops, or mail-order houses. Ditto with base oils.

Massage oils: For an aphrodisiac massage oil, add 6 drops cedar wood, 8 drops geranium, 2 drops ylang-ylang, 10 drops clary sage, and 5 drops sandalwood to 6 ounces of sweet almond oil.

Or 10 drops rose, 2 drops ylang-ylang, 8 drops lemon, and 10 drops palma rosa in 6 ounces of any vegetable oil.

Or 10 drops jasmine, 5 drops nutmeg, 5 drops black pepper, and 10 drops mandarin in 6 ounces of vegetable oil.

For a massage oil designed to relieve general stress, try 9 drops bergamot, 11 drops geranium, and 10 drops ginger in 6 ounces of vegetable oil.

Another relaxing blend is 7 drops neroli, 3 drops lavender, and 20 drops lemon essential oils in 6 ounces of vegetable oil.

Another general blend is 15 drops grapefruit, 11 drops rosemary, and 5 drops palma rosa in 6 ounces of oil.

Baths: For a wild and tropical shared bath, add one 10-ounce can of unsweetened coconut milk, 10 drops gardenia oil, and 10 drops of oil of amber to warm water. Hang wind chimes at the open window, slice pineapple and mangoes to eat while in the tub, and imagine yourselves in a tropical jungle.

Slide into this bath on a hot summer day or night. Two hours or more before bathing, place 2 drops of peppermint oil in enough water to make a tray of ice cubes. (You might want to make two or three trays.) Freeze. Prepare cool drinks, like hard apple cider with lemon twists, iced cappuccino, or tall frosty mugs of beer. Run hot water, and drop in 15 drops of magnolia oil, 10 drops of orange blossom oil, and 2 drops of peppermint oil. Put your drinks and the ice cubes by the side of the tub. Lie in the tub until you are hot enough to melt, then pick up ice cubes and slowly run them over each other's bodies.

Have you ever considered taking a bath together—in the morning? What a way to start the day. Bathe with eucalyptus soap and a tub filled with 5 drops of eucalyptus oil, 10 drops bergamot, 10 drops lavender, and 3 drops of cinnamon. Lean back, sip your morning coffee, and listen to NPR together.

Another morning bath idea is designed to help with hangovers you might have gotten wining and dining each other the night before. Try 5 drops of grapefruit oil, 3 drops rosemary, 2 drops fennel, and 1 drop juniper in a warm, not hot, bath.

Diffusers: Using essential oils to perfume a room can perk up your life. Various methods: Place essential oils in a potpourri burner (I like non-electric ones) or on a clay or metal ring resting on a light bulb; add oils to a few ounces of water in a spray bottle, and shake before spraying; or pour boiling water in a bowl, and drop in essential oils.

See "Resources" at the end of this chapter.

Two drops of clary sage, 2 drops of geranium, and 1 drop of sandalwood will scent the air and might improve communication during a soul-stroking talk.

See "Soul Strokes."

To create a relaxing mood, use 8 drops geranium, 3 drops clary sage, 5 drops lemon, and 3 drops bergamot.

For those lazy Saturdays when you can't get going but want to, mix 8 drops grapefruit, 4 drops lavender, 4 drops lime, and 2 drops basil, and let it permeate your house.

For romance, diffuse 8 drops palma rosa, 1 drop ylang-ylang, 2 drops clary sage, 2 drops nutmeg, and 4 drops lime into the atmosphere.

Diffusing a drop or two of chamomile or clary sage in the bedroom will help you sleep.

During cold and flu season, diffuse 3 drops lemon, 5 drops bergamot, 1 drop cinnamon, 1 drop clary sage, and 5 drops geranium into the air. It is supposed to kill bacteria in the air.

Establish Your Own Aromatic Traditions

Create your own smells to celebrate or commemorate special times. Experiment using essential oils, dried herbs, fragrant flowers, and perfumes. For example, you might decide that the smell of freesias is your birthday smell. Your partner and you can use that smell on subsequent birthdays to create a special mood as well as to build a bridge between all of your other happy birthdays. It could be waking up to a bouquet of freesias, a bath with freesia oil waiting for you when you come home from work, or a massage with freesia lotion.

Relax the Senses

Take turns. One person lies down, eyes closed, and **Relaxes** while the other person kneels or sits beside. Do this in silence, no music. The person sitting speaks softly, "Relax, eyes, relax. Forget about seeing. For the next few minutes, you don't have to focus, you can relax. Relax, eyes, let go. . . . Relax, nose, relax. Forget about smelling. For the next few minutes, you don't have to smell anything. You can relax. Relax, nose, relax, you can let go. . . ." Repeat with mouth (forget about tasting), hands (forget about touching), and ears (forget about hearing). Finally, end by saying, "And now, you are floating, totally relaxed. And when you return, whenever you're ready, your senses will be completely clear, open, and sharp like never before." Speak rhythmically and very slowly, lulling your partner into relaxation. Repeat with other partner.

See "Moving into Your Bodies: Moving Energy" for another healing meditation.

This is excellent for mothers who often report being "touched out" when they are nursing or for anyone raising young ones at home. Help your sweetie regain her senses.

Touching

Add "Music: Feeling Amorous," "Diffusers" (this chapter), and soft lighting for more pleasure.

Communicate to your partner ten nonsexual ways you would like him or her to touch you.

Use a different kind of touch with each other than you usually do. For example, if you always hug, shake hands or touch elbows or rub noses. If you always kiss each other on the lips, kiss each other on the hands or neck.

Try nonsexual touching with your sexual partner. Decide on an equal period of time for both of you (twenty or thirty minutes apiece is nice). Take turns touching each other any way you want except sexually (no genitals) and without conversation.

Arrange to have a massage together, lying side by side. Visit a day spa or have two massage therapists come to your home!

Resources:

Aphrodite: A Memoir of the Senses, by Isabel Allende (Perennial, 1999). Read and cook together, and see what is stirred up.

Aromatiques: A Sensualist's Guide to Aromatic Oils, by Eva-Marie Lind (SOMA Books, 2002). A highly visual aromatherapy primer, appealing not only to the sense of smell, but also sight, touch, and imagination.

Romantic Sensations Card Game—A romantic card game that combines your senses of hearing, taste, smell, touch, and sight to create a romantic experience with your partner. Available from http://www.timefortwo.com.

Secrets of the Spa: Fifty ways to Pamper and Revitalize Yourself at Home, by Catherine Bardey (Black Dog and Leventhal Press, 2002). A set of fifty-two cards, each featuring a recipe and detailed instructions on one side and a color photo on the other.

Scents and Scentuality: Essential Oils and Aromatherapy for Romance, Love, and Sex, by Valerie Ann Worwood (New World Library, 1998). Use your nose to get into your partner.

Spa: Pamper Body and Soul with Ideas from the World's Best Sources, by Karena Callen (Rizzoli Press, 2001). An inspirational yet accessible guide that is both useful and beautiful.

Erotic Delights

You'll Need:

Sexy music. See "Music: Feeling Amorous."

Massage oils.

All manner of sensual delights, like hot fudge, ostrich feathers, silk boxer shorts, and erotic stories. (See "A Sensory Banquet" for more ideas.)

Your couple's journal or paper, and pens.

Time required: Endless luscious hours of passionate, timeless consummation.

See "Women and Men Nurturing Each Other."

When to Do It:

- When you are sexually bored, detached, or frustrated.

- When you would love to experiment with sex toys, edible underwear, or erotic videos.

- On a special occasion like an anniversary or birthday.

- If you have always wanted to use hot fudge in new and exciting ways.

What Is It?

Imagine pleasuring, satisfying, exploring, and sating your partner's deepest emotional needs through the alchemy of bodies colliding. Imagine losing yourself momentarily in the ecstasy of oneness. Envision rolling around in hot fudge and licking it off each other. Erotic delights can be so many marvelous things.

Boredom is the principle issue in long-term sexual relationships. You might hear yourself saying, "Where did the passionate, juicy, take-me-to-the-moon sex go?" "I never thought this would happen to us!"

To arouse your sexual appetite, start by nurturing your relationship in other areas. Putting more attention (even small amounts) into your relationship will almost always help ignite your sexual fires. However, there is a catch-22 here: if you nurture your relationship *only* in the hopes of getting more sex, it will backfire on you. Sex is a by-product, not the direct result, of caring for your partner.

Next, overcome the myth that if you've been together for more than a few years, you are doomed forever to boring sex. This is not true. I repeat, *this is not true.* Indulge yourself in some positive thinking. Repeat "The best is yet to be," "Wild sex can happen with us," or "I am attracted to my partner, and my partner is attracted to me." Work together on believing new wonder and excitement are not only possible, but *will happen*.

Adjust your attitude, and start paying attention to your partner outside of the bedroom: these are mandatory preliminary steps to renewed sexual intimacy.

This chapter is not meant to address sexual problems but, like the rest of the book, is meant to alleviate disconnection, boredom, and ho-hums. However, the resource section lists places where help for difficulties is available.

If you are having difficulties, please know that there is help available, and often a problem that has been bothering you for years can be eliminated more easily than you imagine.

What to Do:

Explorations: Sexual Talk

Sharing your beliefs, fears, and desires around sex in a loving, open manner is a very simple and amazingly potent way to refuel your passion.

Complete the sentence stems below by either writing or verbalizing as many responses for each question as you can allow yourself to share. Or bring home a book about sexual enhancement, look at it together to break the ice, then use the questions for further exploration. Or answer each question by using your body to *show* your lover your answers.

The thing I love most about having sex with you is . . .

When I am afraid I won't be good in bed, I . . .

When I was growing up, I learned that sex was . . .

I feel guilty about sex sometimes because . . .

I find you sexually attractive when you . . .

One of my fondest sexual memories with you is . . .

When I want to make love and you don't, I feel . . .

A sexual fear I have is . . .

To feel "in the mood" I need . . .

When we have oral sex, I feel . . .

The way I would like to be touched by you is . . .

If you could do one thing to me next time we make love, I would like you to . . .

I feel like not having sex when you . . .

I am afraid to talk about sex with you because . . .

A sexual secret I am afraid to share with you is . . .

The way I've been blocking love in my life is . . .

If you are too inhibited to talk about sex, imagine the worst thing your partner might do, feel, or think if you revealed yourself fully to him or her. Also, conjure up the best thing that might happen if you had a frank discussion about your sex life. Better sex happens not because of better technique, but because of true intimacy. Intimacy comes from revealing the real you.

Sexual Fantasies

Sharing sexual fantasies with your lover intensifies your level of intimacy because you are exposing your deepest desires. It also empowers you. By telling your partner what you would like, you take responsibility for your desires, which prevents resentment and sexual mind-reading games.

In detail, write a sexual fantasy that you would like to have fulfilled by your lover. Sometimes, partners don't fantasize about each other. If that is the case, take one of your favorite fantasies and insert your partner. If you feel too embarrassed to dream, complete the sentence "A sexual fantasy I would like to act out with you is . . ."

Share your fantasies, then take turns expressing what you found exciting in your partner's sexual daydreams and how, when, and where you would like to enact it.

A *general note about fantasy:* There is debate about the use of fantasy during sex with your partner. Many sex therapists believe that if fantasy helps you have a pleasurable experience, go for it. Others believe that fantasy can be used to block true connection and intimacy. One compromise is to use fantasy only for self-pleasuring or to get yourself in the mood (say during a simmering sexual day, see below) and to not fantasize while making love with your partner. Another is to use fantasy during sex only if you are fantasizing about your partner. Whatever you do, don't disclose your fantasies without warning or to arouse jealousy in your partner.

Another Version

If sharing fantasies doesn't appeal to you, try making a list of ten things that make you pant, wriggle with pleasure, and otherwise become aroused. Share your lists, and next time you make love, incorporate a couple of your partner's items into the experience.

Simmering Sexual Feelings

If one partner is often more in the mood than the other, or if one partner complains about lack of foreplay, try this exercise.

Starting in the morning, roll over and caress your mate while whispering in his or her ear, "I want to make love to you tonight like lions mating on the veld." (Or something like that.) Don't squelch this by saying, "But tonight's the PTA meeting." If tonight isn't a good time for you, then lick your lover's ear and gently propose an alternative date. *Stick to that date!*

Throughout your day, massage your anticipation. Make whispered illicit phone calls about what you are going to do to each other that night; have lingerie, silk boxer shorts, scented massage oil, or a canister of whipped cream delivered to work with a naughty note; meet for lunch and pretend you are illicit lovers. Your imagination is the only limit. Spend the day simmering your excitement. Read erotica on your lunch hour, pleasure yourself while the kids are napping, or on the commute home fantasize about a fantastic sexual encounter you and your partner shared in the past. Once together in the evening, keep building the tension. Rub against each other "accidentally" while you're cooking dinner, go out to dinner and feed each other, take a shower together, take time to arrange the atmosphere in your bedroom, and then, finally, time for love. (Yes, you can do this with children. Five minutes of sexual innuendo over dessert while the kids watch TV, ten minutes of foreplay while the kids are in the bath, fifteen minutes of intercourse after the kids fall asleep. Be creative; it doesn't have to be one continuous encounter!)

See "Music: Feeling Amorous."

If you are concerned the buildup will be bigger than the payoff, start with a one- or two-hour buildup, say over dinner. And if you really want to pack a wallop, go away for a weekend and delay sex until Saturday night or Sunday morning.

Getting in the Mood

See "Massage" for additional directions if necessary.

These simple ways of touching can be used singly or in creative combination to help you when you sort of want to have sex but aren't raring to go.

The sandwich press: The lighter partner lies on top of the heavier, stretching out and matching arm to arm, leg to leg. Turn your heads to the side, and lie cheek to cheek. Breathe deeply. The person on the bottom imagines himself or herself sinking into the mattress or floor, while the person on top concentrates on melting into the lover.

The brain press: Place your right hand behind your partner's head at the base of the skull, and your left hand over the forehead. Press firmly, and hold for a count of twenty. Both of you breathe deeply, with your eyes closed, and concentrate on letting go of tension and worries.

Back body sweep: One partner sits with back straight and arms relaxed at the sides. The other partner stands behind and places one hand on each shoulder, about an inch away from the skin (you don't actually touch). Sweep the hands toward the opposite buttock, crossing mid-back. You are making an X across your partner's back. Move quickly. Repeat three times.

Whole body sweep: One partner lies down, eyes closed, arms and legs slightly apart, breathing deeply. To relax: The partner giving the sweep starts at the hands and sweeps up the arms and down the side of the body to the toes, again with hands one inch away from the body. Repeat two more times, then do the same sweep on the other side of the body. To revitalize: Sweep from the toe to the hand along each side of the body three times.

Standing sweep: Stand toe to toe, hips close together. Both partners place their hands on either side of the base of the other's spine (right above the buttocks). Press deeply, then run your fingers all the way up to your partner's neck, pressing firmly on the muscles on either side of the spine. Return your hands to the base of the spine, and repeat two more times. (This is wonderful naked but can also be done anytime, anywhere, as a sensuous pick-me-up.)

Ask and Ye Might Receive

Without specific information, your sexual partner is lost. Our bodies, our tastes, and our preferences are always changing. There is nothing wrong with telling your partner exactly what you want, as long as you do it when he or she is open to it.

The point of this exercise is to enable each of you to experience being totally passive during sex as well as totally active. Decide who will go first, approximately how long the encounter will last, and when you will meet again to satisfy the partner who gives this time.

One person becomes the receiver and one becomes the giver. The receiver's role is to relax and try to experience as much sexual gratification and arousal as he or she is capable of while giving explicit instructions to the giver. The giver concentrates on being as artistic and lavish a lover as he or she can be.

As receiver, gather any aids you would like the giver to choose from: massage oil, aromatherapy oils, feathers, or a vibrator (or two). Get comfortable, taking a few deep breaths. Tell the giver where to start on your body and what to do. For example, "Please start by lightly tickling my entire body with your fingertips, but avoid my breasts and genitals until I tell you. . . . That's perfect. I'm going to breathe and enjoy this for a few moments. . . . Now massage my feet using the massage oil. . . . You can touch me a little harder. . . . Great." Keep giving instructions, as specific as possible. Offer encouragement, but be very clear in your own mind that this is your time to receive exactly what you want. Don't worry about the other person's needs.

As the giver, follow the receiver's instructions as explicitly as possible. Concentrate on staying relaxed by breathing deeply and checking in with your own body. How does it feel to be giving without receiving anything back? Breathe into any feelings of tension or performance anxiety. If you feel unsure about an instruction, do it and then ask, "Was that okay?" or "Did that feel good, or would this feel better?" You can add your own creative touches, but primarily focus your energy on trying to fulfill your partner's requests.

When you are finished, talk about what this was like for each of you. End by reaffirming the date and time when the giver will become the receiver. Above all, stick to this appointment!

A variation on this exercise is to show your partner how you like to be made love to by pleasuring yourself in front of him or her in such a position that they can see what you are doing. The point is not to have an orgasm (although if that happens, fine) but to teach your partner exactly how you like to be touched.

For many people, this might be a daunting or embarrassing assignment. Candlelight, a talk beforehand, stimulating yourself with your eyes closed, your sense of humor, and the knowledge that your sex life could improve might encourage you.

No Sex

A common complaint many women have is that all touching or hugging has to lead to sex. Decide on a time when you will hug, touch, kiss, and even do some "heavy petting" but you will not have actual intercourse or achieve orgasm. Try massaging the entire body but *not* the genitals. Focus on being able to be touched by your partner without having to concentrate on climaxing or "performing."

A Tantric Way to Begin

Ancient Tantra is a spiritual system in which sexual love is a sacrament. By beginning sex with a more conscious attitude you can elevate it to the level of spiritual nourishment.

Sit facing your partner, gazing into each other's eyes. As you inhale, bring your palms together in a gesture of prayer. Close your eyes. Exhale, bending forward, keeping your back straight but not rigid, until your foreheads touch. Hold here, focusing on the contact between you and your partner. Then inhale and come up, opening your eyes, looking into your partner's eyes, and saying, "The God in me salutes the God in you." (You can of course substitute whatever word conveys reverence for you: Goddess, Great Spirit, my soul, Higher Power, the best of me.) After the salute, the rest is up to you.

Nurturing Each Other Through Desire Differences

What do you do when one person wants to have sex more than the other? What do you do when one partner complains the other never initiates sex? That is, besides ignoring the problem and letting resentments pile up? (I am addressing this subject not to give solutions to deeply rooted problems but to suggest additional ways to nurture each other sexually. If these are recurring problems for you, seek professional help to deal with the underlying issues.)

If frequency of sex is a troublesome issue for you both, try agreeing to not initiate or even talk about sex for two weeks. Write the end date on your calendar. During this time, nurture each other every day in small ways, and hug and cuddle a lot. Two days before sex could resume, do the "No Sex" exercise. On the day that sex can resume, do the "Simmering Sexual Feelings" exercise.

When one person wants to have sex and the other doesn't, ask each other, "What, besides sex, would make you feel loved right now?" Act on the ideas given. The idea is to find other ways to nurture each other that are equally valuable. Sometimes, this is enough. Other times it opens an important dialogue. Other times it leads to heartfelt sex. Experiment.

Do the "Releasing Resentment" exercise.

If it feels healthy and possible, nurture your partner either by leaving him or her alone and not asking for sex for a few days or by initiating sex out of the blue, say at 4 A.M. If you feel resentment about either action, ask yourself why. Don't tune out and give unconsciously. Instead, use the opportunity to give wholeheartedly to your partner while learning about your own relationship issues. (Yes, it is hard to pleasure your lover while you are psychoanalyzing yourself. Play with it and see what happens.)

Heterosexual Sexual Nurturing

Consider the subject of oral sex, frequency of sex, and who initiates what from a "man's" point of view. Consider the statement "But I'm a man. I have needs!" not as a tired cliché but as a call from the male spirit saying, "I can totally relax only during sex. It is the only way I know to communicate with you. I want to be as close to you as you want to be with me, but I want to do it with my body. I want to know you desire me and that I please you. Nothing makes me feel more alive than making you come or knowing that you desire me enough to take me in your mouth without my having to ask."

Consider the subject of oral sex, frequency of sex, and who initiates what from a "woman's" point of view. Consider the statement "All you ever want to do is have sex" not as a tired cliché but as a call from the female spirit saying, "I give and I give to everyone until I feel like one big breast. I need to be given *to*. I feel sometimes like I'm an object, only a body to be looked at and touched, instead of a whole person. See and desire all of me; connect with my mind and soul first, then my body."

As a woman, what would happen if the next time your mate wants to have sex, you consider this not as a confirmation of your status as body and eternal nurturer but as a request for communication from him, a desire to connect with you in the way he knows best, and an opportunity to give him what would most deeply nurture him at this moment?

As a man, what would happen if the next time your mate wants to touch but not have sex, you consider this not as a rejection of your deepest self but as a request to be loved and valued as more than a sexual object, and as an opportunity to connect both physically *and* verbally, and as an opportunity to give her what would most deeply nurture her at this moment?

It can become a dance between your different needs if you reframe these differences as opportunities to increase your understanding of each other, instead of indictments of each other's insensitivity.

(Note: Again, these are generalizations; that is, highly dangerous statements. They are examples of possible starting points. They are not in any way meant to illustrate what is universal or "normal.")

Some Specific Ideas

Start at a woman's feet, and very slowly work your way up by caressing her thighs and the backs of her knees, but do not touch her genitals. Or do the same from her head without touching her breasts.

Suck your lover's fingers and toes. Toes have more nerve endings than genitals. Dip digits in hot fudge, fruit juice, or whatever other fluids appeal to your taste, and lick them clean.

Dribble water across a stomach and then blow gently.

Surprise your partner by decorating the bedroom. You could fill the room with balloons or flowers or light candles, play wild, tribal music, burn musky incense, and cover the bed with a fake animal throw.

Write down three brief, erotic fantasies, put them in a hat, and have your partner pick one to enact.

Radio psychologist Barbara De Angelis recommends kissing your partner for at least twenty seconds with no plans of having sex. She believes this gives you time to feel physically connected, to "get the juice flowing." Three twenty-second kisses a day keep the passion bubbling.

Take a walk in the woods and gather flowers to later adorn your partner's genitals with.

Sex in the kitchen adds new luster to the room faster than a remodeling job. Feed each other mango. Hold ice in your mouth while sucking parts of your lover's body. The kitchen table might be just the right height to lie back on while the other person stands or kneels. . . .

Blindfold your partner and make love while whispering everything you find attractive, arousing, and beautiful about him or her.

Reenact the first time you made love. Recreate details of the setting if you can't be in the setting itself, the time of day, any music that was playing, smells (what kind of soap or lotion or perfume did you have on?), but most importantly, concentrate on recreating how you acted, what you talked about, how it actually, finally happened!

And

Analysis of early Kinsey research showed that 92 percent of women who regularly spent twenty-one minutes or longer on foreplay consistently experienced orgasm. But most couples spend an average of fifteen minutes. So slow down. Decide together to take lots of time making love. Remember to relax, and take lots of deep breaths.

Resources:

For Each Other, by Lonnie Barbach (Anchor, 1982). Excellent, clear help, especially for women who can't reach orgasm.

Good Vibrations Catalog, on-line at http://www.goodvibes.com or call
   800–289–8423, or visit 1210 Valencia St., San Francisco, CA 94110.
   The store's number is 415–974–8980.

Hot Monogamy: Essential Steps to More Passionate, Intimate Lovemaking, by
   Dr. Patricia Love (Plume, 1995). Dr. Love proves that becoming sen-
   sually and "sexually fluent" is a skill that can kindle the flames of passion regardless of how long a couple has been together.

Intimate Kisses: The Poetry of Sexual Pleasure, by Wendy Maltz (New
   World Library, 2001). A collection of poems to inspire couples to
   deeper physical intimacy.

101 Nights of Grrreat Romance: How to Make Love with Your Clothes On,
   by Laura Corn (Park Avenue Publishers, 1996). How to make love
   with your clothes on.

Secrets of a Passionate Marriage, by David Schnarch, Ph.D. (Sounds True
   Audio). A revolutionary approach thousands have used to take their
   relationships to new and lasting heights of sexual ecstasy and intimacy. Audio.

Sexplay Board Game—A game board with six spinners. Starting with the
   first spinner, you set up what you get to do to your partner. Explicit
   and really inventive. Available on the Web; search by title.

*The Sex-Starved Marriage: A Couple's Guide to Boosting Their Marital
   Libido,* by Michelle Weiner-Davis (Simon and Schuster, 2003). This
   book comes very highly recommended from several of my newsletter
   readers. Good for mismatched libidos.

The Unmade Bed, edited by Laura Chester (HarperCollins, 1992). Quality
   erotica for married couples.

Music: *Best of Sade* and *Lover's Rock* by Sade, *Live in Dublin* by the Coors,
   All-Time Greatest Hits by Barry White, *Voodoo* by D'angelo, *Love Sen-
   suality Devotion* by Enigma, *The Hits 2* by Prince, *Let's Get It On* by
   Marvin Gaye, *Heart Shaped World* by Chris Isaak, *Love Songs* by Billie
   Holiday.

Massage

You'll Need:

Vegetable oil (sunflower, safflower, almond, *not* peanut).

Essential oils for scent (optional). (See "A Sensory Banquet" for massage oil recipes.)

Relaxing music like Coyote Oldman's *Tear of the Moon*.

A quiet, comfortable place.

Time required: Ten minutes on up.

When to Do It:

- After a difficult day at the office, a hard workout, an exhausting fight with a teenager, or chasing a toddler around the house.

- To get in the mood to make love.

- On the beach, in the woods, in the backyard.

- As a transition between work time and play time.

What Is It?

Everyone loves and appreciates the magic of a tender touch. You can be having a terrible day, and your sweetie can rub your neck for ten minutes, and voilà! Peace and perspective!

The secret to a good massage is *not* your technique but your ability to be fully present and listen to the messages from your lover's body. Don't let your fears that massage is too difficult or detailed for you to learn keep you from trying. These massages are especially made for busy people, and the benefits to your relationship, peace of mind, and health are incredible!

What to Do:

Sensual Extras

Use oil with all the massages. Keep some near your bed. Warm it by rubbing your hands together. Repeat all movements five to ten times. Mix up the instructions. *There is no right way.* For a longer massage, combine hand with face or back with foot. Improvise! To ensure equal time, decide how long each person will be massaged (say ten minutes for you tonight, ten for me tomorrow).

Center Yourself

The person being massaged, **Relax.** The person giving the massage, breathe deeply, eyes closed. With each exhalation, visualize your breath moving down into your hands until, after four or five breaths, you can begin to feel your exhalation streaming out through each of your fingertips. Imagine this exhalation emerging as tingling, healing energy. Slowly open your eyes and begin the massage of your choice.

Back Relaxes

Place your palms on your lover's back and make large, leisurely circles around his or her shoulders.

Starting slow and light and gradually squeezing harder, knead the shoulder muscles that curve from the neck to the shoulders. These are the trapezius muscles. Use your thumb and fingers, doing both sides at once.

Massage the muscles on either side of the spine with small circular motions, using your thumbs only. Work down, then up. Experiment with light and deep pressure.

Working from the waist up, place your palms on either side of the waist, fingers pointing toward the spine but not on it. Firmly slide your hands up the entire back. When you reach the shoulders, reverse your hands by making a circle over the shoulders so that the heels of your hands are now pointing toward the spine and your fingers are on the sides of the body. Now bring your hands down the back, firmly enough to move your partner toward you. Reverse when you reach the hips, and repeat.

Finish with featherlight strokes up and down the back.

Foot Massage

Because feet are often sensitive, you might want to use extra massage oil.

Stroke the foot with your palm, using a circular motion and working from the toes to the ankle. Continue around to the sides and bottom of the foot. Focus on warming and loosening the muscles.

Place your thumbs on the top of your lover's foot just below the ankle, so that your fingers curl under and rest on the sole. Squeeze firmly while dragging your hands toward the toes. When you reach the toes, slide your hands back and begin again. Repeat several times.

Make a fist with one hand, and steady the foot with the other. Use your knuckles to massage the arch with small, steady circles. Use firm pressure. Continue by moving across the bottom of the entire foot.

Place the heels of both your hands against the top of your lover's foot while your fingertips press into the sole. Press down firmly with your palms while at the same time you press up with your fingertips into the arch. Next, slide the heels of your hands apart so that you end up grasping the sides of your partner's feet, pulling gently.

With one hand, steady the foot while, with the thumb and forefinger of your other hand, you grasp the base of the big toe. Firmly pull up on the toe while at the same time you twist your fingers in a corkscrew motion. Do each toe gently.

Sandwich the foot between your hands. Imagine breathing your energy into your partner's foot. Repeat on the other foot.

Hand Massage

Hold your mate's hand between both of yours. Breathe!

Make a fist, and massage your partner's palm in circles using your knuckles. Repeat on the other hand.

Firmly hold your partner's hand with your thumb pressed into the soft area between the thumb and forefinger. Press with your thumb while you rub your fingers back and forth, and up and down, across the back of the hand.

With your thumb and forefinger, lightly grasp the base of your partner's thumb. Pull your thumb and forefinger firmly from base to top of the thumb, making a corkscrew motion as you go. Slide off the tip. Repeat gently with each finger on each hand.

With one hand grasp your partner's wrist, and with the other pull the hand toward you, using thumb and forefinger to trace the lines between the knuckles all the way to the webs between the fingers. Knead each webbed pad between your thumb and index finger.

Place your thumbs together on the top of the hand. Stretch the back of the hand by pulling down with your thumbs all the way to the wrist.

Turn the palm up and stretch the palm back the same way, by pulling to the sides with the heels of your hands.

Finish by making a V with your index and second fingers and pushing it between your partner's fingers.

Face and Neck Massage

Sit with your partner lying in front of you, feet pointed away.

Make small circles all over the scalp. Spend extra time on the large bones behind each ear, drawing your fingers up and over until you reach the temples.

Place your thumbs together lightly in the middle of the forehead, where the "third eye" is located. Press lightly while you rotate your first three fingers around the temples.

Press down on the forehead using the entire hand. Use your other hand on top to add pressure. Maintain even force for ten seconds. Release very gradually.

Lay your hands on your partner's cheeks with your fingers pointed toward the chin. Rotate the flesh slowly. Press down on the chin.

Take your little finger and place on the inside corner of each eyelid. Pressing very lightly, move your finger over the closed eye and under the eyebrow, bringing the next finger into place and repeating until you are using all four fingers, moving very slowly across the eyes. Repeat on the bottom ridge of the eye.

Hold your partner's head with one hand under the chin and the other behind the skull. Lift the head slowly just a few inches. Rotate very gently and slowly in an arc from side to side. When you feel tension, stop, never pushing your partner's neck past the point of tension.

Finish by stroking the big bones behind the ear again, this time using four fingers on either side moving down to the large band of neck muscles and into the shoulders.

Resources:

Living Arts Massage Practice for Couples (Living Arts, 2000). A thirty-six-minute demonstration video with massage techniques designed specifically for men and for women. Video.

The New Sensual Massage: Learn to Give Pleasure with Your Hands, by Gordon Inkeles (Arcata Arts, 1998). Written in a reassuring and intimate tone, lavishly illustrated and beautifully designed, this book can prepare you in a single evening to give a wonderful massage.

Moving into Your Bodies

When to Do It:

- When you feel like a moldy couch potato.

- On a spring afternoon, when the sun is shining, the breeze is fragrant and mild, and somewhere inside you is a small child who desperately wants to come out and play.

- When you or your partner unwinds best by being active.

What Is It?

Do you ever feel like doing something physical together? Besides sex? Dancing together, getting sweaty, or healing each other by sharing energy are great ways to enhance your relationship by becoming more in tune and at peace with your physical selves. As you become more grounded, you become more sure of your boundaries, which is a key issue in intimate relationships. Moving together can help you release passion-polluting stress and free up blocked energy. Liking your body frees you to be more physically intimate and comfortable. Finally, experiencing bodily pleasures together deepens your connection to that "place beyond words" and helps you communicate in nonverbal ways.

What to Do:

Part 1: Take Inventory

Select two relaxing pieces of music (roughly four to six minutes each) back-to-back on a tape or CD. Sit or lie down together, close your eyes, and **Relax.** Begin to notice where your body is touching the bed, floor, or chair. . . . Notice which parts of your body move as you breathe. . . . Taking your time, breathing deeply, let your attention drift slowly through your body. What parts feel very alive? What parts of your body feel less

You'll Need:

Clothes and shoes you can move in.

Music that makes you want to shimmy, shake, bump, and grind.

Space and privacy to safely get wild in.

Time required: Many ideas can be done in fifteen or twenty minutes. One section requires up to forty-five.

alive or energized? Do some parts feel lighter than others, warmer, more tense, tingling, relaxed, or cold? Can you feel the base of your spine? Can you feel the back of your head? Your fingers? Keep taking your personal inventory until the first piece of music ends.

As the second piece of music begins, focus on your partner. Where do you think he or she is most alive in his or her body? Slowly and gently reach over and touch the place on your lover's body where you think there is the most connection and feeling. Take a moment, then let your hand drift to a place where you feel there is the least feeling. Alternate touching alive and less alive places for the rest of the music. Be gentle, move slowly, and don't speak.

When the music is over, come back slowly and talk about what you learned about your own body, what you learned from where your partner touched you, and whether you agreed with the selections. Or move to the next part, or make brief notes about what you've experienced to share later.

Part 2: Moving Energy

Sometimes moving energy brings up feelings of grief, anger, or fear. Allow yourself to feel whatever comes up by breathing deeply and communicating with your partner about what you are feeling.

Decide who will "receive" first. Receiver, communicate what parts of your body you would like "enlivened." Pick parts that felt dead or blocked in part 1, or rely on past experiences or your intuition. Then lie down and **Relax.** Your job is to breathe deeply and allow yourself to take in the healing energy being given to you. Nothing more. No worrying about your partner or about giving back.

The "giver" gets comfortable, perhaps sitting on a pillow beside the receiver, and begins with the breathing exercise in "Massage: Center Yourself." Spend a moment feeling the healing energy in your hands. When you are ready, gently bring one hand to rest on your partner's fore-

head and the other on her or his belly. Visualize your healing energy traveling down your arms, into your fingers, and flowing into your mate's
belly. Visualize your energy traveling up your mate's spine and into the
neck and head until it reaches your other hand, and you receive it back
up your arm as you inhale. Then, as you exhale, feel your energy moving
down your arm, into your mate's belly, then through the body and back
into your hand that is resting on the head, establishing a continuous cycle
of healing energy. Apply firmer pressure as you sense the energy soothing,
removing any blocks, opening and healing.

Now, *slowly* move one hand to one of the areas your partner asked to be
enlivened while leaving your other hand on the belly or head (whichever
is most comfortable). Take several minutes to visualize the energy circling
between these two areas. Slowly apply firmer pressure. Slowly release and
move to another area while keeping one hand on the previous area. The
idea is to move slowly down and around the body, creating healing circles
between two points, always keeping one hand on the previous point. For
example, head and belly, head and chest, chest and hip, hip and knee,
knee and foot—whatever combination feels right.

End by touching head and belly again. You might want to think or say a
prayer or positive thought. If the giver feels spacey afterward, place your
hands on the floor or ground and do the same healing circle visualization
with the Earth's energy.

Switch roles, and repeat. You may have to wait if one partner is too wiped
out. Afterward, discuss whether your body feels any different. What sensations did you feel? Did any images or colors appear to you? It can be
worthwhile to note any gender differences. For example, did one partner
have a harder time giving? Did one partner have a harder time receiving?
Did anyone feel unworthy? Uncomfortable? Sexually aroused? Open a
dialogue, or have each partner record his or her experience in your couple's
journal.

These exercises get better with repetition and are especially healing when
one partner is stressed out or ill.

Dancing

Choose some music that makes you want to dance, or try doing this without music. Decide who will lead first. Stand facing each other with your
eyes closed, fingertips touching. The partner leading uses his or her hands
to express an emotion: nurturance, love, freedom, passion, desire, or
whatever feels right. Do two or three different emotions while your partner tries to guess the feelings. Repeat with the other person leading. You
can also use your entire body or just your feet (touching big toes, for
instance).

Sports

If your partner is passionate about a sport, once, just once, try it, no matter how silly you feel. The purpose is to experience what your partner
finds enjoyable, without having to do it right or well. No criticism
allowed, which includes criticizing yourself. Several times during this
experience, ask yourself how your body feels. Play with timing your
breathing to your actions. Talk afterward about how it felt.

Motivation

If neither of you is active now, then choose four (two apiece) different
physical things to experiment with, fun physical activities you've always
wanted to try. Forget heart rate or being able to keep it up. Just pick two
fun, moving activities. (Run at dawn; do yoga with a videotape; canoe
across a lake; chop wood; sit opposite each other with your legs open,
hold each other's wrists, and stretch back and forth; roller-skate; jump on
a pogo stick; fly a kite; plant a tree.) Sit down and make four firm dates
for one month to do these activities together. *Make a firm commitment.*
Entropy steals your relationship because you let it. Be realistic. If you can
get together only every two weeks, extend this plan for two months. Talk
together about what you expect your obstacles will be: "I'll be too tired,"
"We never have racquetballs," no child care, staying late at work, and so
forth. Plan for your obstacles.

Inner Calm

Run or walk together while imagining a wave is behind you, gently carrying you forward, lifting you, cooling and refreshing you like your own mini-ocean.

Walk together silently, imagining yourselves as two still, small points of light, moving quietly and effortlessly through space.

Walk or run together while concentrating on your breathing. Try inhaling for three steps, exhaling for three steps. Or whatever rhythm works for you.

See "When Life Is Too Crazy" for more relaxing ideas.

Release

Stamp your feet together. Share and exaggerate your frustration, anger, or tension by shouting while you stamp. For example, you might yell, "I had a horrible day," while stamping around the living room. Your partner answers, "I hate everything!" You'll feel silly at first, but if you let go even a little you quickly get into a rhythm that will help you both release lots of tension. Playing rousing music or closing the windows might help you let go.

See "Letting Go."

One of you comes home in a bad mood. You try to talk about it, but your conversation and the evening are quickly degenerating into miscommunication and anger. Stop, face each other, and have the same conversation while making ridiculous, horrible, or absurd faces and speaking total gibberish—animal noises, made-up words, honks, wheezes, whatever. Do this for *at least* three minutes. Express what you are truly feeling without getting stuck in words.

See "Daily Communication: Nonverbal Communication."

Read this to each other, giving each partner a turn:

Stand with your feet roughly shoulder-width apart, toes turned inward a little. Take a moment to center yourself by breathing three times, very deeply. Make your hands into fists, and push your knuckles into your lower back, right above your hips. Lean as far back as you can, keeping your head in line with your spine. Try not to tense your neck. Breathe ten

See "Erotic Delights" and "A Sensory Banquet" for more body delights.

long, slow, deep breaths as far down into your belly as you can. Make a sound every time you exhale. Allow each sound to last as long as it wishes. You may begin to feel your body vibrate. Now, bend forward from your waist, letting your head and arms dangle. Breathe another ten long, deep, slow breaths, making any kind of sound you wish with each exhalation. Let whatever you feel wash through your body and out.

This is a great exercise to do before a massage, after a tense day, or before making love. It may sound awkward, but it feels great.

Fantasy

What are you waiting for? Life is short, that much we can be sure of. Fulfill a physical fantasy. Canoe the Amazon, climb Mount Shasta (renew your vows at dawn before the climb), raft the Colorado, visit the mud baths in northern California (or a day spa and have massages side by side), hike the back country of Yellowstone or the Appalachian trail (even for a day), bike from Maine to Seattle (or do fifty miles in one day in your area), dive the Great Barrier Reef (or learn to snorkel), kayak with whales in British Columbia (or canoe a local river), visit hot springs in New Mexico in the wintertime (or hot tub for twenty minutes and then lie on the snow naked for a minute). Fantasies can come true. It can happen to you!

Resources

Om: Yoga in a Box for Couples: Beginner Level, by Cyndi Lee (Hay House, 2002). A sixty-five-minute CD with a beginning yoga class for two and seventy-one flash cards demonstrating each yoga posture, not to mention a candle, incense, and an all-music CD. Very well done.

The Diet Cure: The Eight-Step Program to Rebalance Your Body Chemistry and End Food Cravings, Weight Problems, and Mood Swings—Now, by Julia Ross (Penguin, 2000). One of the best organized books on using diet and supplements to help with mood.

Music

When to Do It:

- When your life is filled with teeth-grinding noise.

- When you want to enhance any nurturing activity or any aspect of life, especially erotic and sensual experiences.

- When one or both of you needs to get out of your head and into your heart.

What Is It?

Many studies have explored the power of music, from its ability to calm us when we're stressed or lift us up when we're down to how music influences our blood pressure and the level of stress hormones in our blood. Music has been used to reach autistic children, help cancer patients endure chemotherapy, and reduce anger at mediation talks. One study found that participants enjoyed music more than sex!

All in all, music is an effective, easy, inexpensive way to add grace and beauty to time spent together. Music can transform the mundane into the sublime (dinner), the sublime into the spiritual (making love), the spiritual into the ecstatic (meditating together).

What to Do:

Finding Music

Throughout this chapter, I will give suggestions of music that might meet a certain need, like music to pick up your spirits. However, music is a very personal choice. Go through your current music collection, and make notes about what music you might play to enhance or change a mood. Go

You'll Need:

Music selections of your choice.

Stereo or boom box.

Simple instruments.

Tape recorder and tapes.

Walkman or head-phones.

Time required: One to thirty minutes.

on excursions to music stores together, especially stores that let you listen.
Keep a section in your personal comfort book to note musical ideas.

Change the Mood

Imagine a fight is brewing. Both of you are sure you are right. Or both of
you want to be couch potatoes but you also want to exercise. Instead of
fighting or feeling guilty, let music change your mood. Select a piece of
music that will transform your mood—fast, lighthearted music to motivate or soft, slow music to calm. The associations and subtle variations
are endless.

Holding hands, lie down with your feet near your speakers. Let the music
you choose wash over you for ten minutes or longer. Concentrate only on
the music. When thoughts about how tired or angry you are come to the
surface, turn your focus back to the music. After the piece is finished, sit
in silence for thirty seconds or so, breathing and checking in with yourself. If you feel different, let your mate know with a smile or a few words.

Note: Don't use this to drown out your partner or run away from an
important discussion.

If you want to be soothed, listen to Bach's Concertos for Two Pianos or
check out a Windham Hill collection. Need energy? Maybe Tchaikovsky's
Swan Lake "Waltz" or Gabriel Roth's *Totem* or Brahms's Piano Concerto
no. 1 or Chopin's *Preludes* or some heat from the Red Hot Chili Peppers.

Morning Music

Don't wake up to screeching morning DJs! This may sound obvious, but
tuning your clock radio to a classical station set just loud enough to
slowly stir you to consciousness can put an entirely different slant on
the day.

Music to play in the morning: Vivaldi's Flute Concertos, Mozart's Clarinet Concerto, or James Brown (especially "I Feel Good").

Music to start the day with a sense of fun or if you have kids: "When You Wish upon a Star," "Whistle While You Work," soundtracks from *Winnie the Pooh*, *Fantasia*, and *The Jungle Book*, or Haydn's Symphony no. 45.

See "Everyday Rituals" for more about starting the day.

You can use morning music to get a laugh out of your partner, help her or him prepare for a stressful day, or send a gentle message saying "I know how you feel." For example, play *Chariots of Fire* when your sweetie is having a hard time getting out of bed, or if you feel like starting the day on a spiritual note, try listening to *The Virgin's Lament* or *Vox De Nuve*, both by Noirin Ni Riain and the monks of Glenstal Abbey, or *A Feather on the Breath of God* by Gothic Voices with Emma Kirkby or Libana's *Fire Within* or *Clannad: The Magical Ring*.

Influential Sounds

Sound in our environment affects us and our relationships, often without our noticing. Tune in to your environment. You will probably notice loud, irritating sounds first: garbage trucks, crying babies, phones ringing. Observe how these sounds make you feel. Do you feel tension erupting in your body? See if these noises influence how you treat your partner. For example, my sister works in an office with phones ringing constantly. At home, whenever the phone used to ring, she would become suddenly irritable and sometimes snap at her husband. By becoming aware of the noises around her and their effect on her mood, she became less irritable toward him because she knew the source.

Next, move past the obvious, and pay attention to how subtle and distant sounds affect you. For example, the distant sound of a train whistle makes me miss my parents, and I go looking for a hug from Chris. Observe yourself with loving detachment, and look for connections between feelings and particular sounds. Share this information with your partner.

The third level: listen for silence. Where are the silences in your relationship right now? Where are they comfortable? Where are they tense?

How do you and your partner use silence? When? No judgment, just loving self-observation and then communication.

Music and What to Do on Friday Night

Sit in the dark with the windows open, and listen to Beethoven's Symphony no. 3, the "Eroica." Loud. This is especially great on a warm, windy night. Listening to any great piece of music outdoors, even in your backyard, especially at night, can be very pleasing.

Do you feel like an exhausted slug but need to get ready for a night out? Put on some loud, rousing music, and dance your way through the shower, getting dressed, feeding the kids. Old Bruce Springsteen, B-52's, Dvořák's *Czech Suite*, Rolling Stones's *Love You Live* or Spanish flamenco music stirs tired bones.

Or play relaxing music to balance yourself. This especially helps when the kids are crazy and you *have* to go to this company dinner. Try Beethoven's Symphony no. 6 (first and second movements), Bach's *The Well-Tempered Clavier Book 1*, Neil Young's *Harvest Moon*, or Enya's *Shepherd Moon*.

Making Beautiful Music Together

Buy a couple of inexpensive hand drums, and drum together. Play with the kids too. It may sound silly, but it is a very powerful way to release tension. Yes, your neighbors might think you've gone New Age Cave Person on them, but you'll be feeling great. Don't worry about technique; just let your natural rhythm take over and mingle with your lover's. Breathe and relax your shoulders.

You can use drums during an argument. Imagine you are talking about buying a new car. You were using one of the methods in the "Negotiating" chapter, but you've disintegrated into entrenched positions over who wants what. Stop. Ask your partner if he or she is willing to take a break and drum. If agreeable, break out your drums, and take turns pounding out your opinion on the subject at hand. Mimic with your drumming what you were trying (unsuccessfully) to express with your mouth. See if you can reach a satisfying conclusion. If not, it is guaranteed to clear your head and release your rigid attitude. Note: Don't use drumming to avoid talking.

See "Negotiating."

Another enjoyable idea: Visit a craft store or fair together, and look for simple instruments. One couple I know in Cleveland Heights keeps a beautiful wooden xylophone on their coffee table. My sister has "Eggs"— egg-shaped noisemakers that sound like maracas. We have a rain stick (when turned, it sounds like rainfall), a harmonica, chimes, and hand drums. Always an alternative to TV, always a quick way to jumpstart the creative spirit or at least drive the dog crazy. Also fun when guests visit.

Express Your Love

My dear friend Eric records cassettes of favorite music to give a voice to how he feels about his sweetie (and his friends, too). Push past familiar songs. Experiment with new music that tells her or him how you feel. Eric has a huge music collection; most of us don't, so borrow from friends and the library to increase your expressive choices.

Feeling Amorous

The longer you are together, the harder it is to find time to make love and the less often you are both "in the mood" at the same time. Use music to "warm up" and synchronize your ardor.

This is truly an area for experimentation to find the right music. A piece that works for me (but my sweetie has to use it sparingly) is Chopin's "Les

Sylphides" waltz. (We danced to it at our wedding.) One couple wrote me that when they want to get "in the mood," they play a compilation of opera arias. "The CD plays while we go about putting the kids to bed, taking showers, locking up. The sexual tension slowly builds. We meet in bed as the recording ends!"

More suggestions for getting in the mood or "necking" on the couch: "Something" by the Beatles; "Can't Help Falling in Love with You," Elvis; "The First Time Ever I Saw Your Face," Roberta Flack; "When a Man Loves a Woman," Percy Sledge; "If" by Perry Como; Mozart's 21st Piano Concerto; almost anything by Johnny Mathis; "Sexual Healing" by Marvin Gaye; *Tears of Joy* by Tuck and Patti (Windham Hill); Sade's *Love Deluxe*; Anita Baker's *Rapture*; Kenny G's *Silhouette*; Stanley Jordon's *Acoustic Alchemy*; Lyle Lovett's "Nobody Knows Me Like My Baby."

Experiment and find a new set of "your" songs. Spend a Friday night browsing in a music store, then go home, put on your selections, and see what happens!

Resources:

The Power of Sound: How to Manage Your Personal Soundscape for a Vital, Productive, and Healthy Life, by Joshua Leeds. (Healing Arts Press, 2001). Book and CD using sound to heal and enhance.

The Roar of Silence: Healing Powers of Breath, Tone, and Music, by Don G. Campbell (Theosophical Publishing, 1989). Campbell is one of the pioneers of using sound to heal.

The Singing Cure, by Paul Newham (Sounds True, 1998). A course in theraupetic singing. Audio.

Websites:

Healing Music Organization
    http://www.healingmusic.org

National Public Radio—music heard on NPR
    http://www.npr.org/music/index.html?loc=homebutton

Sounds True
    http://www.soundstrue.com

Nesting

You'll Need:

Beautiful, beloved things.

Various organizational helpers: baskets, boxes, filing cabinets.

Soft lighting, sensuous bedding, a good mattress.

Paper and pens.

Time required: Thirty minutes to several days.

When to Do It:

- When you are fighting because of irritations caused by your home, for example, tripping over shoes, no closet space, no reading light in the bedroom, and so forth.

- When you crave a richer feeling of home.

- When you want more beauty and order in your life. (Who doesn't?)

What Is It?

If comfort is associated with anything (other than food), it is associated with home: cozy spaces to retreat to, warm beds to snuggle in, cheerful kitchens, bathrooms set up for pampering and bathing together, tranquil gardens with a bubbling fountain . . . are you nauseated yet? The *reality* of home is often no place to put anything, chipped furniture, dust balls, dead grass, cat hair on everything—not very serene or comforting.

But a deep craving for a home is one that shouldn't be denied. The popularity of movies such as *Gone with the Wind*, *E.T.*, and *Places in the Heart* speaks to this craving within many of us. Whether it is a longing for roots or a refuge from the world, the creation of home is intricately linked to the creation of a relationship. Creating a place where you can both relax, a place that expresses each of your tastes, a place where you experience both the mundane moments of day-to-day life as well as the big signposts and celebrations—all of this provides a container for your life together, a foundation. Explore this aspect of your life together. Making a home doesn't just mean choosing curtains or paying the mortgage on time.

What to Do:

Explorations: Home

Answer the questions below, either verbally by taking turns or in writing, sharing your responses later. Don't think too much. The less you ponder, the more easily you can get past the obvious and into more personal revelations.

Free-associate with the word *home*. Name everything that comes into your mind around this word.

Name a story or movie or TV show that evokes a strong feeling of home for you.

When you were a child, did you create any play homes? Name a few. (Examples: a tree house, friend's bedroom, basement.)

Have you ever experienced a feeling of homelessness? What was it like?

Write a list of words about your ideal home. Don't limit yourself to reality or convention.

Share your answers, and see if they inspire you to deepen, reinvent, or newly appreciate your home.

Identify the Irritants

For the cries of joy in our house (lasting well over a week) you would have thought we had won the lottery. In fact, Chris had installed a light in our bedroom. For almost two years, the only light in the bedroom had been a single reading light by the bed. Doing anything in that room at night (besides sleeping) subtly irritated me simply because I couldn't see. These organizational details affect your life together significantly!

Sit down together and make a list of similar annoyances in your home. It may include insufficient lighting, messy closets, or cabinet doors that don't close. Arrange your list in terms of priority: what would you most like to change? Tackle the number one priority by breaking it into small steps (pick out the light fixture, get the hardware, hire someone to install it). Set a realistic timetable for action, and divide up the labor fairly. (Too simplistic? If working on the house is an area of conflict for you, see "Negotiating" and "Forgiveness" for help.)

Creating a Spiritual Center

A home needs a center, an expression of its soul. To create this, write a mission statement for your home, an explanation of what your home stands for. Examples include "a sanctuary for all who enter," "a meeting place for friends and family," "a place where neighborhood kids hang out." Get together with your partner and all other members of the household. It might help to make a list describing the ideal mood, feeling, and attitude you wish your house to embody. From this list, compose a prayer, poem, or pledge. Or find a quote or paragraph that describes the feeling you wish to express. Post your statement somewhere in your home.

Another way to express the spiritual aspect of your home is to physically create or find a symbol that reminds you of the deeper life being lived around you. Fifteenth-century philosopher Marsilio Ficino advocated an image of the cosmos, either a model of the universe or a painting of the heavens on the ceiling. It doesn't have to be a fixed or solemn symbol or one connected to religion. You could hang a corkboard in the kitchen and tack up letters, drawings, and family photographs as a living collage of special moments and thoughts. The top of a cabinet in our home serves as an ever-changing spiritual display where, when we feel like it, we create shrines to remind us of the seasons, our goals, whatever feels right. When we are busy, the cabinet reflects that as well: empty and dusty. Selecting a painting or poster invoking the spirit of your home is another possibility.

See "Natural Nurture: Discovering Your Local Landscape" for ways to connect to your homeland.

Beauty

Thomas Moore, a New England psychotherapist and author of *The Care of the Soul*, believes, as did Renaissance Platonists and Romantic poets, that the soul needs beauty like the body needs food. This is not a particularly popular idea today. Beauty has become a narrowly defined sales tool. But that isn't true beauty. True beauty arrests us, brings us up short, giving us cause to pause and step outside of our practical life. Have you ever stopped to contemplate a moment of beauty in your home? Whether a flower arrangement or the head of your daughter glistening in the sun, it is beauty that speaks to you.

Consider your soul when buying things for the house. We recently bought a dining room table that has this quality of soul—beautifully made, solidly constructed, caressed by the hands of other families over the last ninety years. Next time you purchase anything for your house, ask yourself, "Does this nourish my soul?" From tea towels to sofas, this question can short-circuit consumerism and put a lid on fights over taste. Other good questions to ask yourself when making purchases for your abode are: "Will I still like this in a year? Five? Ten?" Or simply, "Why do I like this item?"

Study your surroundings together. Consider where you can give beauty a more prominent role in your life. Create your environment so that it appeals to your shared aesthetics. You could plant geraniums around your front door, make a still life of fruit on your bedside table, organize the neighbors to paint a less-able neighbor's house or clean up a vacant lot. You don't need sterile perfection or money or "style," but beauty that absorbs you, inviting you to slow down and be in the moment together.

See "Divine Sustenance" for more.

Organization

On the more practical side, how can you control the endless flow of stuff that threatens to bury you alive?

Designate a big basket with handles as the errand basket. Books to be returned, prescriptions to be refilled, dry cleaning—all that clutter goes inside.

Store children's bath toys in a mesh bag on a hook hanging over the bathtub.

Mail, magazines, bills: ugh! Flip through your magazines once a month, cut out anything you want to save, and cache the clippings in cardboard boxes or file folders with headings such as Dream House, Recipes, Craft Projects. Read the mail by the recycling bin, and throw out as you go along. Clip pages from catalogs, jot the ordering number on the page, and throw the rest of the catalog out.

See "The Art of Gift Giving."

Consider implementing a regular simplifying ritual. One family sets aside a time every two weeks, puts on the same rock 'n' roll CD, and spends several hours tackling household projects. Afterward they go out to eat. A seasonal ritual of storing winter or summer clothes can help closets do double duty. You can buy or make all kinds of storage boxes and create an extra closet in your attic or garage.

The Inviting Bedroom

Consider how you can improve your bedroom from the standpoint of your love life. First, the room itself. Is there another bedroom that might suit you better, in terms of privacy or proximity to a bathroom? Improving soundproofing can directly improve your sex life. Everything from lining the walls with bookshelves, hanging heavy drapes, putting down carpet or an area rug, even padding the walls with batting and covering that with fabric can help you feel less inhibited. Banish chattering televisions, children's toys, children, stale socks, and home offices from your bedroom. Watching TV or worrying about work are not conducive to sleep or erotic interludes.

Next, the bed. Is it comfortable for both of you? Would a larger, firmer, or softer mattress help? Do you suffer from the passion-squelching horror of squeaky bedsprings? We spend almost half our lives in bed: invest in a good one when you can afford it. If you can't buy a new one, fix the old one. Take the mattress off and put it on a platform. Pile extra blankets or comforters on the mattress to make it softer.

Next in importance is lighting. Keeping candles and matches handy, putting a dimmer on an overhead or bedside light, even experimenting with colored lightbulbs might spice up your love life.

If you use sex toys or erotica, designate a special drawer or cupboard that can be locked to keep out prying eyes and little fingers.

Consider the use of fragrance and music to create a transition between regular life and your relaxing, being together, intimate time.

See "A Sensory Banquet" and "Music: Feeling Amorous."

Resources:

A Home for the Soul: A Guide for Dwelling with Spirit and Imagination, by Anthony Lawlor (Random House, 1997). Make every area of your home—even your closets—a place of beauty, solace, and joy.

Facing the World with Soul, by Robert Sardello (Lindisfarne Press, 1992). Approaching the mundane concerns of life with an eye on soul.

Home Sanctuary: Practical Ways to Create a Spiritually Fulfilling Environment, by Nicole Marcelis (McGraw-Hill, 2000). Create a home that fits you.

In a Spiritual Style: The Home as Sanctuary, by Laura Cerwinske and Matthew Fuller (Thames and Hudson, 1998). Lush pictures of spiritually inspiring private spaces.

Move Your Stuff, Change Your Life: How to Use Feng Shui to Get Love, Money, Respect, and Happiness, by Karen Rauch Carter (Fireside, 2000). Some cheesy humor, but I like this book best because much of feng shui seems far too serious for me.

Sharing a Place Without Losing Your Space: A Couple's Guide to Blending Homes, Lives, and Clutter, by Regina Leeds (Alpha Books, 2003). A practical approach to arranging "stuff" and decorating with a minimum of stress, strain, and argument.

The Care of the Soul, by Thomas Moore (HarperSanFrancisco, 1992). Inspiring exploration of how to cultivate depth in everyday life.

Shared Sanctuary

You'll Need:

A private space, either inside or outside your home.

Paper and pen (optional).

Some favorite things for both of you, like spy novels, down pillows, the smell of fresh-cut grass, photographs of blissful moments.

Time required: An hour or so to create your sanctuary, then however long you can steal away.

When to Do It:

- When you often say, "We never have any time alone."

- When you feel you need to "get away" on a regular basis to recharge and reconnect.

- When you both crave peace and quiet.

What Is It?

A shared sanctuary is a place where you both can leave your worries behind; a nook where no talk of work, kids, or problems is allowed; a private area where communication and peacefulness flow between you. A beach on a remote tropical island? That's one possibility. But another is a space in your home, a place you make sacred by dedicating it to the essential goal of nurturing your relationship.

Why create or dedicate a special place? Because creating a sanctuary establishes a *physical reminder* of your intent to nurture each other and the relationship. A shared sanctuary says, in effect, "This relationship is important, and this space is dedicated to that." A retreat place can also forge peace of mind. During rough or busy times when you don't see much of each other, you can relax a bit knowing your haven is waiting for you, that you have a place to go to catch up together. Your shared hideaway can be a neutral zone where you leave behind a nagging fight. There are a multitude of possibilities.

What to Do:

Creating a Sanctuary

This exercise on creating a sanctuary is a playful one, so do it in a relaxing space: in a hot tub or bathtub together, with a glass of wine and takeout on a Friday night, around a campfire in the woods, lying in bed with your eyes closed while pleasant music bathes you.

Let the questions below provide a gentle guide. You could read them and take turns fantasizing, while one partner makes notes. Use them to help you come up with a list of what you want in a sanctuary and what the intent of your sanctuary will be. It will most likely encompass more than one thing. For example, my needs for our sanctuary are uninterrupted time together and the full attention of Chris. Chris's needs are to break through the barriers we sometimes erect between us and no talking about money. We both want to treat each other with a feeling of respect and special attention. All can be accommodated.

The only rule is *don't let reality stop you*. Let your imaginations fly. And no killjoy remarks or frowns from the peanut gallery.

What do the words *shared sanctuary* evoke for me?

If this refuge could be anywhere, where would I have it? What would it look like? Smell like? Sound like?

What do I *not* want in this place?

What is the single most important thing for me to get out of creating and sharing a sanctuary with you?

Finding the Actual Space

The actual space is less important than the mood, the feeling you evoke when you are in it together. You can create a hideaway as elaborate or as simple as you please.

Think about your answer to the questions, "If this refuge could be anywhere, where would I have it? What would it look like? Smell like? Sound like?" Decide what elements are most important, comforting, or fun. Then find a space in your home where you can get at least a taste of these elements.

For example, Chris imagined a Swiss Family Robinson tree house, outside, close to nature. I wanted a warm, underground nest with a fireplace and lots of pillows, filled with the smell of herbs. We both wanted quiet. We decided on two sanctuaries. (Note: We live in a very small house in an urban area.) The tree house is a large hammock near the garden. My nest is our bed.

Chris wanted the sound of the woods, so we got an environmental tape to play on our portable tape player. I wanted the smell of herbs, so I spray essential oils to scent the air. We open the windows in the bedroom, push the play button, and together create a magic bubble, a haven from the world, if only for ten minutes.

Dedicating the Space

The word *sanctuary* means "sacred or holy place." Nurturing the relationship can be holy work, and as a place to do this work, your sanctuary can become a sacred place. Creating a simple dedication ceremony can help make your special place sacred. Sing a song together. Hold hands and meditate. Read a poem aloud. Pray. This also helps if space is a consideration and you end up creating your sanctuary in a regular room used for many purposes. By playing music you can blot out noise and evoke a comforting mood, or you can designate a certain word or phrase to signify the living room is no longer the living room but your personal territory, or you can observe a minute of silence together or recite a prayer to switch it into a space for connection and relaxation.

If you have children or elderly parents living with you, you might include them in the creation of your sanctuary so that they won't feel excluded when you retreat there. Instead, they might understand what you're trying to do and how important it can be.

Privacy

Establish clearly what the rules for interruptions will be. What will you allow? What really bugs the other person? Does petting the dog or playing with the cat constitute an interruption? Will you answer the phone? The door? What will you tell your children, housemates, or even neighbors about this special place and time?

Children under the age of four probably won't understand your sanctuary. The only time to retreat is when they are occupied by a sitter or asleep. (If you have kids under four, you're having a hard enough time reading this page, let alone creating a sanctuary.) For children four and up, introduce the concept of quiet time, and use a timer to give it focus. Explain that everyone needs quiet time. Tell them how long quiet time will last. Start in small increments, and build up. Ask your child what he or she would like to do during this time; an art project or listening to music is a possibility. Then set a timer for five minutes, explaining that he or she may not disturb Mommy or Daddy until the timer goes off. If the child does come into your sanctuary before the five minutes are up, call a family meeting to discuss the issue of privacy further.

Locked doors are essential with children. You can begin as early as two and a half to teach your children that when the door is shut they should knock, and that you will always do the same for them. For children of reading age, it might work to post a sign on your bedroom door that says "Quiet Time" or to leave your door open most of the time so they know that when it is closed, they need to knock.

Using Your Sanctuary as a Neutral Zone

Using your sanctuary as a neutral zone may be the trickiest use of your retreat. As with many ideas in this book, the neutral zone works best if you spend a few minutes setting up clear and conscious ground rules. For example:

Define *neutral zone* together. Does it mean no fighting, no mentioning taboo subjects (sex, money), or talking about these subjects using only the soul-strokes method or some other ritual?

Will you use your sanctuary in the middle of a fight, as a cooling-off zone? Or will you go there only when you are both cool and collected?

What if one person wants to go into the sanctuary and cool down, and the other person is too filled with hate or anger to do so?

Can one partner refuse to retreat without causing more fighting?

Conceivably, you could imbue your sanctuary with such a feeling of love and respect that you could use it as a tool for getting out of stuck situations. Say you've been fighting for the hundredth time about the same old subject, and one of you calls for a retreat to your sanctuary. You go, sit in silence for a few minutes, and gain enough perspective to see a way out of your "stuckness." (Note: This is an ideal example, perhaps more suited for a Gandhi than a Louden or Smith. But possible. . . .)

Finally

Your sanctuary, retreat, place of quiet and rest, whatever you what to call it, can be anything you make it. Just keep in mind what you *both* want it to be and what you want to accomplish by going there.

And

The ideal situation is for every member of the family to have a "room of one's own." Foster privacy and time alone in your household, and you will find the time you share that much sweeter.

Resources:

Sanctuaries, by Jack Kelly and Marcia Kelly (Bell Tower, 1996). A guide to lodgings in monasteries, abbeys, and retreats in the United States.

Staying Put: Making a Home in a Restless World, by Scott Sanders (Beacon Press, 1994). A spiritual exploration of home.

The Woman's Comfort Book, by Jennifer Louden (HarperSanFrancisco, 1992). Includes a section on creating a personal sanctuary.

Romantic Illusions
What Did You Expect?

When to Do It:

- When you have a hard time seeing your partner for who he or she really is.

- When you are confused about the difference between romance and love.

- When you insist on being a knight in shining armor or a damsel in distress.

- When you are plagued by an ineffable sense of disappointment in your partner or relationship.

What Is It?

Romantic illusions are one of the most dangerous aspects of Western relationships. These confusing expectations leave us feeling empty, disappointed, yearning for more. Why?

Because of a tradition called courtly love. Originating around A.D. 1200, courtly love was about a *spiritual* relationship. A knight fell in love with a lady with great, consuming, holy passion. He worshiped his lady and performed great feats to exemplify the sense of greatness she inspired in him. He worshiped her as a symbol of the divine. But take note: knight and lady *never* married, nor did they ever have sex. They kept their passion at a fever pitch, without letting it fall into the realm of the mundane. (*Mundane* meaning diapers, budgets, and morning breath.)

Courtly love gave meaning to the lives of the people in feudal Europe. It connected them to the ecstatic experience of being united to something larger than themselves. Today we search, often unconsciously, for just such a joyous experience to give meaning to our lives. It used to be that ritualized experiences like courtly love provided us with feelings of purpose

You'll Need:

Courage to see past the illusions.

Relaxing music like *In Medicine River* by Coyote Oldman.

Time required: Twenty minutes.

and connection. But not only does this no longer work for us, few of us have found anything else that does. So what have we done? Unconsciously, we have taken the fantasy of courtly love, the desire to identify with something larger than ourselves, and combined it with the reality of a day-to-day relationship. Then we wonder why our flesh-and-blood partners never live up to our expectations, why we are confused by the difference between romance and love, why the line between commitment and personal fulfillment is so blurred.

Think about the words people use to speak about the experience of love. We are "swept off our feet." We become "one with our partner." We adore our lover. We are in heaven. *We are trying to find spiritual meaning through our relationship*. We are using our human, worldly relationship to touch the divine. This becomes a problem for three reasons: One, we aren't aware of what we are searching for or what we are hoping to find. Two, we are human, so when reality rears its ugly head, we become disillusioned, and we look for another person with whom to fall in love, so we can once again experience this feeling of meaning, mystery, and ecstasy. Three, it is impossible because as Dr. Nathaniel Branden wrote in *The Psychology of Romantic Love*, "No one can think for us, no one can feel for us, no one can live our lives for us, and *no one can give meaning to our existence except ourselves* [italics mine]." Love for another human being can help us find meaning, but it cannot be the meaning of our lives.

This is not to say romantic love is wrong. It is a tremendously vital, powerful force—a direct connection with our soul. What is wrong is how we have unfairly burdened our relationships. It is possible to gently begin to untangle the *real* relationship from the passionate web of romance, without losing the spark that helps us stay put, stay involved and committed.

What to Do:

Examine Romantic Convictions

The best defense against romantic illusions is to explore your convictions or beliefs about romance. Hold up to the light what your unconscious self believes about romantic love.

How strongly do you believe or disbelieve the following romantic plati-
tudes? *Quickly* give each statement a rating. Don't debate with yourself,
don't give the "right" answer, but say what you *feel*.

1 = Never True	2 = Sometimes True	3 = Very True

PARTNER 1   PARTNER 2

_____   _____   Love at first sight is not only possible, it
means you've found your soulmate.

_____   _____   Good sex happens no matter what if you
really love each other.

_____   _____   Marriages should be arranged.

_____   _____   People fall out of love for no reason.

_____   _____   True love is forever.

_____   _____   Love gets better the longer we are together.

_____   _____   Love hurts.

_____   _____   Arguing is healthy and good.

_____   _____   People can live happily ever after.

_____   _____   All relationships burn out.

_____   _____   It is almost impossible to stay together
forever.

_____   _____   We shouldn't have to work at our relationship if we are really meant to be together.

_____   _____   We should be able to get everything we need
from each other.

_____   _____   Romance is essential for a relationship to
stay alive.

Compare your responses with your partner's. Talk to each other about how your beliefs are affecting your relationship. This is deep stuff, and little will change or be resolved with one quiz and one discussion, but you will find new connections bubbling to the surface in the coming days, connections between your deeply held beliefs about romance and your actions, needs, and frustrations. For example, let's say you panic over even little fights with your mate. Perhaps now you can see that is because you believe it is true that all relationships burn out, and your panic is a product of your fear that your relationship is ending. Perhaps now you can glimpse that fear for what it is: a belief that can be changed. Keep teasing it out, be patient, and watch out for arguments that can be triggered by examining these sacred cows. Strive to be conscious and open with your partner when something occurs to you.

See "Acceptance" for help.

Seeing Beyond Our Projections

Gently seeing who the real person is beyond your romantic illusions is the goal of this guided visualization, based on the work of Cleveland-based therapist and workshop leader Belleruth Naparstek.

Set aside twenty minutes and a private space. No interruptions! If you do it together, take turns reading the instructions very slowly while playing relaxing music. Or you can record the instructions and play them back while having the experience together.

Relax. Pay attention to your breath. Send wonderful, healing, deep breaths to all the uncomfortable places in your body. . . . Let your breath take you to the center of your being, where you are relaxed and safe, fluid and open.

(In the following paragraph, substitute *him* if appropriate.)

Now take another deep breath. Follow your breath until you find yourself calling to mind this other, this special person that you are in a relationship with. Let this person enter your awareness. . . . A picture of this person, see her in whatever posture, in whatever setting, whatever clothing.

Let yourself experience a sensory awareness of her and her surroundings. Feel the air around her. Move around her, see her from every angle. . . . The back, the sides. . . . Now, dissolving the boundaries, enter her awareness, allow yourself to move into her. . . . Note whatever resistance you may or may not have to doing this, and soften the edges of your resistance or fear, so for just a short while, you can enter her consciousness, breathe her breath, feel what it is like to be in her body. Look down and see her hands, her feet, her clothes. Feel what is happening in her heart. . . . Her belly. . . . The muscles of her back and neck. See through her eyes what the world looks like, sounds like, as you breathe her breath. And feel her feelings. . . . Perhaps even see yourself from over there. See yourself with her eyes. What you look like to her, how you seem, from this body, from this consciousness. . . . Feel what it is like to be looking over at you, breathing this breath. Stay with that for a while. Then, very gently, softly and easily, whenever you are ready, return to your own awareness, to your own body, reinhabiting your body, fully and easily, breathing your own breath once again. Feel your own feet on the floor, your own bottom on the chair or the bed.

Whenever you are ready, jot down your impressions of what this experience was like for you.

Then share with your partner what you learned.

Becoming Best Friends

When 351 couples married fifteen years or longer were asked by *Psychology Today* what had kept their marriages going, the most common reasons given were "My spouse is my best friend" and "I like my spouse as a person." Yet how often we act just the opposite, holding our partners hostage to a ridiculously high set of expectations, expectations we would never submit our friends to. Have you ever considered how much more tolerant you are of your friends than your partner? Loosen the hold of romantic illusions, and strengthen your relationship by fostering a spirit of friendship.

See "Ease into
Nurturing Each Other:
No Change for the
Day."

See "A Couple's
Journal" for explanation
of stream-of-
consciousness writing.

Step back before criticizing your partner, and ask yourself, "Would I say this to my friend?" Or when you are demanding something from your mate, ask yourself, "Would I demand this from a friend?"

Ask yourself every morning for a week, "How can I treat my mate as a friend today?" Act on whatever comes to your mind, no matter how small or silly.

List in your shared journal fifteen ways you can treat each other like friends, using stream-of-consciousness writing. Select five items that appeal to you most. Combine them into a list of ten, a pledge of friendship. Post this where you can see it often.

Further Help

There is no way these exercises are going to change your notions of romantic love completely. It is a very complex and ongoing process, one that author and Jungian analyst Robert Johnson calls the "most difficult task of consciousness that any man [sic] can undertake in our modern Western world." Try these suggestions:

Read the books in the "Resources" section together, or listen to the audiotapes listed.

Redo these exercises in six months or a year.

Study the media, especially popular music and Hollywood "romantic" movies, for examples of how the myth is perpetuated. Share your detective work. You could make a category in your journal for recording your findings.

Watching movies from the perspective of how they are fueling your romantic illusions puts a whole new spin on Friday night.

Explore the chapter "Divine Sustenance" for suggestions for connecting with spiritual meaning.

Explore "Releasing Resentment" and "Forgiveness" for healing from romantic expectations.

Resources:

Can Love Last? The Fate of Romance Over Time, by Stephen A. Mitchell (W. W. Norton, 2002). A case for the death of romance.

Dreams of Love and Fateful Encounters, by Ethel S. Person (Penguin, 1988). An analysis of love. Amazingly well researched.

He's Scared, She's Scared: Understanding the Hidden Fears That Sabotage Your Relationships, by Stephen Carter and Julie Sokol Coopersmith (Delacorte Press, 1993). Ready to face your fears in order to find a genuinely intimate romantic relationship?

Intimate Partners: Patterns in Love and Marriage, by Maggie Scarf (Ballantine, 1988). The bestseller that pushes beneath the surface of marriage to explore the depths of true intimacy.

Oxford Book of Marriage, edited by Helge Rubinstein (Oxford University Press, 1990). A compendium of poems, essays, and stories on all aspects of marriage. Good for dipping into and reading aloud.

Permanent Partners: Building Gay and Lesbian Relationships That Last, by Betty Berzon (Plume Books, 1990). Offers clear, compassionate advice and counseling on the internal and external problems faced by two men or two women as they create a life together.

The Truth About Love: The Highs, the Lows, and How You Can Make It Last Forever, by Dr. Patricia Love (Fireside, 2001). Great advice for everyone who says, "I love him/her, but I'm not in love."

We, by Robert Johnson (HarperSanFrancisco, 1983). Johnson uses the myth of Tristan and Isolde to explain romantic love and clear up our illusions.

We Love Each Other, But . . .: Simple Secrets to Strengthen Your Relationship and Make Love Last, by Dr. Ellen F. Wachtel (St. Martin's Press, 1999). Offers practical tips to help restore your relationship when you feel like giving up.

Divine Sustenance

You'll Need:

Couple's journal or paper, and pens.

Time required: Twenty minutes to an hour or more.

See "Romantic Illusions."

When to Do It:

- When you yearn to connect your relationship to a greater whole.

- When you seek an end to a power struggle.

- When the idea of relationship as one avenue to experiencing the divine intrigues you.

What Is It?

A relationship will not work as an end in itself for spiritual fulfillment. But it can function as a challenging path *toward* spiritual fulfillment. A *relationship will not give meaning to your life, but it can help you find meaning in life*. In other words, you cannot find the meaning for your life in another person, but you *can* gain access to the experience of meaning by opening yourself to the rigors of being in relationship.

Think about it. A committed relationship challenges us to draw on the best parts of ourselves, to operate out of love, compassion, and patience, all on a *daily* basis. A committed relationship forces us to squarely confront our ugly side, our failings, all the aspects of our personalities that we hate. Love allows us to experience the essential duality of life—how you can love a person one minute and despise him or her ten minutes later—as well as the ultimate paradox—the more you love, the more you have to let go. It is through love that we can most truly experience life and, by doing so, nurture each other's souls.

What to Do:

Explorations: *What I Believe*

The questions here are designed to help you clarify what you believe. They work best if scrutinized over a period of time. The aim is for you to share your inner beliefs, even redefine them, if necessary, for yourself.

Even in spiritually active families, there are often areas of belief that are unexamined or not shared. Here is a chance to rectify that.

Come up with as many responses as you can for each question, either verbally or in writing. If you do this verbally, either make notes for each other or record your responses.

When I think of God (Goddess, Creator, Higher Power), I think of . . .

When I think of my soul, I think of . . .

My partner could nurture my spiritual growth by . . .

My purpose in life is . . .

The beliefs from the religion of my childhood that no longer make sense to me are . . .

The beliefs that I now experience as truly important are . . .

The beliefs that comfort me during times of grief and loss are . . .

My life has the most meaning and purpose when . . .

My moral code is . . .

In order to allow myself spiritual nurturing, I would have to . . .

See "Natural Nurture: Going Farther."

The Need for a Spiritual Practice

As much as being in a relationship provides a place to grow spiritually, it must never substitute for a genuine spiritual practice. The relationship provides lots of opportunities to grow and develop the essential parts of yourself, but you must find other ways to directly experience what you personally consider meaningful. Psychologist Abraham Maslow believed all human beings need to experience certain values that give meaning to life—truth, beauty, justice, and playfulness, among others. I humbly agree this is true.

Experiment together. Visit new churches if yours no longer speaks to you. Meditate together. Read spiritually oriented books that interest you—*A Course in Miracles*, quantum physics, *Be Here Now* by Ram Dass, the Bible. Spend time with great art and music. Learn to play an instrument

See "Community
Context"; "Nesting:
Creating a Spiritual
Center"; "Music:
Making Beautiful Music
Together"; and
"Creative Connection:
The Inner Relationship"
for more spirited ideas.

or paint together. Climb a mountain, and stay awake all night watching
the stars. Attend lectures on spirited topics. Best of all, make a regular
time each day for a few minutes of prayer or meditation or silence
together. Breathing and centering together each day will do more for your
inner self than perhaps any other single act.

The Higher Purpose

Every relationship has a higher purpose. *Your* relationship has a higher
purpose. What an astounding thought! What if the connection you form
with your beloved is about something greater than your day-to-day struggle
to make a living, respect each other, and raise your children? What if your
relationship is part of your singular contribution to human evolution?
What if the person you love has come into your life for a reason that goes
beyond great sex?

See "About Relaxing"
and "Creative
Connection: The Inner
Relationship."

Every relationship has a higher purpose. Explore what yours is. **Relax**
next to each other, and consider the question, "What is our relationship's
higher purpose?" Allow ideas, images, colors, and sounds to float into your
consciousness. After a few minutes of meditating on this magical question, discuss what occurred to you or write a story together or create a
collage.

These exercises are
especially wonderful to
do on a retreat. See
"Natural Nurture:
Going Farther."

Also, look for clues in your life. Ask people who are in couples (who
won't scoff at your question) what their higher purpose is. This is a wide-
open, completely individual quest, to be defined only by the two of you.

Sacrificing to the Marriage (or Any Committed Relationship)

An indispensable part of being in a committed relationship is the practice
of sacrifice. Yet too often we perceive this act of sacrifice as losing, giving
in, or crying "uncle." What if you reframed this act into a spiritual practice? Mythologist Joseph Campbell said, "Here I am, and here she is, and
here we are. Now when I have to make a sacrifice, I'm not sacrificing to
her, I'm sacrificing to the relationship." When something has to give,
when you want one thing and your mate wants another, you give in *not*
for the other person, but *for the relationship.*

Notice the word *sacrifice* comes from the Latin word "to make holy." It is in this spirit you give of yourself. For example, if you give up your hockey game to pick up the kids so your mate can play racquetball, and you do this while feeling, "There is another life here, the life of the relationship, and this must be tended and kept alive. I'm giving up my game not for him but for this thing called our marriage" you feel spiritually nourished instead of taken advantage of.

If you decide to miss your game with a tit-for-tat feeling, "I will give him or her that and then later I will expect this," you end up feeling resentful and bitter, playing out the role of martyr. Or if one partner is always renouncing his or her desires (especially if this partner is a woman in a heterosexual marriage) and the other person rarely, if ever, does, the concept of sacrifice is not working. While an even score is neither possible nor necessary, the only way this will work is if both partners are using it as a ruling principle. Trust is implicit here.

How to tell when sacrifice is not okay? When you are giving up your essential self, when you are distorting yourself or trying to please or placate out of a need to feel loved. Sacrificing doesn't mean becoming a saint or suppressing your feelings. It is a different act in each situation and for each person. Experiment with surrendering your stubbornness, your desires, your pushing and pulling to the larger container of your marriage.

Reclaiming Your Shadow

One place in love that is ripe for growth is recognizing that the things your partner does that drive you crazy are exactly the things you most dislike about yourself.

The next time he or she does anything that annoys you, angers you, makes your eye twitch spasmodically, sit down. Right where you are. Take a couple of deep breaths. Ask yourself, "How does this remind me of myself?" *Give yourself time to hear the answer.* Trust whatever floats into your consciousness. Bless this aspect of yourself, try to own even for a moment that you might be imperfectly perfect. End by blessing your partner, either silently or aloud, for allowing you this opportunity to learn.

Yes, this does sound like something a perfect person does. It ain't easy, but it is very powerful.

Love and Fear

Make a list of your current fears, an accounting of worries, anxieties, phobias, everything you dread.

Set up a comfortable, safe environment, perhaps your shared sanctuary. Start with some deep breathing. One partner reads one fear from his or her list. Pause, take a deep breath, look into each other's eyes, and visualize his or her fear being bathed in love. Imagine this any way you like. Next, your partner verbally applies love to your fear. *However your partner chooses to apply his or her love is valid and miraculous.*

Switch and repeat with an item from the other partner's list. Work your way down both lists. Remember to pause, breathe, and visualize love. Your visualization may be vague, it may spontaneously change, or it may include auditory or sensual aspects. Whatever happens is right. An example:

PARTNER 1: I fear not being good enough at what I do.
(Pause, take a deep breath, look into each other's eyes, and visualize this fear being bathed in love.)

PARTNER 2: I love the doubt in you because it makes you strive to always do better work, to always be prepared.

PARTNER 1: I fear never being successful.
(Pause, take a deep breath, look into each other's eyes, and visualize this fear being bathed in love.)

PARTNER 2: I love you just the way you are. I love your level of success right now.

Love can transform *anything*.

Commitment: Accepting Our Failings

It is impossible to always live up to the ideas presented here as well as to all your own ideas about morality, love, and loyalty. It is unreasonable to expect to. Learning to forgive each other, and yourself, is probably the most daunting spiritual discipline of all, so daunting I've given it a chapter all its own.

See "Forgiveness."

Resources:

Gratefulness: The Heart of Prayer, by Brother David Steindl-Rast (Paulist Press, 1990). Connection to the Divine through opening to the blessings that await us in everyday life.

Essential Spirituality: The Seven Central Practices to Awaken Heart and Mind, by Roger Walsh (John Wiley & Sons, 2000). Seven common practices drawn from the world's major religions to create a guide to contemporary spirituality.

If the Buddha Married: Creating Enduring Relationships on a Spiritual Path, by Charlotte Kasl (Compass Books, 2001). Buddhist principles applied to committed relationships.

Marriage as a Path to Wholeness, by Harville Hendrix. Order from Sounds True Catalog. Call 800–333–9185 or visit http://www.soundstrue. com. Funny, brilliant, and helpful. Audio.

Ordinary Magic, edited by John Welwood (Shambhala, 1992). Welwood brings together essays about spirituality in everyday life.

The Future of Love: The Power of the Soul in Intimate Relationships, by Daphne Rose Kingma (Main Street Books, 1999). Kingma explores the idea that the form of our relationships is changing to offer us new gifts for soul's growth.

The Power of Now: A Guide to Spiritual Enlightenment, by Eckhart Tolle (New World, 1999). A highly cogent and effective call to live beyond ego and mind chatter, to unite with the eternal Now.

The Seeker's Guide, by Elizabeth Lesser (Villard, 2000). A personal journey and a wonderful selection of spiritual practices from one of the cofounders of Omega.

The Spirit of Intimacy: Ancient Teachings in the Ways of Relationships, by Sobonfu Some (Quill, 2000). Some distills the ancient teachings and wisdom of her native village to give insight into the nature of intimate relationships.

The Subject Tonight Is Love: Sixty Wild and Sweet Poems of Hafiz, by Hafiz, translated by Daniel Ladinsky (Penguin, 2003). The fourteenth-century mystic is brought into this West through the modern, inspired, embodied translation.

Websites:

Belief Net
  http://www.beliefnet.com

Enlightenment
  http://www.enlightenment.com

Naked Integral
  http://www.integralnaked.org

Soulful Living
  http://www.soulfulliving.com

Spirituality and Health
  http://www.spiritualityhealth.com

Creative Connection

When to Do It:

- When you are restless or bored or are trying to avoid raiding the refrigerator.

- When you wish to learn about and give expression to your relationship.

- When you need to express emotions that feel "beyond words."

What Is It?

What does being creative have to do with nurturing your relationship? Painting and messing around with clay is something only kids or artists do. Who has the time?

Just consider the benefits of exploring this neglected area of life. Studies have shown that relationships that last have several things in common, one of which is playing together. Being creative is a fantastic way to play together. In addition, the act of creating can convey a feeling of personal renewal and joyful self-esteem; it can help you to feel more alive.

Inventing, playing, creating, messing around together can allow you to see each other and the world with new eyes, enlarge your base of communication, give you something to do with children on a rainy day, and give you new experiences to share. All these healthy, enjoyable feelings will flow into and revitalize your relationship when you create together.

(And it can be very sensual to slide your fingers through paint, plunge your hands into cool clay, spread vivid colors across a piece of smooth paper. . . .)

Note: Avoid the words *artist* and *art*. Beauty, final results, perfection, and competition have *no place* in these exercises. The focus should be on learning about each other and having fun, not producing something nice. Please don't take this seriously!

You'll Need:

Drawing paper. Any kind.

Pens that are easy to draw with.

Other creative materials, like crayons or watercolors.

Finger paints or clay.

Gentle, relaxing music like *Rosamystica* by Therese Schroeder-Sheker or creative, soulful music like *Skeleton Woman* by Flesh and Bone.

Time required: Thirty minutes to an hour or more.

What to Do:

The Questioning Mind

Mystery and wonder are very renewing. Renewal is an integral part of relationship and self-care. Hence, love is strengthened by contact with mystery and wonder. Try these suggestions:

Each day for a week ask each other, "I wonder what would happen if . . ." I wonder what would happen if we didn't watch TV tonight? I wonder what would happen if we moved to New Zealand? I wonder what would happen if we went for a drive in the country instead of going to this party?

Pretend you are a camera and your partner is the photographer. Camera, close your eyes. The shutter button is your left shoulder. Photographer, guide your camera around, position her or him to record scenes in your environment that you would like your partner to see *as if for the first time*. When you are ready to take a picture, tap the shutter button (your partner's left shoulder). Camera, open and close your shutter (your eyes) very briefly, no more than one second, and record what you see on your film (in your memory). Do this for either a twelve- or twenty-four-exposure roll. Afterward, talk about what you learned. What was it like to see without expectations? Repeat with your partner. This is especially fun to use when you are on vacation and want to see an area for the first time. It is also effective to help heave you out of a rut or to reframe your point of view during a worn-out fight.

See "Ruts."

Go on a wonder walk. Point out everything to each other that sparks wonder, curiosity, delight, or the "can you believe that?" feeling. Focus on one leaf or one puddle at a time. Get close to it, see it as a world unto itself.

Creative Communication

Talking is not always the most effective, wise, or revealing way to communicate with each other. The following exercise was drawn from the work of Dr. Shelly Van Loben Sels, a gifted therapist based in West Los Angeles.

Get your drawing paper and pens. Put on some gentle music, and take a few deep breaths. Stand or sit side by side, with your bodies touching. One person starts by making a single stroke on the paper—a squiggle, a line, whatever occurs to you. Your partner adds to your stroke, just as he or she would add a comment in a conversation. Switch back and forth. The only rule is to build on what the other has drawn.

See "Daily Communication: Nonverbal Communication" for more ways to communicate without words.

When you are finished, talk about your experience. What did you learn? What were you "talking" about? What was your partner "talking" about?

This exercise is fun to do with any of the questions in the "Exploration" sections of different chapters. It is also useful to use in a "discussion" around an issue you are stuck on. Experiment with watercolors, paints, crayons, or any medium that appeals to you.

Artistic Anger

Rose and Virginia, Topanga Canyon filmmakers, shared with me how they use the creative process to help them understand and transcend anger. After a fight, separately, they draw about their feelings of anger and fear. (Neither is an artist. Stick figures, nonrepresentational blobs of color, and symbols all work equally well.) When they are feeling more trustful, they share their drawings, using them as a way to share their deepest fears and be vulnerable with each other. They sometimes use their pictures to prevent fights about the same subject.

See "How to Have a Nurturing Fight."

The Inner Relationship

Get two large pieces of drawing paper. Use any drawing tool you like.

Draw a circle that fits the full size of your paper. Sit quietly, holding hands, and **Relax** while meditating on the question "How can I nurture my partner's inner self?" Don't look for answers. Instead, simply let the question sit inside of you. When you are ready, create an image in the circle. Don't think about it, just let it flow out of you. Don't worry for a second about art, representational images, or the final product. When you are finished, you might like to write a few words around the outside of the circle.

See "Massage" and "Divine Sustenance: The Higher Purpose."

Display your images side by side. Study them for a few minutes. Have a soul-stroking talk about what you see in yours and what you see in your partner's.

It can be very nice to begin or end this exercise with a massage.

Sex and Painting

This exercise combining sex and painting was inspired by the work of artist and educator Adriana Diaz.

Reserve an hour to be alone in a private space. Choose art materials you can use your hands with; clay or finger paints work well. Set up an inviting environment, one that will allow you to be comfortable naked *and* work with messy materials. An old sheet on your bedroom floor is one possibility.

Sit facing each other, naked or partially clothed, however you feel most comfortable. Study each other, taking one aspect of the body into your attention at a time. Start with the head and face, and work your way down. Touch your partner. Use different parts of your hand: little finger, palm, knuckle. Pay attention to how your partner's skin and bones feel under your hand. Sink into the magnificence and godliness of this body. Pay attention to the details: the back of the neck, the curve of a shoulder, the belly button.

When you have spent *a lot* of time treasuring the unique wonder of your lover's body, turn to your materials. Move very slowly. Immerse your hands in the paint or clay. Rub it between your fingers. Contemplate how many times these same hands have touched your partner. Close your eyes. Lose yourself in the sensuous textures of your materials. Let your hands explore viscerally and nonintellectually the link between the materials and your lover's body. Don't think about making anything on the paper or with your clay, just experience. When you feel finished, you are.

Resources:

Intimate Creativity: Partners in Love and Art, by Irving Sarnoff and Suzanne Sarnoff (University of Wisconsin Press, 2002). An exploration of romantic partners successfully engaged in the production of collaborative art and how the relationship affects the collaborative process and the creative process affects the relationship.

The Creativity Book: A Year's Worth of Inspiration and Guidance, by Eric Maisel (Jeremy P. Tarcher, 2000). A wonderful day-by-day year's journey into deep creativity.

Writers and Artists on Love: A Quotable Muse Journal, by Eric Maisel (New World Library, 2004). Brief quotations on each page delve into the nature of love—both as a romantic endeavor and as a fuel for creativity.

Nurturing During Crisis and Loss

You'll Need:

Your shared sanctuary or another comforting, safe place.

Paper and pens.

Time required: Two minutes to several hours.

When to Do It:

- Before a crisis happens.

- When you want to commemorate the anniversary of a loss.

- When you are feeling grief for losses or recent changes in your life.

What Is It?

Times of crisis and loss are times of great growth, tests of our ability to give to each other. This is a call for courage during those difficult times.

All relationships, all lives, go through periods of nearly unbearable pain and sorrow, as well as a multitude of moments of stress and garden-variety crisis. In both types there exist powerful opportunities to test how much you can love, support, and comfort your partner.

What to Do:

A Grief Story

Natasha and Jono had been friends for years and lovers for about a year when Natasha began to have seizures. When the results of her first brain scan came back "with something on it," Jono looked Natasha in the eye and told her, "I will stand by you every step of the way." He realized that all judgment and expectations for the relationship had to be put aside and total commitment and support given to Natasha during the upcoming uncertainties. During the following long and extraordinarily grueling process of discovering exactly what was wrong with Natasha, she and Jono developed ways to deal with their grief and fear. First, they realized they still had to take care of themselves. Jono immersed himself in work when he could concentrate, kept his friendships alive, and discussed everything with his family. Natasha threw herself into the job of getting well, knowing she needed to be as responsible and active as possible in her treatment. "I knew I couldn't burden Jono with everything because although there were times when I just wanted to be totally dependent, I knew I had to take care of myself to some degree if I was going to survive." They worked to keep each other from burning out, taking turns being the strong one, taking turns keeping life organized. They arranged for backup support (day nurse, maid service, family that could fly in) if they should need it after the subsequent surgery. During the convalescence, they built in time for Jono to leave and see movies, have a little fun. They had friends come in to entertain Natasha. They planned a trip to Jono's hometown for after the surgery so they could have something to look forward to. Most of all, they tried very hard not to succumb to their grief, rage, and fear and not to dump these emotions on each other.

I tell you this story because they dealt so well with one of the toughest situations you can face—the unknown illness of a loved one, an illness that might be terminal or might turn your beloved into someone you can't communicate with. The following ideas were inspired by Jono and Natasha's ability to adapt and deal with their experience. (P.S. Natasha has fully recovered.)

Develop Your Skills

Acknowledge that you already possess the ability to deal with crisis. Retreat to your shared sanctuary or create a safe, cozy environment. Talk about past struggles and losses. How did you help each other? What worked? What didn't work? Were there any bad habits you got into that you would like to avoid in the future? Compose a list of actions and encouraging thoughts to draw on in the future. Part of this list might include action you can take now: investigating life insurance and wills; deciding to act on a long-cherished fantasy; strengthening your present support system so you can get help if a child or your partner becomes ill; talking to other people about how they are prepared for emergencies; starting a special savings account.

*See "Community
Context: Exploration."*

Designate a special section in your couple's journal for recording these ideas.

Offer Encouragement

One couple wrote to me about their practice of writing positive messages to each other on cards or sticky notes, then hiding these cards in surprising places. An example: "I'm so proud of the way you are handling this project. You are creative and meticulous. I love you." You could also note what you appreciate about your lover; write positive statements to help him through a tough day; cite a quote to inspire her; tell him how attractive he is. (During a crisis, you often forget you are a beautiful and sexual being.) Tailor the messages to your situation.

See "Nurturing
Merriment: Outrageous
Acts."

Light at the End of the Tunnel

Give yourselves something to focus on besides the crisis at hand. This is especially effective during a long separation or grueling work schedule. Natasha and Jono (see above) used the promise of a trip to give them something to focus on besides brain surgery.

Sit down with your calendars. Mark the date when whatever you are going through will be over. Decide on a superb treat to celebrate. Create a representation of this reward—a rough drawing of your dream house; a clipping from the newspaper describing your vacation; a photo from a happy trip you plan to repeat. Seal this in an envelope, and print the date on it. Put it someplace where you will both see it occasionally.

If you don't know the exact date when the rough time will be over, write a description on the envelope instead of a date. "When you graduate from medical school." "After brain surgery." "When we are transferred out of here." If the real end is too far away or vague, use this technique to give yourselves mini-rewards along the way.

Relax

Remind each other to breathe.

See "Rhythms of
Rapport: A Reconnect-
ing Ritual."

Take ten minutes before bed to play some relaxing music, hold hands, and breathe deeply. Imagine the stress of the day leaving your body.

A variation: do this outside, lying on the Earth, looking up at the stars. Imagine you are breathing out your problems and sending them into the universe, where they are transformed into light.

Taking care of yourself becomes even more important during prolonged strain. When you wake up every morning, ask yourself, "What can I do to nurture myself today?" then "What can I do to nurture my partner today?" Try to act on the ideas that come to you, or at least the essence of them. If you decide the best way to nurture yourself today is to kidnap your partner, take the day off, and go to a beach, do it! If it is impossible, perhaps a lunch date by a lake or fountain would be possible.

See "Self-Care in Relationships."

Be Present

Becoming overwhelmed by grief, illness, or pain comes partly from projecting into the future or lingering in the past. Help each other to stay focused on the present. Immerse yourself in simple activities like chopping wood or scrubbing the floor. Postpone big decisions if possible. Meditate together. Spend time walking in nature, immersing yourself in the physical world around you. Do this by pointing out details to each other and using all of your senses.

See "Creative Connection: The Questioning Mind."

A Healing Visualization

When your partner is ill, depressed, or otherwise unhappy, sometimes you can help, and sometimes you can't. Situations where helping is not possible might include waiting at the hospital while your beloved has surgery; watching your mate battle a long bout with depression; or simply knowing your partner is unhappy at work on a particular day. These are all perfect situations for this simple visualization.

Find a quiet place where you can relax for five minutes. Take a few deep breaths, allowing yourself to let go of tension, allowing yourself to let go of expectations. There is no right way to do this. Keep breathing deeply and rhythmically.

Allow your image of the Divine Healer to come into your mind. It could be God, Jesus Christ, white light, Goddess, a wise teacher; any image that spontaneously occurs to you is perfect. Picture this Divine Healer standing in or near water; whatever body of water you see is perfect. Breathing deeply, take just a moment to feel the love and total healing ability of your Divine Healer. Now, see the person that you love and wish to help in the arms of your Divine Healer. See him or her being held and comforted. All the suffering and pain begins to flow out of your lover's body. Your Divine Healer hugs your partner. You can see the pain, the grief, the illness melt away as the compassion of your Divine Healer, the compassion that you too feel for your lover, flows into his or her heart. Hold this image as long as it feels good, then bless your partner and thank your Divine Healer in any way that feels good to you.

See "Moving into Your Bodies: Moving Energy" for another healing technique.

Resources:

See "Everyday Rituals: Bedtime"; "When Life Is Too Crazy"; and "Empathy" for related ideas.

Fire in the Soul, by Joan Borysenko (Warner, 1994). How to transform crisis into spiritual opportunity.

Silver Linings: The Power of Trauma to Transform Your Life, by Melissa Gayle West (Fairwinds, 2002). West shows how to create meaning from life-shattering events—however you define life-shattering.

Writing Out the Storm: Reading and Writing Your Way Through Serious Illness or Injury, by Barbara Abercrombie (St. Martin's Press, 2002). An inspirational handbook for anyone coping with serious illness or injury—yours or your loved one's.

Website:

Healthy Place
http://www.healthyplace.com

Letting Go

When to Do It:

- When your jaw is aching and your hands feel like claws because you've been holding on to life so tightly.

- If, when you are very connected and intimate, you feel there is still room to be even closer.

- When you are trying to increase trust in your relationship.

- If, when things have been going well, you or your lover inevitably picks a fight to destroy the closeness.

What Is It?

Letting go means trust, acceptance, loosening the deadening mask of perfection, putting a lid on nitpicking criticisms, and trusting your partner to love, support, and nurture you. It is trusting yourself enough to relax and go with the flow. It is allowing yourself to feel good and enjoy your time together even though everything in your life isn't perfect (because everything in your life will never be perfect).

Do you believe you must maintain control or something terrible might happen? Do you let yourself experience love all the way down to your toes, until your entire body shivers with delight, or do you always hold back just a little? How often do you stop yourself from feeling glorious, either internally by criticizing your delicious feelings or by sabotaging the intimacy through picking a fight about a minor fault of your partner's? What happens to your relationship when everything is going great?

Can you imagine moving into a more trusting, feeling place? It is frightening, sometimes even terrifying, to loosen your white-knuckle hold on life, even for a few minutes, and experience the abandonment and

You'll Need:

Relaxing music like *Timeless Motion* by Daniel Kobialka.

Room to move around.

Paper and pens.

Courage.

Time required: Ten minutes to twenty or thirty.

fulfillment of trusting love. But what could be more comforting than to let your partner see you and accept you *as you are*, the real you, not the mask of beauty or successful businessman or great lover? To step into the moment and be with your lover, without giving up who you are, is truly letting go.

What to Do:

See "Nurturing Merriment" for a definition of silly.

(Note: The first step in trusting each other is to allow yourself to be silly.)

Falling

One person stands in front of the other, closes his eyes, relaxes, and falls backwards. Take *several* deep breaths before you let yourself go. As you are falling, name what you are feeling, either aloud or to yourself. (Aloud requires more trust.) Repeat with each person a few times, then talk about what you felt and learned. See if you can relate what you felt to a memory or a belief about life. Use this exercise whenever you are feeling defensive and closed off.

Blind Walk

See "Natural Nurture: Better Living Through Hiking" for more trusting exercises.

Have your partner close her eyes. Take her hand, and lead her around the house briefly, then outside into increasingly foreign territory. See how long she can keep her eyes closed. Afterward, discuss how this felt for each of you. This is also great to do in the wilderness.

What Is Holding You Back?

Alone, sit down with paper and pen and complete the sentences below either by writing as many completions to each question as you can think of (try for five for each question) or by facing each other and verbally giving your answers. Say or write *whatever comes into your mind*, as quickly as possible, without self-criticism or censorship. Accept that you will feel resistance. You will feel you have nothing more to say. Keep going.

I can't let go because . . .

I am holding on to . . .

I can't trust my partner because . . .

If you can, share your answers with your partner. Learning about your hidden fears is the first step to being free of them. The next step is talking about them, applying as much love as you can, and never, never making fun of your partner.

See "Divine Sustenance: Love and Fear" for a way to transform your fears.

Guided Meditation for Releasing Resistance

Limiting beliefs that bubble just under our happiness hold us back from being fully present in our relationships, pollute our good times, and shut down our flow of life energy.

Decide who will go first. One person lies down, with paper and pen nearby. The other person leads the first through the meditation below. Begin by reading the instructions in "About Relaxing." Play restful music softly and speak very slowly.

Breathing deeply, let your mind wander back to a recent positive experience in our relationship, a time when you felt very close. . . . Very loved. . . . Very secure. . . . Picture the scene, take in the details. . . . Let yourself remember how good you felt. . . . Luxuriate in the good feelings. . . . The sights. . . . The sounds. . . . The feelings of being close. . . .

Very gently, move your attention to what is happening underneath the happy feelings. Can you hear any negative thoughts? These negative thoughts could be worries that something is going to go wrong or self-criticisms or criticisms of me. Or you might not hear any thoughts but perhaps you can feel an undercurrent of panic or tension. Or perhaps you feel a little afraid. Or perhaps it just feels like you are holding back a little bit, not letting yourself relax totally, not completely taking in these pleasurable feelings. Spend a moment sensing and feeling the undercurrent. . . .

Now slowly focus your awareness on your body. Sense where in your body you might be holding these negative beliefs and feelings. Take a couple of deep breaths. . . . Focus in on an area of your body that feels less alive. . . . Or feels tight. . . . Or painful. . . .

Imagine there is a fist closed around this part of your body. Feel how this fist holds in your pain, your negativity, holds it in and exaggerates it. Feel the tension, the resistance. This stubborn fist won't let go. It won't let you relax and enjoy, truly enjoy, feeling loved, feeling good. Can you feel the tension radiating out from this area? Can you feel how you hold yourself back?

Take a deep breath and gradually begin to breathe into the closedness. Softening just a little bit, feel how even a little letting go frees you. The fingers open, one by one, very slowly. . . . Sensations and feelings float out and into your awareness. . . . You aren't trying to deny the feelings or push them away. Just let the feelings be. Feel the resistance dissolving, softening at the edges, letting go in softness.

Remember to breathe deeply, allow yourself to feel good. . . . And as any remaining resistance springs up in your heart or body, breathe into that, allow yourself to be in the moment. . . . Focus on being content and relaxed. . . . Focus on moment-by-moment letting go. Breathe and let go. Let go and breathe. Allow yourself to feel your feelings, allow yourself to feel good. . . . Feel loving-kindness for yourself, for me, for the people you love. Breathe and let go. . . .

End with a hug. Often, after this meditation, a person needs a few moments to "come back." It can be helpful to jot down a few notes about the experience. When you are both ready, switch and repeat.

Trusting in the Moment

What happens if in the moment of feeling close and in love, you start to shut down? How can you let go to the moment? Try these suggestions:

Communicate about how you feel using the method in "Daily Communication: Catching the Inner Dialogue in Action."

Discuss a signal you can use to express a feeling of holding back when you can't yet verbalize what you are feeling. Instead of continuing whatever you are doing (fighting, not connecting, not enjoying yourself), use this signal and agree to a time and date to get together to talk about what happened. This allows for learning from the moment, opens communication, and keeps you from feeling alone and cut off.

Deep breathing is the central part of letting go. If you find yourself tensing up in a moment of joy, focus on your breathing for a moment. Breathe deeper, all the way down into your belly. Often, when you do this, a thought or feeling will occur to you. Share this with your partner. It doesn't have to be a big deal, just breathing and brief sharing.

Recognizing that you picked a fight as a way to stop from letting go, and admitting this to your partner, opens the way for dialogue. In other words, it is never too late to say, "Hey, yesterday I was feeling really good, and then I shut down. That is why I said what I said."

Resources:

Destructive Emotions: A Scientific Dialogue with the Dalai Lama, by Daniel Goleman and Dalai Lama (Bantam, 2003). Dialogues between the Dalai Lama and a small group of psychologists, neuroscientists, and philosophers that explore the question: Can the worlds of science and philosophy work together to recognize and change destructive emotions such as hatred, craving, and delusion?

Faith: Trust in Your Own Deepest Experiences, by Sharon Salzberg (Riverhead, 2002). I love how Salzberg defines faith.

The Language of Letting Go, by Melody Beattie (Hazelden Information Education, 1996). A powerful way to break free from limiting behaviors.

Releasing Resentment

You'll Need:

Time required: An hour the first time. Ten minutes on a regular basis.

When to Do It:

• When your stomach is churning, your shoulders are tense, and you can't sleep.

• When anger has taken over your relationship.

• When you can't seem to carry out any of the exercises in the book or otherwise nurture each other.

• When you haven't had sex in a long time.

What Is It?

The biggest and most dangerous obstruction blocking your ability to nurture your partner and your relationship is your resentment and the anger underlying that resentment. We all have it. We hoard it, recalling each and every disappointment, unkind word, and human failing, not to mention enlarging the really big mistakes, until our partner has become the most horrible, hateful person on the planet.

Resentment, anger, hatred, and contempt block your ability to be present in your relationship and undermine your efforts to nurture each other. The best way out is *through* the anger and hurt. By recognizing and releasing how you have hurt each other you can heal. You cannot move into forgiveness until you have fully experienced and communicated your anger and even your hatred.

Resentment work must be done often. *Resentments build up on a daily basis.* All those little things you try to ignore or the big ones that you don't have time to discuss can stockpile themselves into ugly, stinky, sticky piles of hate that plug up your ability to love. In a nurturing relationship, you must recognize and release your resentments as often as you can, starting now.

What to Do:

About Resentments

Think of resentments as neither good nor bad but simply pieces of information you have stored that influence the way you think and feel about your lover.

Resentments are choices. You choose to resent your partner. You choose how you interpret an event. She can ignore you because she had a bad day, or she can ignore you because she is a selfish, self-centered, work-obsessed &#@!*#.

No partner is more hurt, cheated, bad, or good than the other. *You must accept this if you are to move forward*. Otherwise, you will do the following exercises with the attitude "I'm more hurt than you are, and I'm going to rub your nose in it."

Any part of this exercise can be done on a regular basis. It may seem petty to mention pet peeves and small grievances, but please try it. Releasing your frustrations works like a miracle tonic to restore vibrant connection.

Part 1: Resentment List

Alone, construct a list of ten items you resent about your partner by finishing the sentence stem "I resent you for. . . ." It is imperative that you both have the *exact same number*. If you want to do more or less than ten, that's fine, as long as both of you agree to do the same number.

When you have your lists, sit facing each other. Close your eyes, and take a deep breath. Take turns sharing the items on your list. It doesn't matter who goes first. One person shares one item by saying, "Name, I resent you for. . . ." Using names makes this exercise more powerful. After a short pause, the second person shares one item from his or her list in the same manner. Go back and forth, all the way down your lists.

Here is an example:

> Bob, I resent you for working such long hours.
>
> Randy, I resent you for not helping fix up the house.
>
> Bob, I resent you for not putting your hairbrush away. (They don't have to be big things.)
>
> Randy, I resent you for talking to me when I'm on the phone.

When you are finished, give each other a hug or say something positive about each other, even if you don't feel like it.

Keep going with the next part if this is the first time you've done this exercise or if you still feel resentment.

Part 2: Beliefs

Separately, read over your resentment list, then one by one, convert each resentment into a negative belief you hold about your partner using the sentence stem "I feel. . . ."

For example: "Bob, I resent you for working such long hours" becomes "Bob, I feel like your work is more important than me." "Randy, I resent you for not helping fix up the house" becomes "Randy, I feel having a home together isn't important to you." "Bob, I resent you for not putting your hairbrush away" becomes "Bob, I feel discounted because putting your hairbrush away doesn't matter to you even though it is important to me." "Randy, I resent you for talking to me when I'm on the phone" becomes "Randy, I feel like my privacy isn't as important to you as your need to talk."

When you are finished, take turns sharing each belief back and forth. *Do not comment on what your partner says*. This is not about reality or defending your honor. It is *only* about clearing the air.

This part of the exercise can also be repeated on its own. Keep going if this is the first time through for you.

This time make a list of ten items by completing the sentence "When you _____, I want to hurt you by _____." If you find it difficult to link your retaliation with a specific event, just complete the last part of the sentence.

For example:

> When you drive too close to the center line, I want to hurt you by telling you you're a bad driver.

> When you watch TV instead of talking to me, I want to hurt you by going to bed early and not having sex.

Share in the same way as each of the previous steps.

If this is the first time you have done the exercise, please do one of the exercises in the "Forgiveness" chapter together now. It will bring a sense of release and closure. Or have a talk about what doing this was like for you.

Resources:

A Meditation to Help with Anger and Forgiveness, by Belleruth Naparstek (Image Paths, 2002). Another winning imagery tape and affirmations.

Be the Person You Want to Find: Relationship and Self-Discovery, by Cheri Huber (Zen Meditation Center, 1997). Sound, refreshing, Zen-ish relationship advice.

Divorce Busting, by Michele Weiner-Davis (Simon and Schuster, 1993). Practical and insightful help.

The Couples Companion: Meditations and Exercises for Getting the Love You Want, by Harville Hendrix (Atria Books, 1994). Meditations and healing exercises for healing and enhancing your relationship.

How to Have a Nurturing Fight

You'll Need:

Private space you can make noise in.

Time required: Who knows? Some battles are five hot minutes; others are hours.

When to Do It:

- When you are experiencing "chasing your tail" fights: the same old fight, over and over again, without any resolution.

- When you want to solve a problem but you can't get past your anger and finger pointing.

- When the way you disagree now hurts you.

- When you have a feeling that your fights could be transformed into acts of love if you knew how.

What Is It?

Moments of throat-choking, fist-clenching, mind-blowing anger offer some of the richest, most growth enhancing, and most difficult opportunities to nurture your lover. Just when you hate him most, or just when she is expressing to you how much she can't stand you, this is the moment in which your love can blossom into increased maturity and depth.

Isn't a relationship better off if no one rocks the boat? Many of us learned that it is very bad to feel angry, to disagree, to become flushed with anger. As a woman you might have been taught to always please your partner, even if that meant denying your self. As a man, you might have learned it was your responsibility to handle everything perfectly, and if your partner is unhappy, it is because you haven't done your job well. *Anger is neither good nor bad, it just is.* Fighting is *not* something that only bad, stupid, uncouth people do. People who disagree stay together, *if* (and this is an all-important *if*) *you can learn to disagree in a supportive, nurturing manner, if when you are angry and when anger is being directed at you, you can find it in your heart to nurture your partner.*

To fight in a nurturing manner means you express your anger fully without assassinating your partner's character. Fighting in a nurturing manner means you are willing to acknowledge your partner's anger, not run from it or minimize it. It means you are willing to listen, not judge or defend yourself, because in listening and *allowing* your partner's anger, you perform a deeply nurturing act. And perhaps most importantly, it means *you realize you can never change or control another person, especially through your anger.* Anger and conflict will be transformed into a nurturing act of relationship and self-growth when you give up your desire to get your partner to do it your way and focus instead on what you can do to change the situation.

Note: My understanding of anger has been deeply influenced by the brilliant work of Dr. Harriet Goldhor Lerner, author of *Dance of Anger,* and Dr. Shelly Van Loben Sels.

What to Do:

Before You Fight, Drain Off Excess Anger

Anger becomes a problem in two ways. First, it will be a problem when you don't allow yourself to feel it. Your feelings control you when you ignore them. Next time you start to feel angry, *allow yourself to feel the anger, but do not take it out on your partner* because the second way anger gets out of hand is when you spew your anger at your partner like battery acid, scarring your mate's soul with words that never should have been uttered. Harriet Goldhor Lerner states that attacking your partner with an enraged tirade "may serve to maintain, and even rigidify, the old rules and patterns in a relationship, thus ensuring that change does not occur. When emotional intensity is high, many of us engage in nonproductive efforts to change the other person, and in so doing, fail to exercise our power to clarify and change our own selves." Our fights become toxic and useless when we vent rage at our partners and stay focused on trying to change him or her, instead of trying to change ourselves.

So feel your anger, but don't stab your partner with it or use it to withdraw. Tell your partner, "I am angry (or confused or I need to sort my thoughts). I want to talk about it. I'll be back in a minute." Go off alone, and let your anger out in a safe way. Sit in a chair, grip the edges, and repeat to yourself, "This won't last forever. It is okay to feel this way." Or stamp your feet and make loud "Aha" noises. Or put on some thumping, intense music and dance your anger out, making lots of noise, or scream into a pillow. Or count to ten while breathing deeply and allow yourself to feel the range of your feelings. Go for a run, play handball, pour your anger out in a letter and then burn it. However you choose to do it, when you are enraged, drain off some of your anger before attempting to communicate.

Question Yourself

Use moments of uncomfortable, irritating pain to learn about yourself and to take responsibility for your own life. Ask yourself, "Honestly, why am I angry?" Anger is often (but not always) a cover for another emotion. Mixed in or underneath your rage might be the real reason you are upset. Tease this out so you can communicate clearly with your lover. "I'm angry because you didn't fix the door like I asked you" is one level. Pausing in your anger and asking yourself, "Honestly, why am I angry about this door situation?" might help you see that you are angry because you can't get him to do what *you* want when *you* want it, or you feel like your desire to have a nice house doesn't matter to her, or if he really loved you he would do what you asked. You might be able to see you are trying to control her and that you don't feel loved or heard and that you do have choices besides being chronically angry about the door not getting fixed. This doesn't mean you blame yourself for being angry. Anger is neither good nor bad, but it is almost always a learning experience.

The next question to ask yourself is, "What, specifically, do I want to change, and what can I do?" In the case of the unfinished door, you might want to change the feeling that the house will never be finished. To do this in a nurturing manner, you have to give up trying to control what your partner does. That doesn't mean you can't ask him to fix it, but it does mean you can choose to ask him, wait one week, then fix it yourself, forget about it, or hire someone else. Choose these alternatives *only* if you can do so without making little snide remarks about how she never does anything around the house or martyr remarks like, "Oh, my aching back. I really hurt it today putting that door in." The crucial difference is that you act to make yourself feel better but not to hurt, irritate, or anger your partner.

Sometimes, employing these questions only leaves you feeling more confused and angry. It is impossible to always be clear about feelings or what you would like to have happen. Don't be alarmed if questioning yourself only makes things more fuzzy. Sit with the fuzziness. Don't run away from it. Don't jump into acting on your anger. Struggle with it. Engage it. Allow yourself to slow down. To quote Dr. Lerner again, "Anger is a tool for change when it challenges us to become more of an expert on the self and less of an expert on others." Chew on that next time you feel fuzzy.

Guidelines for a Nurturing Fight

Read and discuss these guidelines for a nurturing fight ahead of time. You won't remember all of them. You won't have a nurturing fight every time. Learning to fight in a nurturing way is a never-ending process, never perfect but always illuminating and better than below-the-belt, cruel, or repetitive fighting.

Agree that when one of you has a bone to pick, you will both stay together *in the same room* until each of you feels the discussion has been brought to a satisfactory resting point.

Agree not to do anything else while talking. Get out of the habit of fighting in the car, while doing the dishes, while one of you is watching Monday night football. If you are angry at one of these times, note your feelings and agree with yourself to hold your tongue until a more appropriate time. It is in this moment that you can best practice sacrificing to the marriage. It takes great spiritual self-control to allow yourself to stay in touch with your emotions and yet postpone expressing your hurt. But it is an essential act of a mature love relationship.

See "Divine Sustenance: Sacrificing to the Marriage."

Agree to try to avoid words like *always, should, never,* and *ought.* Use the all-important "I" statement. "*I* feel angry that you *sometimes* come home late from being out with your friends," not "*You* make me sick, you *always* come home late, and you *never* want to have sex with me, and it *shouldn't* be this way."

No judging or defending. Nothing escalates a fight faster than when either partner, especially the partner whom the anger is being directed at, starts saying, "But I was late because . . ." or "I don't do that. You do that."

*See "Negotiating" and
"Recognizing Your
Needs."*

A nurturing fight is *not* a problem-solving or a negotiating session. Sometimes the problem at hand gets solved, but that shouldn't be your main purpose. Focus on expressing your anger, hurt, and disappointment without blowing your partner's self-esteem away, *without trying to change him or her.* If it is your turn to listen, focus on listening and being with your lover's anger, not trying to take it away or solve it.

Start and end with a positive statement. For example, "I love you, and I need to share some difficult things. Can you listen, please?" A possible reply might be, "I love you, and I am willing to listen." And to finish, "Thank you for hearing my anger and frustration." In reply, the other partner might say, "I heard your anger and frustration without judging or disliking you"—a nice way to close the argument.

While fighting, one person speaks at a time, without interruptions. The person who started the fight concentrates on getting out his or her anger, "taking it down to the end of the end of the end," as Dr. Van Loben Sels says. When the person who has started the fight seems finished, it helps if the listening partner says something like, "Is that all you need to tell me about how you feel?" or "Is there anything else? I'm willing to hear it all." Note: Getting it all out doesn't mean you won't want to bring it up later.

The listening partner listens and reassures his or her lover of that fact by repeating back key phrases. Period. *No blaming, defending, or trying to prove oneself right.* Wait your turn to fight. Hold your stuff back, and stay focused on your partner. Don't rehearse your retort in your head. This helps each person feel heard, which is crucial.

Breathing deeply helps immensely.

An Example

Carlos and Martya are fighting about working out a budget. It is an old fight that always ends in an angry stalemate.

MARTYA: I love you, and I need to share some difficult things. Can you listen, please?

CARLOS: I am willing to listen. I trust you.

MARTYA: I'm so angry that you won't finish the computer work on our accounting program so that we know where we stand in terms of what we have spent for the year. It makes me feel anxious, uncared for, and exposed.

CARLOS: I hear you saying how anxious you feel because I haven't kept the accounting work up to date.

MARTYA: Yes. I feel crazy not knowing whether I can afford to buy a book or whether we can go out to dinner on the weekend. I feel helpless and confused and worried about the future. I feel like a dependent child.

CARLOS: I hear you saying you feel you can't spend any money because you don't know where we stand.

MARTYA: Yes, and that makes me feel horrible, like working doesn't have any point because I can't enjoy the money. I'm so sick of this situation!

CARLOS: Is there anything else? I'm willing to hear it all.

MARTYA: Just that something has to change. I love you, and I'm glad you listened to me.

CARLOS: I heard you, and I'm glad I listened.

Now it is Carlos's turn.

CARLOS: I love you, and now it's my turn to share some difficult things. Can you listen, please?

MARTYA: I love you too, and I am willing to listen. I trust you.

CARLOS: I feel like it is totally my responsibility to do the budget. You've had more experience with money than I have.

MARTYA: I hear you saying you feel overwhelmed.

CARLOS: No. I feel like it is totally my responsibility, and I don't like that.

MARTYA: I hear you saying you feel that it is totally your responsibility to handle all the money.

CARLOS: Yes. I feel inadequate to do this job and pressured by you, which makes me feel more inadequate. I hate money, and I don't want to do it alone.

MARTYA: I hear you saying you feel pressured and pushed, and you don't want to do this alone.

CARLOS: Pretty much. Let's negotiate who does what tomorrow.

MARTYA: Okay.

CARLOS: I love you, and I'm glad you listened to me.

MARTYA: I heard you, and I'm glad I listened.

Yes, this is a perfect fight and no, it won't happen this way, but it is worth trying. It is extraordinarily nurturing if you have a fight and it didn't go well, to have the courage to go back to your partner later and say, "That fight last night didn't go well. Let's try again." It is a wonderful statement of connection and caring about your partner to want to try again to hear him or her.

What Next

When you have finished a nurturing fight, you may want to do one of the exercises in "Forgiveness" (if you both feel tender) or one of the problem-solving techniques in "Negotiating" (if it feels unfinished but you are no longer angry). Or you may want to spend time being together. Or apart.

To Repeat the Directions

1. Allow yourself to be angry, but on your own. Ask yourself, "Honestly, why am I angry?" and "What, specifically, do I want to change, and what can I do?"

2. Don't use anger to change your partner. Use it to learn about yourself and the relationship.

3. Stay put, don't judge, take deep breaths, make "I" statements.

4. Start with a positive statement. Listen without giving your side or rehearsing your retort. End with a positive statement and a hug.

5. Go on to negotiating or forgiveness if desired.

Keeping It Current

Fighting gets crazy because of stockpiling grievances and anger until you develop a hair-trigger response. Your lover says he or she doesn't like your haircut, and suddenly you are screaming about the time he or she left you stranded in a bus station ten years ago.

To avoid "kitchen sink fights," you need to *stay on the subject you are fighting about*. At all costs, avoid bringing up old issues. It helps if you keep current in expressing your grievances. When you are angry about something, discuss it as soon as you are calm enough. Resentments will pile up anyway. Do the first exercise in "Releasing Resentment" often.

Resources:

Crucial Conversations: Tools for Talking When the Stakes Are High, by Kerry
   Patterson, Joseph Grenny, Ron McMillan, Al Switzler (McGraw-
   Hill, 2000). Teaches the tools to handle life's most difficult and
   important conversations and achieve positive outcomes.

*Fighting for Your Marriage: Positive Steps for Preventing Divorce and Preserv-
   ing a Lasting Love,* by Howard J. Markman, Scott M. Stanley, and
   Susan L. Blumberg (Jossey-Bass, 2001). Based on the highly
   acclaimed PREP® (Prevention and Relationship Enhancement Program) approach. Use the strategies to handle conflict more construc-
   tively and reduce the odds of breaking up.

The Dance of Anger, by Harriet Goldhor Lerner (Quill, 1997). A brilliant
   book about changing the patterns of anger. Written for women, but it
   includes many ideas men will find useful.

Tongue Fu!: How to Deflect, Disarm, and Defuse Any Verbal Conflict, by
   Sam Horn (St. Martin's Press, 1996). Constructive alternatives for
   turning hostility into harmony.

Forgiveness

When to Do It:

- Anytime you want to transform your relationship to a more open, accepting, and loving one.

- After "Releasing Resentment" or "How to Have a Nurturing Fight."

- When you are so choked with bitterness, you can't open up to your mate.

- When you've been together for a long time and need to erase the history book.

What Is It?

Forgiveness "is a letting go of the painful resentment that naturally arose between different desire systems," according to Stephen Levine, author of many books about living a mindful life. Forgiveness allows a stillness to be created at the center of our selves. It allows us to lessen our clinging to past disappointments and harsh beliefs that make our partner look like a terrible person. Forgiveness allows us to lighten our hearts and open our eyes to the person we are in relationship with. Forgiveness works not only as a specific process, forgiving yourself and your lover for each transgression you have been chewing on, but also as an act of opening, softening, and letting go of free-floating guilt, hurt, and bitterness.

Forgiveness doesn't mean forgetting. It doesn't mean tuning out in a denial fog in front of the TV or losing yourself in a buzz of activity. Nor does it mean forgoing your boundaries or giving up your ability to say no. In fact, forgiving above all means accepting each other for who you really are—with separate needs, desires, and identities. Before you can forgive, you have to allow yourself to feel your anger and hurt, perhaps through some negotiating. Don't shove your pain under forgiveness. Forgiveness can be the last or the first step, as long as you don't use it as a martyr would—to punish yourself.

You'll Need:

Soft, spiritual music like Z by Marcey.

Paper and pen.

Time required: Fifteen minutes for each partner for the meditation. Fifteen or more for the writing exercise.

See "Negotiating" and "How to Have a Nurturing Fight."

What to Do:

Forgiveness Meditation

Find a comfortable, private spot, perhaps your shared sanctuary. Put on some relaxing music. One partner reads the instructions slowly and with feeling, while the other partner lies back, eyes closed, and gets comfortable. Because you will be using your hands, it helps to position the book in such a way that you can read it without having to hold it.

Begin by reading the instructions in "About Relaxing." Read very slowly and pause often, especially at the ellipses (. . .). Then read to your partner:

Bring a picture of me into your mind's eye. Gently allow an image, a feeling, a sense of me to form. . . . Now think back to an incident in which I hurt or disappointed you, or just allow yourself to get in touch with a general sense of anger, resentment, or pain you feel toward me. . . . It is okay with me. Allow yourself to deeply feel the anger, the resentment, the hurt. (Pause thirty seconds.)

Now, tune in to your body. . . . Can you feel where the anger, hurt, and resentment are located in your body? (Pause.) Feel for areas of tension, tightness, a feeling of stuckness. Don't think, just sense. When you find such an area, rest your hand on it.

(When your partner indicates an area, gently place your hand on your mate's.)

I rest my hand on yours in a gesture of love and acceptance, and I ask you to forgive me for whatever pain I may have caused you in the past, intentionally or unintentionally, through my words, my thoughts, or my actions. However I may have caused you pain in our past, I ask you to forgive me. . . .

(Keep your hand on your partner's, and imagine sending warm, healing energy, loosening and softening the pain and tension. Breathe deeply, and focus only on sending healing energy. Do not become preoccupied with what he or she may be feeling or experiencing.)

I send healing, loving warmth into this tight area while I open my own heart in forgiveness of myself. . . . Feel the energy I'm sending you. Together, breathing deeply, opening our hearts to forgiveness.

Begin in this spot in your body to let go of any bitterness, any anger, any pain, slowly relaxing into forgiveness. And spreading out from this spot, expanding your attention slowly throughout your body, releasing all the pent-up emotions, the pain, the tension. . . .

Gradually move into your emotions, into your emotional self, breathing deeply, slowly releasing. Saying to yourself, I forgive you for whatever you may have done that caused me pain, intentionally or unintentionally, through your actions, through your words, even through your thoughts, through whatever you did, through whatever you didn't do. However the pain came to me through you, I forgive you. I forgive you.

Allow me to just be in the stillness of your heart, in the never-ending warmth and compassion that exists at the center of your being. . . .

Feel this spot in your body opening, softening, lightening, mercifully lightening. Feel your whole body lightening. . . . Feel the love I am sending you rippling and radiating throughout your body. . . . (Long pause.)

Saying to yourself, I forgive you. I forgive you. . . .

Now gently bring to your mind's eye an image of yourself, any way you choose to see yourself. . . . Recalling in your own way incidents you feel guilty about. . . . Things you regret. . . . Feelings of shame. . . . Recalling everything you would like to let go of. Feeling the hardness in your heart, hearing the critical voices telling you how ashamed you should be, how terrible you are.

Now where in your body can you sense some of this guilt and pain? Can you feel a place in your body that feels stuck, dead, blocked? Put your hand there when you find it. (Pause.)

(Again, gently place your hand over your partner's. Imagine sending heal-ing love to this spot and slowly throughout his or her body.)

Take a deep breath and say to yourself, "I forgive you." Call out your name in your heart, saying to yourself, "I forgive you."

Breathe into this tight spot in your body, feel my love warming you, feel your own love for yourself. I open my heart in forgiveness of you. I love and accept you. . . . Feel the energy I'm sending you. Together, breathing deeply, opening our hearts to forgiveness.

Begin in this spot in your body to let go of any bitterness, any anger, any shame you hold toward yourself. . . . Slowly relax into forgiveness. And from this spot, expand your attention slowly throughout your body, releasing all the pent-up emotions, the pain, the tension. . . .

Gradually move into your emotional self, breathing deeply, slowly releas-ing. Call to yourself by name, "I forgive you. I forgive you. I forgive you."

Allowing yourself to just be in the stillness of your heart, in the never-ending warmth and compassion that exists at the center of your being. . . .

And slowly, you begin to feel a very soft, warm, cleansing rain falling on you. It smells like spring as this rain bathes your skin and then moves past your skin and into your body, moving to all the places in your body where emotions need loosening, where beliefs still need freeing, until you easily and effortlessly begin to feel lighter. And now you feel the rain moving into your heart, calling your first name, saying, "_____, I forgive you and I forgive (*your name*)."

If the mind offers up hard thoughts that it is self-indulgent to forgive yourself, if it judges, just feel the rain softening that judgment, freeing that density, bathing you with forgiveness. Allow yourself back into your heart. Feel the warmth and care that wishes your own well-being. See yourself as if you were your only child. Let yourself be embraced by this mercy and kindness. Let yourself be loved. See your forgiveness forever awaiting your return to your heart. Allow yourself to be loved. Allow yourself to feel happier than you have in a long, long time.

Slowly the rain evaporates, leaving you feeling totally cleansed and refreshed. Your heart is open, my heart is open, our hearts exist perfectly in harmony and together in forgiveness.

Give your partner plenty of time to come back into the room. When you feel ready, switch positions and repeat.

Forgiveness on Paper

A simpler, slightly more pragmatic exercise, forgiveness on paper is to be done alone. This one appeals to the more rational partners and also works well as a keeping-the-forgiveness-muscles-in-shape practice. This exercise is also good for forgiving people besides your lover: family and friends, living or dead.

Across the top of a piece of paper write the sentence:

"I forgive _____ for _____. I release you and myself."

The most successful way to do this is to keep rewriting the sentence for each item. The repetition helps you remember more items (nothing is too petty, no one will see this but you) and gives the exercise a ritualized feeling.

Next, write across the top of a new sheet of paper:

"I forgive myself for _____. I release myself."

Repeat, rewriting the sentence for each item, large and small, that you would like to be released from your soul. Again, continue for five or ten minutes. Allow your feelings to flow; don't hold back tears or joy, just note the feelings and let them go.

When you are finished, you might want to end by: burning your papers; putting them in a balloon, blowing it up, and watching it float away;

---

ripping the paper into tiny pieces and flushing it down the toilet; burying the papers; ripping them to shreds and releasing one or two tiny pieces into the ocean, lake, or stream. Taking a shower or bath after this process can also provide a satisfying conclusion.

Resources:

Forgiveness, by Sidney Simon (Warner Books, 1991). Another excellent guide.

Forgiveness Is a Choice: A Step-by-Step Process for Resolving Anger and Restoring Hope, by Robert D. Enright (American Psychological Association, 2001). Far from a quick fix, this is the definitive well-researched, truly effective guide to healthy forgiveness.

Guided Meditations, Explorations, and Healings, by Stephen Levine (Anchor, 1992). Collection of meditations you can use on a daily basis. Inspired the forgiveness meditation and many of the meditations in this book.

How Good Do We Have to Be?, by Harold S. Kushner (Back Bay Books, 1997). Combining psychology and spirituality, Kushner employs acceptance to overcome perfectionism.

The Art and Practice of Loving, by Frank Andrews, Ph.D. (Jeremy Tarcher, 1991). One hundred forty-four practices to help you become more loving.

The Art of Forgiveness, Lovingkindness, and Peace, by Jack Kornfield (Bantam, 2002). A collection of age-old teachings, modern stories, and time-honored practices for bringing healing, peace, and compassion into your daily life.

Negotiating

When to Do It:

- When you continue to have a "chase-the-tail" fight, even after trying the nurturing fight technique.

- When the word *compromise* is not in your vocabulary.

- When you feel you have been making too many compromises and you have lost sight of your true needs.

What Is It?

Negotiating is the art of compromise. Negotiating is the act of helping each person feel loved and heard while finding a way to meet each partner's needs and wants as much as possible. Reasoning, compromising, and offering trade-offs are the only ways to solve differences of opinion between two people who consider themselves equals. Manipulation, supplication, and disengagement are techniques used by people trying to get their way from someone they believe has more power than they do. Bullying and superiority are techniques used by people who assume they have more power and control. *Only negotiating indicates peership*, and negotiating fosters the growth of a healthy, enjoyable, lasting relationship.

Life in an intimate, equal relationship is a constant give-and-take, a see-saw of compromise. In the early days of your relationship, you wanted to please your partner and you were probably more sensitive to her or his needs and wishes. But time builds up all kinds of distortions, power struggles, unmet needs, and crusty resentments, resulting in a lack of flexibility for each of you. Restoring that flexibility without damaging your emotional needs is what the art of negotiation is all about.

This chapter provides a sampling of techniques for overcoming impasses and restoring your faith and trust in each other. Some are more detailed, others more playful. Try different ones at different times, or perhaps one

You'll Need:

Your shared sanctuary or any comforting place.

Paper and pens.

Time required: Ten minutes or longer.

will appeal to both of you and become a trusted tool. There is no right way, except the way that allows both of you to feel honored, loved, and heard.

Note: Anger and disagreements need to be aired before you can begin to compromise, or you will worsen the situation. If you are angry, have a nurturing fight *first*. If you have resentments, air those before working on compromising.

See "How to Have a Nurturing Fight" and "Releasing Resentment."

What to Do:

Five Basic Steps for Negotiation

Step 1: Separate the personalities from the problem. This might be the hardest step for people in intimate relationships because each time your partner does something that disappoints, hurts, or angers you, you are convinced in your deepest self that your partner doesn't love you. If you think back to each disagreement you have had, you probably can't remember many details, but you can remember your feelings—and at the bottom of those feelings is almost always a feeling of not being appreciated or not being heard or not feeling loved.

Before you begin *any* negotiation session, reaffirm your love. There are many ways to do this. Start by telling your partner five things you appreciate about him or her. Or do the empathy meditation in "Empathy." Or ask yourself, "How is my partner feeling right now?" Or state to each other your positive intentions: "I love you no matter what." Above all, trust that your partner is not out to get you.

See "Daily Communication: Developing an Open Heart."

Step 2: State the problem from both sides clearly. After reaffirming your love, use the process of mirroring to state the basic problem *until you agree on what the problem is*. One person makes a *short* statement of the problem at hand as he or she sees it. The partner listening repeats this statement back. If the first person isn't satisfied with this version, then he or she restates the original statement and asks the partner to repeat it again. Reiterate this process until each partner is assured the other understands. You only need to do mirroring in the beginning, but if you get bogged down later, it can be useful to mirror back what you think your partner is saying.

This may seem tedious, but it stops the cycles of misunderstanding that block compromise.

Step 3: Address your deeper needs, and create a win-win situation. To do this, you have to get out of thinking your way is the only way. After stating the issue and mirroring back, ask each other this eye-opening question: "What do you want that you are not getting now, that would give you the experience of being loved more deeply?"

After you learn the answer, ask each other, "How can I help that happen?"

Don't negotiate with the idea you want to win. This isn't business, this is love. If only you win, the person you love loses, and that means the relationship loses too. The way around that is to increase the size of the pie so that when you do divide it up, the pieces are bigger.

Step 4: Pay attention to keeping the process fair. If the way you negotiate together meets both of your standards of fairness, then the fact that one person is giving in more or getting less doesn't matter because it has been arrived at in a fair and equal manner.

Tactics to avoid:
Manipulation. Being positive is good, but wheedling, using sex as a motivator, or pretending to be weaker than you are—these are all bad news.
Punishing. Threats, violence, taking away your affection—all of these will ruin a love relationship faster than living with your parents.

Step 5: Be clear about what you decided. End your talk by parroting back what has been decided and writing it down, perhaps in your couple's journal or someplace else where you can see it and be reminded. Too many disagreements happen because both parties aren't clear on what was agreed upon. *Write it down!*

One way of putting it all together. Jody and Sue are negotiating who does the grocery shopping. They have had arguments too numerous to mention over this subject. They meet in their shared sanctuary a day after having a nurturing fight about the subject. They sit facing each other, taking a couple of deep breaths.

SUE: I want you to know I love you, and I want to work things out.

JODY: I love you too. I trust you, and I know we can work this out together.

SUE: What are we working on?

JODY: The problem as I see it is you keep forgetting to go grocery shopping, and we have nothing to eat and I get angry.

SUE: (Mirroring back her statement) Jody, the problem as you see it is I keep forgetting to go shopping, and we have nothing to eat and you get angry.

JODY: Yes, that's right.

SUE: (Now stating her version of the problem) As I see it, I'm too busy to go shopping every week, and I think you could help out by going when I'm too busy.

JODY: The problem as you see it is you are too busy to go shopping every week, and you think I should help you by going for you?

SUE: I think you should help me by just filling in sometimes.

JODY: (Trying again) The problem as you see it is you are too busy to go shopping every week, and you think I should help you by just filling in sometimes?

SUE: Yes, that's correct.

JODY: What do you want that you are not getting now, that would give you the experience of being loved more deeply?

SUE: I need to feel you appreciate me for what I'm already doing and for the times that I do get to the store. I need to feel less pressured and more in control.

JODY: How can I help that happen?

SUE: Tell me more often how much you appreciate the work I do. Maybe we can sit down together on Sunday and look over our schedules for the week and decide who is going to do what chores. You know, be less rigid?

JODY: I would consider that, but first I need you to hear me.

SUE: Okay, what do you want in this situation that you aren't getting now, that would give you the experience of being loved more deeply?

JODY: I need to feel you understand how much work I do. I just feel so resentful when you don't help me. I need to feel understood and appreciated, and I need more time for myself.

SUE: How can I help that happen?

JODY: If we agree to divide up the chores differently every week, you have to do your share and not forget and not need to be reminded. I hate having to nag you, and I hate being disappointed. I need to know you are in this relationship with me, and I need to know you will sometimes take the initiative on Sunday nights to get us to sit down and plan the chores for the next week.

SUE: I can do that.

JODY: So what are we agreeing on?

SUE: On Sunday nights we will sit down together and go over the coming week and agree to what household chores we will each do. We will be equally responsible for making sure that meeting happens and that we follow through. We will show more appreciation for what we are already doing.

JODY: (Repeats what Sue just said while writing the statement down.)

SUE: I love you. I trust us to make this work.

JODY: I appreciate you for sitting down with me and taking this seriously.

You can use this guideline any way you choose, but often couples find it is good to start out with a more rigid structure because this helps prevent backsliding into old battles.

A Rating System

See "Recognizing Your Needs: Compromise" if you get stuck.

A simple idea from two friends of mine: When they both want different things, they carefully and honestly rate what they want, and whoever has the higher number (they use a scale from one to ten, ten being highest) gets to do what she or he wants. They don't keep score, and they don't abuse the system. To tune into their true needs, they sometimes close their eyes and ask themselves silently, "How much do I need this right now?"

Either-Or Day Ritual

An either-or day ritual can be very useful for stopping chronic fights and overcoming impasses, and it is especially effective when children are receiving conflicting messages from parents. It allows you to see, without giving up your power, what will happen if the other person is allowed to do what he or she wants.

The process is very straightforward. When you and your partner are struggling with a difference of opinion or beliefs, try dividing up the week. On Monday, Wednesday, and Friday, your partner's point of view prevails *without argument,* and you agree to listen and learn what you can about his or her way of wanting to do things. On your days, Tuesday, Thursday, and Saturday, the same goes. You do it your way without any comments from the peanut gallery. On Sunday, sit down and have a soul-stroking talk about how it felt.

Creating Negotiation Rituals

By experimenting with ritual actions, you can often hasten the way to mutual understanding. Try designating a specific negotiating area in your home, a nearby restaurant, a park, a place that the act of visiting signals you are both willing to see past your established positions. Selecting ritual objects that symbolize your position on the disagreement at hand is another possibility. Sometimes symbols speak louder and clearer than words. Evan Imber-Black and Janine Roberts write about a couple who created a board game together to express and negotiate their differences. The very act of creating the board game helped them understand each other. Chess, Battleship, or other battle-oriented games might be helpful for releasing your mutual anger and gaining perspective.

Resources:

"A Ritualized Prescription in Family Therapy: Odd Days and Even Days," by M. Selvini-Palazzoli, L. Boscolo, G. Cecchin, and G. Prata, *Journal of Family Counseling* 4, no. 3 (1978), pp. 3–9. The either-or day ritual is from this article.

How One of You Can Bring the Two of You Together: Breakthrough Strategies to Resolve Your Conflicts and Reignite Your Love, by Sue Ellen Page (Broadway Books, 1998). In a power struggle? Hear yourself saying, "If only she/he would . . ."? Then buy this book!

The Divorce Remedy: The Proven Seven-Step Program for Saving Your Marriage, by Michelle Weiner-Davis (Simon and Schuster, 2001). Simple and obvious action steps, no intimidating discussions or emotional letter writing. If your marriage is in danger, get this.

The Relationship Toolbox: Tools for Love, Healing, and Personal Empowerment, by Robert Abel (Valentine Publishing House, 1998). Seventy universal tools you can use to deepen your relationship.

The Seven Principles for Making Marriage Work, by John M. Gottman (Three Rivers Press, 2000). Hate the idea of sharing every thought and feeling? Perhaps total honesty isn't the answer.

Ruts

You'll Need:

Various unrutlike items, like marshmallows, National Geographic, wax museums, miniature golf courses.

A full-length mirror.

Time required: One minute to whatever it takes to change your mind-set.

When to Do It:

- When you experience everyday bouts of boredom, twinges of tedium, lulls of listlessness.

- When faced with making leisure plans, you repeat over and over again, "I don't care," or "I'll do whatever you want, *dear*."

- When you are experiencing a strange feeling of not being able to focus on your partner's face; your mate is so familiar she or he almost blends into the wallpaper.

- When you don't feel like doing anything *but* your same old routine.

What Is It?

Ruts. You don't see them coming, you just wake up one day and look at your loving partner and realize "we're in a rut." The telltale signs: everything looks gray around the edges, there is a heavy, plodding feeling in your body, food all tastes the same, and when you think back to what you had for breakfast yesterday, you can't remember *anything*.

That's a rut.

Why do ruts happen? Because we haven't been paying enough attention to the pleasures in life. Because we become prisoners of the routines we created to give us a sense of reassurance and stability in a difficult world. Because we haven't been filling our deepest needs or listening to our innermost self. Sometimes because we have been avoiding a serious problem in the relationship in order to keep life wrinkle-free.

What to do? For most ruts, the antidote is to shake things up a bit. A vital part of life is growing, investigating new things, learning from unusual or challenging experiences. Infuse your relationship and daily life with change. Even *small* changes (I'm not talking about selling the house, moving to Costa Rica, and opening a surf shop) can allow you to experience renewed energy, passion, creativity, and love for your partner, your life, and even your job. And a small change can help open the way to dealing with larger problems by helping you see the situation differently.

What to Do:

Taking Responsibility

It is tempting to hope something out of the blue will appear to enliven your relationship and your life. Dreams of winning the lottery, being kidnapped by your mate and taken to Rio without a moment's notice, even small fantasies of coming home to a clean house, the kids fed and in bed, soft music playing, and a bottle of wine on the table—all of these great fantasies share a common theme: *someone else* jolts you out of the drowsy malaise of rutville. This attitude perpetuates the rut phase. *You have to rouse yourself.* It is inviting to blame your partner or wait for him or her to do something, but it won't get you anywhere. In fact, it only makes things worse. This doesn't mean you have to jump in and fix everything or be hyperresponsible for the state of your relationship. It does take two. But it does mean (once again) you are responsible for the quality of your life. You can only change your own experience and hope your partner comes along.

See "Self-Care in Relationships."

Start Small

Do something new *every day*, like:

Kill your TV. Nothing perpetuates a rut like zoning out in front of the TV. Put it in a closet, unplug it, rearrange the furniture so watching it requires craning your neck and contorting your body.

Almost everyone has a TV-watching routine. You turn it on during dinner and then keep watching "for just one more program" until the evening is lost. Break that routine! Eat dinner in the backyard, have a conversation on the front porch for thirty minutes, then watch TV, if you still feel like it. Make love first, then watch *Northern Exposure*.

Switch roles with your mate for an evening, a day, an hour. Carry it all the way through. Do things the way she or he would, strive to see life from your partner's perspective.

See "Divine Sustenance" and "Getting to Know You" for thought-provoking questions.

Have a conversation about something other than your work, your kids, or what to have for dinner. Read an article from *National Geographic* or *The Nation* or a classic short story together, and discuss it afterward. Discuss politics. Discuss spiritual beliefs.

See "Everyday Rituals: Evening."

Change your daily routine. Pick up a pizza on your way to a drive-in movie. Meet after work someplace different: a state park for a picnic, a museum for some beauty, a cave for some spelunking. Come home, put on loud music, and dance together before dinner.

See "Nurturing Merriment" for more silliness.

Stand face-to-face with your partner, knees bent slightly, feet about shoulder-width apart. Maintaining eye contact at all times, hold your belly and begin gently bouncing up and down. With each bounce, say "ha." Continue to bounce faster, continuing saying "ha" until you are full-out laughing. Laugh for a minute. An entire minute, no cheating.

For more ideas check out "Everyday Rituals."

Sleep on your partner's side of the bed.

Do Something Crazy

Stand up when you eat dinner. Cook topless. Cook something for dinner or breakfast that you never eat, like pasta in the morning or peanut butter and banana sandwiches for dinner.

Act on an impulse. If you feel like taking off your shoes and jumping in a fountain, do it. If you hate what you made for dinner, grab your coats and go out. Fun ideas are constantly trying to wriggle into your consciousness, but the dim fog of the doldrums cuts them off. Listen to them and act!

Have a food, water, shaving cream, or marshmallow fight in the kitchen. Nude. Clean up the mess *much* later, still nude. If you have kids, skip the nude part but involve them.

Put down a sheet of plastic in the living room, rub yourselves with lots of massage oil (you have to be naked to do this), and wrestle. Also lots of fun with the sixties game Twister.

Make love someplace very different: an elevator, in the wild, in your backyard, at your office after hours, or in your office during lunch hour with the door locked (this won't work if you work in a cubicle).

See "Erotic Delights" and "Natural Nurture: Wild Love" for more ideas.

Next time you are out together, even just doing errands, whisper lewd comments in your partner's ear. Follow up on them.

Skip wearing underwear for the day, and call your mate midday to tell him or her. Or buy some super out-of-character underwear and wear it on an ordinary day. Silk boxers with little poodles or a leather teddy . . .

Change Your Leisure

If you *always* go out to dinner on Friday night or you *always* order in pizza and watch a video, throw caution to the wind and *do something different* without planning, without worrying about crowds or parking. Agree to change, to support that change, and not to blame the other if everything doesn't go perfectly. Check out line dancing at that country bar you always drive by, walk on the beach, drop in uninvited on friends, take the kids camping in the backyard. Break your regular pattern.

See "But There's Nothing to Do" for more possibilities.

Regular Vacations Are Essential

Everyone needs regular vacations. If you only have an afternoon, fine. Attitude is key. Don't do anything but relax and be together in a different place. Many couples who wrote to me swore by the magic of regular weekend trips to recharge their relationships, especially if they have children. What? You say you have no money and three small children? Have a vacation at naptime. Or a nightly vacation after the kids go to bed. Or do what Anne Mayer, author of *How to Stay Lovers While Still Raising Your Children*, recommends: Go to bed at the same time your children do, then set your alarm to go off one hour earlier and have some quiet time before the kids wake up.

Emotional Risks

Initiate a soul-stroking talk with your partner around the question "Are you satisfied with our relationship?" or "What would you change about our relationship?"

Together, reach out to someone you are estranged from or make friends with someone new. Put yourself on the line emotionally by opening up and going first. Express your appreciation to your best friends or family by writing a letter telling them all the things you like about them.

See "Acceptance" and "Letting Go" for more risky ideas.

Stand in front of a full-length mirror together, naked. Tell each other what you love about each other's bodies. Let the other person complain about what he or she hates about himself or herself, then respond with a loving compliment contradicting your mate's negativity. (This takes courage.)

Quagmire—More Serious

Ben and Sophie from Chicago have discovered that their ruts are sometimes caused by not dealing with an emotional problem. They also have found they must wait until they reach a certain level of frustration before they can locate the energy to confront their problems. But sometimes the torture of waiting is too much. In other words, what do you do when you want to move out of your rut but you lack the energy? A perspicuous catch-22. Try:

Releasing anger by pounding each other with encounter bats (foam-covered sticks for martial arts); making a "ha" noise while jumping up and down; getting a massage from a body worker who is schooled in helping you release trapped emotions; breathing together; focusing on the positive things about your relationship for a day. All of these can help move your energy into a new place where you have more courage and vision to deal with problems. Finally, reassuring each other that you aren't going anywhere, your love is here to stay, is the best way to "unstick."

Long-Term Changes

Making long-term plans together can help you shift your energy. Pick a shared goal to work toward—fixing up the bedroom, planting a garden in pots on your balcony, reading James Joyce, running in a 10K, building a deck, or planning and saving for a special trip.

From Lynn and Grant in Oregon: "We've been married ten years and we've not been in a rut yet, but we work daily and weekly to brainstorm. . . . We find when we focus on creating projects together, we stay excited, alive, and growing."

See "Cocreators" and "Couple Customs" for ideas.

If you feel your apathy might be caused by ignoring problems in your relationship, consider seeking outside help. Consider what Sylvia Weishaus, Ph.D., a therapist who has been married for over forty years and who teaches classes at the University of Judaism, believes: "One of the most nurturing things that couples can do is get a mental health checkup periodically. Psychotherapists are not threatening. It is perfectly okay to ask for help when you have a question." Therapy is often more successful as a preventive measure or early intervention. Do you wait until you have pneumonia before you go to the doctor? Waiting until you have a crisis in your relationship is not nurturing, and it perpetuates ruts. Working on your problems as they come up is comforting and rut defying. Often, because of the nature of intimate relationships, an issue that might have been driving you both crazy for years can be worked out in just a few visits to an objective, trained couples therapist. "You go for a physical every two years, go for a mental health check-up every three years!" Yes, therapists are expensive, but so is dinner out, and think how much better you might feel afterward. There are low-cost alternatives to therapy. Training clinics can offer quality counseling for much less. Group therapy is cheaper too.

See "But There's Nothing to Do: Relationship Growth."

Shaking Yourself Up

Sometimes a rut doesn't lie so much in a stale relationship as it does in your own personal disaffection with life. For instance, when my work is going badly, suddenly everything about my life is meaningless. So part of getting out of the stuck mode is shaking yourself up, then bringing your freshness back to the relationship.

Indulge a dream. Ask yourself, "What have I always wanted to do just for me?" Dare yourself to fulfill the dream or at least take one step toward it.

See "Self-Care in Relationships."

Ruts can spring from being hyperresponsible for everyone else. Do something to nourish yourself today. Many of the women who wrote me about their relationship ruts said they use the time to work on their independence skills. If things feel stuck, they don't worry about the relationship crashing, and they don't jump in to fix things. Instead, they take some time out to be with themselves and find out what they need.

Change your everyday routine. Park in a different parking spot. Take lunch alone. Walk outside during the day and touch nature. Get up an hour earlier or stay up an hour later.

Call a friend you haven't talked to in a long time. Find a friend who has disappeared.

See "Community Context: Friendships Outside the Relationship."

Plan an all-women or all-men night out with friends.

Rent a cabin in the woods for the weekend—by yourself. Examine your goals, read an inspiring book, eat what you want when you want. Or spend half the time alone and then have your mate (and perhaps kids) join you later.

Zen and the Art of Ruts

Friends of mine wrote me, "We love our ruts. Our ruts are us. Our ruts tell us who we are and where we're not going." What would life be without ruts? One person's rut is someone else's guiding path.

See "Winds of the Heavens: The Intimacy Two-Step" for help discerning rutted patterns.

Although this was written very tongue-in-cheek, there is something to be said for this attitude. Ask yourself, "What is good about this rut? What are we getting out of it? Why would we want to change? Where did this rut come from?" Step back and observe your pattern, your stuckness. Do you always get into a rut at the same time each year? Do your ruts start during a busy time at work? Can you see any patterns?

There are patterns to life, regular and natural down times that need to be fully lived if you are to fully experience and appreciate the good times. Sometimes the only way out of a rut is to roll around in it, relish the familiarity and comfort of the routine, even exaggerate it. Wear your favorite bathrobe every night. Eat the same three things for dinner. Go to the same restaurant every Friday night. Have sex in the same position for a month. Talk in only shorthand with each other. But do it *consciously*.

Finally

Many couples who wrote me said something like, "Panic and anger are a waste of energy. Eventually, you will be up again. Just remember relationships have ups and downs, and that is all ruts are."

Resources:

Great Moments in Sex, by Cheryl Rilly (Three Rivers Press, 1999). A great read-aloud book.

Snap Out of It: 101 Ways to Get Out of Your Rut and into Your Groove, by Dlene Segalove and Ilene Segalove (Red Wheel/Weiser, 2004). Quick and effective.

There Must Be More Than This: Finding More Life, Love, and Meaning by Overcoming Your Soft Addictions, by Judith Wright (Broadway Books, 2003). Wright helps you transform what I call shadow comforts.

Websites:

News of the Weird
http://www.newsoftheweird.com

Positive Press
http://www.positivepress.com

Story People
http://www.storypeople.com

Community Context

You'll Need:

Volunteer activities in your community.

Time required: From two minutes to write a check to a day or more.

When to Do It:

- When you feel depressed or burned out in your relationship or in general.

- When you feel unsupported, lonely, adrift.

- When you need to put your relationship into a larger context.

- When you have enough love, success, and self-esteem to share with others who don't.

What Is It?

Relationships do not exist in a vacuum. Your love is framed by your circle of friends and family, the community you live in, the region you inhabit, and the world condition. You are affected by community changes, supported or taxed by your family and friends, and buffeted by world events. Recognizing these influences and dealing with them in a creative, nurturing way can produce a sustaining background of support and help prevent burnout.

Being part of a community implies giving, and this act of giving has the capacity to revitalize your relationship. Recent studies have shown that helping others can improve your physical health. One ten-year study conducted by the University of Michigan found that the death rate was twice as high in men who did no volunteer work as in men who volunteered once a week. Helping others can also give you a sense of purpose and well-being, sometimes called the "helper's high." Take this one step further. By working *together* to nurture others, you carry this wonderful feeling into your relationship. This can help you gain appreciation for each other and provide a fabric of larger meaning to wrap your own problems in.

Being part of a community also suggests allowing yourself to rely on others, to transcend the feeling that you only have each other. As a society, we put too much emphasis on being self-sufficient (learned from our pioneer history) and not enough on being part of a larger whole. This unfairly taxes your relationship. Nurture others, and see what happens.

What to Do:

Overcoming Burnout Through Nurturing Others

We all have moments, days, weeks, even months when we "fall out of love" with our mates. We feel bored, stuck, trapped, lonely. There are many reasons why this happens, one of which is the cyclical nature of relationships. Sometimes, this feeling must be addressed with outside help. But I propose that there are times when this feeling of burnout can be remedied by doing service work *together*.

See "Ruts: Long-Term Changes" for therapy advice.

Is it selfish to help others with the sole purpose of helping yourself? I believe it is an *honest* motive, certainly better than a tax deduction. If you are clear about why you are helping others, you won't get caught in what my sister-in-law lovingly calls her "Mother Teresa" complex.

Start small. Pick flowers, and leave them at the door of a friend or neighbor. Make sandwiches for the homeless in your area. Write checks together for charity. Invite an elderly neighbor to dinner. Organize a neighborhood watch together. Join Amnesty International, and write letters once a month. Together, teach someone to read. Have a foreign exchange student live with you. Go to a doughnut shop together and buy coffee for yourselves and for the next ten people who order coffee. Pick a name out of the phone book and write a letter to him or her, as a "random act of kindness," saying what a wonderful person he or she is and asking that person to continue the tradition.

Not enough time because of kids? Volunteer for activities that allow you to spend more time with them and teach them important social values. Take over a class project, teach the whole class a sport, become a leader in Girl or Boy Scouts, or involve the whole family in a community project. Grab garbage bags and gloves, and spend Sunday morning cleaning up a local park or beach. Have your kids go through their toys and clothes, and give extras to homeless children. Deliver the goods together. Stuff envelopes for an environmental campaign. Bake a pie as a family, and bring it to your local police station or give it to your mail carrier. Sit down and discuss how as a family you can limit your impact on the environment.

Whatever you do, make sure you are both *equally* enthusiastic and interested. The healing power of doing good will not work as well for your relationship if one person is dutifully going along with the other partner's pet project.

Exploration: A Support System

A strong support system allows you to have other people to lean on, taking pressure off your relationship. Together, consider the questions and sentence stems below.

> What I look for in a friend is . . .
>
> What I would like in a support system that we don't have is . . .
>
> What I love about our present support system is . . .
>
> What I don't understand about your friendships is . . .
>
> What I look for in our mutual friends is . . .

How does it make you feel when someone does a favor for you?

As a couple, whom do you call when you want to have fun? Do you always socialize with just couples? Why?

Think back to a crisis time when you needed support from others. Was it there? Could you ask for help? What didn't work?

What about when you need a little help fast? An emergency baby-sitter, a ride to the airport, someone to feed the dog? Who helps you in these areas?

How about support services: accountant, lawyer, florist, travel agent. Do you consistently run into problems because you don't have a good one?

Who in your relationship nurtures friendships? Is that honestly okay with both of you?

Do you have any friends of the opposite sex? List each opposite-sex friend. Let your partner comment on how he or she feels about your being friends with them.

Decide together on two areas you would like to strengthen in your support system. Distill these areas into concrete action. Write these on your shared calendar, and do them together. Examples could include: interview baby-sitters; invite new neighbors to dinner; go to a party on Friday night with the express purpose of meeting new people.

See "Togetherness Time: Putting It All Together" for more about a shared calendar system.

Friendships Outside the Relationship

We all need friends, people who can meet needs that our partner can't or won't (someone to play basketball with, talk with about books, or go hiking with). This is a necessity. But several problems can arise. The most common is that many men don't have intimate friendships and rely heavily on their mates for this function, and many women turn to a friend outside the partnership to discuss issues that should be discussed inside.

For men: Nurture friendships with men. Rob Pasick, psychologist and author of *Awakening from the Deep Sleep*, believes making new friends and reconnecting with old ones "is an essential ingredient in men's growth and development. . . . Several recent studies have shown that people who have intimate friendships are more likely to survive heart attacks and less likely to develop cancer and serious infections." Pasick talks about how a man tends to become "excessively dependent on the woman in his life, whom he often views as his best friend. This puts a tremendous strain on their relationship. . . ."

The reality is having male friendships can be very difficult. Competition, envy, keeping score, lack of role models, fear of being labeled "gay" (for straight men or men in the closet), lack of time, the experience of being belittled by men in the past (playing sports is an example) all make having male friendships very difficult. Perhaps just accepting that it is difficult to make friends as a man will make you feel less alone and more courageous. Pasick suggests:

Reconnect with an old friend. Avoid pretending everything is perfect and assuming an "I'm superior because my life is great" attitude. Suggest specific times to get together.

Take a risk with a present friend. Make plans for a special event, and invite him. Have dinner afterward, and talk directly about your friendship and how you would like to improve it.

All relationships need attention. Remember birthdays, call just to say hi, carry through with plans and requests.

Men's groups are not all Robert Bly mythopoetic drum fests. You can find a more conventional group, led by a therapist, usually at some cost. Or look for flyers of leaderless men's support groups around churches, temples, personal growth centers, or mental health clinics. If the idea of a full-blown group freaks you out, what about a regular, monthly commitment to get together with one or two buddies, maybe to play chess, basketball, go for a run, *and* have a good talk?

Finally, don't automatically assume because you are friends with a man, your respective wives or girlfriends have to be close too. This can unduly stress a new friendship and can also keep you from exploring on your own how to be socially intimate. It is healthy to have separate friends. Very healthy.

For women: While we have no problem maintaining connections, sometimes we do have a problem in discussing relationship issues with best friends, mothers, or sisters that should only be discussed in the relationship. The simple guideline for this is if you are telling your friend what you aren't telling your partner, then it won't do any good. While it is imperative to have friends who meet needs that your partner can't or won't, it is not healthy to use friends as a substitute for honest disclosure between you and your mate. If you choose to confide *together* in friends, family, or a mentor couple, that is a different issue. It is going outside the relationship with your problems that creates conflict.

Allowing Others to Nurture You

You or your partner might have received strong parental messages that it is not okay to ask people for help unless you are related to them, and maybe not even then. Even if this is not the case, most people feel uncomfortable asking others for help, especially during tough times like losing a job or a long illness. Some of us have internalized a message that to ask for help is to be weak and dependent, as well as beholden to someone else. Yet how heartbreaking is our isolation if we don't reach out to others and let others reach out to us.

Mentor Couple

Find a couple whose relationship you admire, and ask them to be your mentors in love—your own "fairy god-couple," a couple you can learn from. Too little attention is paid to elders in our Western world. When you are struggling with a problem, you can call your mentor couple and ask them how they would handle it. This is especially wonderful when you have questions about children.

As you read this, are you saying to yourself, "I could never do that. It would mean telling our secrets to someone." But consider: it is precisely this type of isolation, this lack of ties to others, that puts such a strain on our relationships. I think this is what "a breakdown in family" really means—trying to rely solely on ourselves. (And a mentor couple is cheaper than a therapist.)

A Friendship Group

Sylvia Weishaus told me about a chavera, or friendship group, composed of couples who had been getting together for twenty-five years. "There is a cohesion there so that you are not isolated. And not one couple in that group even came close to divorce because having this kind of friendship support is a marital support as well." What could be more wonderful? Talk to your partner about forming a group, with a commitment to meet once a month, for the purpose of having fun and supporting each other. I know what you are thinking—"That sounds great, but who has time?" Or, "I don't know anyone who would do that." You don't *have* to know people—post an ad at a local café, your church, or in your local paper. Use the resource of *Utne Reader* magazine's salon service.

See "Resources."

What do you do once you get a group going? Let the group decide. Keeping it simple, not meeting too often, and everyone sharing responsibility for keeping it alive will help create success.

Resources:

Creating Community Anywhere, by Carolyn R. Shaffer and Kristina Anundsen (Jeremy Tarcher, 1993). Step-by-step plans for finding and creating community.

Living a Connected Life: Creating and Maintaining Relationships That Last a Lifetime, by Kathleen A. Brehony (Owl Books, 2003). A well-written and well-researched coaching for creating and deepening the vital relationships that give life richness and meaning.

Salons: The Joy of Conversation, by Jaida N'Ha Sandra and Jon Spayde (New Society Publications, 2001). *Utne Reader* magazine helped the art of conversation be reborn.

The Healing Power of Doing Good, by Allan Luks with Peggy Payne (uni-iverse.com, 2001). An investigation into the essentialness of volunteer work and what forms will most nourish you.

Websites:

Sustainability
http://www.sustainable.org

Utne Reader
http://www.utne.com

Cocreators

When to Do It:

- When you feel too vague about your future.

- Before you are married, move in together, or otherwise reaffirm your commitment to each other.

- On your anniversary.

- When one or both of you wishes to move, change jobs, have a child, or otherwise radically change your life.

What Is It?

Cocreating is the act of forming a life vision together. You can't get what you want if you don't know what you want. You can't have the kind of relationship you crave if you don't share your innermost fantasies. Cocreating entails discovering what you each want out of your shared life. It is a poetic, intuitive, playful way to nurture each other. More than goal setting, cocreating encourages cooperation on spiritual and emotional planes and allows your unconscious to speak to your partner.

Cocreating does not mean you will cease to have separate goals and desires. It does mean taking care of the shared part of your future, without overwhelming or forgetting yourself as an individual.

What to Do:

Visualize Your Future

One person reads the visualization while the other person **Relaxes.** Remember to speak very slowly (especially at the ellipses) and to prevent interruptions during the experience. Relaxing music helps immensely.

Read the instructions in "About Relaxing." Then read aloud:

You'll Need:

Your couple's journal or paper, and pens.

Magazines of all types that you can cut up.

Poster board.

Crayons, markers, colored pencils—whatever is handy, inexpensive, and appeals to you.

Relaxing music like *Deep Breakfast* by Ray Lynch.

Time required: At least one hour.

I love you. You are safe in this room. You are now going to embark on a wondrous adventure that will give you important information about our relationship. Take another deep breath. . . . See yourself walking alongside a tall fence. . . . Reach out and touch the surface. Feel it against your hand.

After a moment, you come to a door in the fence. The door is very large. You notice a key in your hand. If you are willing and want to, use the key to open the door. On the other side is your vision of our ideal life together. Take a deep breath, unlock the door, and step through.

The first thing you see is us in the morning. Beginning our day together. Take all the time you need to see what we are doing. . . . Note where we live, what kind of house, the details of our bedroom, bathroom, kitchen. . . . How we are communicating with each other. . . . Observe any spiritual practices. . . . Notice how we care for each other, little gestures of love. . . . How we handle the morning chores. . . . How we deal with any conflicts that arise. . . . Take your time, and soak in the positive, loving details. . . . Observe how you feel. . . .

Take another deep, deep breath and visualize our workday. . . . Do we see or talk or work with each other? . . . Feel the rhythms of our ideal day. . . . What do we do? Smell the fragrances of our life. . . . Note the differences from our present life. . . . Do we have lunch together? Can you taste the meal? Notice how we cope with stress and problems. . . . Know that you can remember anything you wish from this journey.

When you are ready, envision our coming home from work to be together. . . . How do we greet each other? What do we say? Do we do anything fun? Are there any smells . . . tastes . . . touches? Are there other people around? Take all the time you need to envision this part of the day. . . .

Now, see our evening together. . . . Taste and smell our dinner. . . . Listen for music. . . . Take all the time you need to taste, hear, smell, and touch your vision of our evening together.

If you would like, visualize the ending of this dream day. How do we say good-night? Do we make love? How does it feel? What is different? How do we sleep? Let this final image sink into your mind's eye.

If you like, spend a few more moments envisioning our ideal life together. Perhaps you can see an answer to an old problem. . . . Or how we can work well as parents together. . . . Or a perfect vacation. . . . Allow your unconscious to send positive images to the surface. . . . Take all the time you need. . . .

When you are ready, you notice you are standing before the door in the fence again. Do anything you need to before opening the door and returning home. You can come back here as often as you like. Lock the door behind you. Focus back on your breath. Come back into the room at (*your address*) with me. I love you.

Be very respectful and quiet as your partner returns. It takes a few moments to truly awaken from a guided journey. Ask your lover to write down everything she or he can remember from the journey. Make sure paper and pen are handy. The questions below might help your partner remember the journey.

What did you enjoy most about this experience?

Did anything surprise you?

What ideas would you like to incorporate in your present life?

How can I support you in this vision?

Repeat the visualization, switching roles.

Making a Treasure Blueprint

(This next section does not have to directly follow the meditation.)

The purpose of this step is to make a visual expression of your current shared life vision, to make concrete what you have each envisioned, and to mingle your dreams and desires. Gather together your magazines and art supplies.

Set up a special environment—candles, relaxing music, sparkling juice or wine, and no interruptions. Read each other your accounts of your visualization.

Spend some time flipping through magazines, cutting out images that express aspects of your visualization or your partner's visualization as he or she reads it to you. Draw or sketch scenes from your vision too.

When you feel you have enough visuals, get out your poster board. Devise a composite of pictures, sketches, symbols, words, and color to form a creative representation of your current shared life vision. *Current* means this vision can change. *Shared* implies your plan doesn't necessarily include personal goals and projects but your combined vision of your life together. *Life* alludes to long-term. *Vision* suggests the act of anticipating what will come.

Creating this collage will take compromise. One of you may have envisioned eating breakfast in bed every morning while the other visualized yoga in the backyard. Incorporate both visions: breakfast one morning, yoga the next, or yoga first and then breakfast. On a separate sheet of paper, create a repository for images that you want but your partner doesn't. This montage can become an icon for your personal goals and pleasures.

Please, don't give a minute's thought to art or talent. All that matters is creating a colorful symbol of your collective future, your *possibility*. When it is finished, talk about it. What do you see? Creating the montage will bring up all sorts of creative ideas. Decide to implement just one tomorrow. Hang the montage where you can glance at it often. Let it remind and inspire each of you how truly wonderful your life is *and* is becoming.

Feeling More Practical?

There are times when we want to create together, in a more spontaneous and practical way. When one of you is feeling this way, have a cocreator date. For example, if your dream is to build a house together, buy a few house magazines, borrow how-to and decorating books from the library, order Chinese food, and spend time imagining what you each want in your dream dwelling. Take notes.

You can do this with vacations, a change of lifestyle, jobs, moving to a new apartment, even how to spend a weekend at home.

To enhance your cocreator date, gather materials that stimulate your imaginations. Use the soul-stroking process so you hear and value each other's dreams. Consider writing your own guided visualization, tailored to your dream. For instance, you could both relax to soothing music, spend a few minutes visualizing your dream house, and then talk, draw, and write about what you discovered. Use your imaginations to strengthen your love and deepen your knowledge of each other.

Resources:

Creating the Work You Love: Courage, Commitment, and Career, by Rick Jarow (Inner Traditions, 1995). Written by one of the pioneers in the work/life movement.

Discover Your Soul Purpose CD, by Suzanne Falter-Barns. A powerful meditation to name the purpose that, once you know it, becomes the center from which to live your life. Available at http://www.how-muchjoy.com.

Living Your Best Life: Discover Your Life's Blueprint for Success, by Laura Berman Fortgang (Jeremy Tarcher, 2002). An excellent life-purpose and get-into-action book.

The Call, by Oriah Mountain Dreamer (San Francisco: Harper San Francisco, 2003). Lyrical, personal exploration of life purpose and yearning. Wonderful.

The Emotional Energy Factor: The Secrets High-Energy People Use to Beat Emotional Fatigue, by Mira Kirshenbaum (Delacorte Press, 2003). A very helpful examination of what drains your energy.

Wishcraft: How to Get What You Really Want, by Barbara Sher with Annie Gottlieb (Ballantine Books, 1986). The first and still one of the best life-purpose books.

Website:

How Much Joy
http://www.howmuchjoy.com

Writing Your Own Comfort Book

You'll Need:

Some kind of receptacle: your couple's journal, a file folder, whatever is handy and appeals to you.

Pens.

Sources of information: yellow pages, guidebooks, chamber of commerce information.

Time required: A few minutes to get set up, then a few minutes on a regular basis to add to your book.

When to Do It:

- When you've exhausted all the ideas that appeal to you in this book.

- When you want to explore your surroundings.

- When you want to surprise your partner.

- Anytime you feel the need to learn more about the needs of your relationship.

What Is It?

A couple's comfort book is a personal sourcebook filled with ideas of things to do to nurture each other and the relationship. After I finished writing *The Woman's Comfort Book*, I realized something: I'm not the expert, you are. You know best how to nurture yourself, each other, and the relationship. But remember the paradox: when you most need to nurture yourself or each other, that is when your creative ideas fly out the door. Thus, the need to create your own comfort book, to gather ideas based on *your* likes and dislikes, needs and wants, to write your own reference book unique to your geographical area, your hobbies, your age, children or not. Because the most important role of this book is to get *you* dreaming about what makes you and your partner feel good.

What to Do:

Storage

You need a physical place to store your ideas. You could designate the back of your journal as your couple's comfort book. If you want to change journals every year, you could keep your comfort book in a separate book, the blank kind you find at stationery, art, or bookstores. An accordion file folder organized not by alphabet but by category—Travel, Eating Out, Exploring, Big Trip Dreams, Gifts—works great if you like to clip newspaper and magazine stories. "Clippers" might also try a decorative cardboard box with scissors attached to the lid.

Create a system that allows each of you to *easily* record any and all new ideas. If you find one system doesn't work for you, don't hesitate to switch.

Being Specific

There are so many moments when we crave connection or a small adventure or a big adventure or just a new way to spend time together, but we can't think of anything. And that is why, when you are writing your couple's comfort book, you must be specific. Vague ideas won't work ("Go out to dinner"), but specific ideas with costs, directions, times open, and specials work well ("Two-for-one special at the seafood diner on Thursday nights between 5:30 and 7:00. Perfect for summer sunset dinner").

Gathering Ideas

Call or write the chamber of commerce and tourist bureau for your area and state. Ask them to send you information for attractions, historical sites, and a schedule of festivals in your area.

Visit a local bookstore, especially one that specializes in books about your area or travel, and check out guidebooks for your area. Good reference books are invaluable. Books listing camping spots, walking tours, restaurant guides, or things to do with kids can be priceless in revving up your life. When you find something you like in a book, mark it with a sticky note, write in the margins, or photocopy the page and file it in your book.

Answer these questions: "Where have I always wanted to explore?" "Where haven't I been since the kid's third grade field trip?" "Where did I go on field trips?" Even in the smallest of towns there are always undiscovered treasures. In Bedford, Indiana, there are the Blue Caves, which my grandmother, who has lived a few miles from there almost all her life, didn't know about until we went for an aimless ride one day.

Browse through your yellow pages. Look for tourist attractions, stores that might offer romantic services, weird restaurants to visit. Let the listings spark your imagination and memory.

Newspapers and magazines are great sources for ideas unique to your area. The problem is finding the time to read them! Once every two weeks, try charging through the paper, scissors in hand, scanning for ideas to clip. Raid regional or city magazines that list local activities for clippings too.

Have a "Writing Your Own Comfort Book" party. Explain the concept to friends and family, suggest a potluck, and brainstorm. Anything goes! Don't limit yourself to reality. Designate someone to write down ideas, then photocopy and mail to participants later. Use questions to get ideas flowing. Examples could include: "What to do on Saturday night?" "What to buy for birthdays?" "Cheap, romantic places to get away for the weekends." "Fun things to do when we are broke." Don't limit who you invite to couples or people who are good at relationships. Good ideas can come from kids, grandparents, and people not currently in a relationship.

Next time you're at a party and are at a loss for what to talk about when meeting new people, ask them what they do for romantic fun or what they do to keep their relationship humming or what they do when they want to show appreciation for the person they love.

Declare one week "New Ideas Week." During that week, each person tries to generate as many new ideas as possible. Set aside some time at the end of the week to share thoughts. The person with the most new ideas gets to decide what to do with your evening.

Adding to your comfort book can be a nurturing thing to do in itself. Next time you're bored or want something to do together, spend an hour or an evening or a Saturday morning adding to it.

A section of ideas for family nurturing activities can be very helpful. Also, generating ideas for what to do with the kids while you are nurturing yourselves can be very, very helpful.

Keep Going

Keep notes in your book about places you like and what you would do differently if you visited again. For instance, if you visited a great bed-and-breakfast but noticed a room that looked nicer, write that down for future reference.

Realize you are always changing, your relationship is always changing, and therefore you need to regularly add to and delete from your book. You could make tending your comfort book a seasonal ritual or a pre-anniversary date. Decide together, and mark it on your shared calendar.

See "Togetherness Time" and "Holidays: Anniversaries."

Resources:

Fodor's Healthy Escapes, edited by Christine Swiac (Fodor's Travel, 2003). Subtitle is *Two Hundred Eighty-Eight Spas, Resorts, and Retreats Where You Can Relax, Recharge, Get Fit, and Get Away from It All.*

Healing Centers and Retreats: Healthy Getaways for Every Body and Budget, by Jenifer Miller (Avalon Travel Publishing, 1998). Greater range of prices than Fodor.

Healthy Escapes, by Bernard Burt (Fodor, 1993). Two hundred forty-two healthy retreats and spas. Just an example of the plethora of interesting guidebooks that are available.

Romantic Antics: Creative Ideas for Successful First Dates, Adventurous Saturday Nights, and Playful Long Weekends, by Joy Decker and Kevin Decker (Adams Media Corporation, 2003). If this doesn't inspire you, just turn on the TV and give it up. Visit their site at http://www.inspirationpoint.com.

Romantic's Guide: Hundreds of Creative Tips for a Lifetime of Love, by Michael Webb (Hyperion, 2000). Low cost, original, thoughtful—more ideas than you can use in your lifetime.

Vacations That Can Change Your Life: Adventures, Retreats, and Workshops for the Mind, Body, and Spirit, by Ellen Lederman (Sourcebooks, 1998). A range of retreat centers and programs.

Final Notes

In writing this book, I participated in the rebirth of wonder and respect for my own relationship. It helped both of us rededicate ourselves to maintaining a conscious connection, every day if possible. It convinced me that being in a relationship is never easy but always immensely rewarding. I learned what it meant to work at a relationship, without making it feel like work. I gained new respect for my parents' marriage of thirty-three years, as well as other successful relationships that surround me.

Writing this book also convinced me that love's worst enemy is stale comfort, and if we have the energy to peek out of old patterns and to look away from the TV or the sixteen-hour-a-day job and look into each other's eyes, then comforting each other can be a vital step back to aliveness and connection.

I wish you patience to love gracefully, courage to love steadfastly, energy to love consciously, and the spirit to have fun doing it.

Please visit me at http://www.comfortqueen.com, and subscribe to my free electronic newsletter, *The Self-Care Minder*. We are creating a lively, grace-filled, flaws-and-all global community of women and men who are exploring how to creatively, joyfully, fully live their lives. Be part of that community! Hundreds of free resources.

You can also reach me at P.O. Box 10065, Bainbridge Island, WA 98110.

May you find the energy, inspiration, and grace to nurture your relationship. May you be at peace.

Acknowledgments

To the remarkable people who opened their hearts and minds (and sometimes houses) to me: Michele Louden Samuelson, Barbra Glascock Clifton and Bill Clifton, Diana and Herb Leifring, Julie and Steve Kearney, Rhonda Foreman Cook and John Cook, Carroll Hodge and Midge Costin, Sara Lou O'Connor and Daniel Hegeman, Nicole Dillenberg and John Cork, Kristina Coggins and Steve Kulchin, John Duvall and Anita Larimer, Anna and Ray Chamberlain, Carol and Terry Kinsey, Lindsay and Craig Olson, Cynthia and David Knudsen, Mary Davies, Rachelle and Sandy Krupp, Paul and Lynn Stubenrauch, Dan and Mary Sutherland, Yvonne and Jack Thomas, Annie and Mike Vosburgh, Barbara Voss and Randy Frakes, John and Julie Waldron, Lynn and Grant Stephens, Willow Green Court Book Club, Mark and Nancy Smith, Melinda Cotrufo and Vince Cox, Debra Marrs, Priscilla Mutter, Mary Mixter, Nancy and Bob Hostetter, Ken and Helen Hazlett, Iris Ferber, Joann and David Greenbaum, Jennifer Taylor, Vivian Cordova, the men in the various groups who gave me their time, my women's spirituality group, and everyone I'm forgetting. Please accept my heartfelt thanks.

For your professional insights, I would like to thank Kay Hagan, Belleruth Naparstek, Celeste Tibbets, Fred Kahane, Sylvia Weishaus, Robin Siegal, Robert Pasick, Kimberley Heart, Garry Diamond, Diane Broderick, and Sandy Silas.

From the warmest place in my heart and for setting me on the path to wholeness, thank you Paula Steinmetz and Shelly Van Loben Sels.

Harper San Francisco has become home to me. Ani, Hannah, Robin, Judy, Lisa, and Mr. Carlson, your support has given me great confidence.

Barbara Moulton, my karma must be very good in the editor department. Your patience with my neurotic episodes, your insight when I'm stuck, and your capacity to make me laugh when I am afraid are deeply cherished.

Acknowledgments Nicole and John, Randi Ragan, Zahra Dowlatabadi, and Eric Wishnie, I shower you with gratitude for the part you played in this project.

Mom and Dad, thank you for the living example of a strong, courageous, honest marriage. Two people who desire each other, have something to talk about, and live together, after more than thirty years—wow.

This book would not exist without my lover, my mate, my best beloved, Christopher Martin Mosio. Chris, you are truly my cocreator. You bring the very best of me into the light. Your patience and courage are so wonderful. Thank you for letting me put our relationship under the microscope and on the page.

Finally, thank you to all the women who found solace in my first book and to the couples reading this one. May you create a nourishing base to sustain you through your long walk on this planet. Namasté.